The Trevi Fountain

THE TREVI FOUNTAIN

John A. Pinto

Yale University Press
New Haven and London

Publication of this book has been aided by a grant from The Millard Meiss Publication Fund of the College Art Association of America.

MM

Designed by Nancy Ovedovitz and set in Garamond No. 3 type by Rainsford Type. Printed in the United States of America by Vail-Ballou Press, Binghamton, New York.

Library of Congress Cataloging in Publication Data
Pinto, John A.
    The Trevi Fountain.
    Bibliography: p.
    Includes index.
    1. Fontana di Trevi (Rome, Italy)   2. Salvi, Nicola.
3. Rome (Italy)— Fountains.   I. Title.
NA9415.R7P5   1986   730'.945'632   85-2480
ISBN 0-300-03335-4 (alk. paper)

10   9   8   7   6   5   4   3   2   1

To my wife, Meg

Contents

6

The Construction History
of the Trevi

7

Salvi's Design for the Trevi:
Evolution, Conflict,
and Compromise

8

Salvi's Iconographical Program
for the Trevi

9

The Trevi and Its Place
in the History of Art

Appendix 1
Documents and Published Reports
Pertaining to the History
of the Trevi Fountain

Appendix 2
Documents Describing the Trevi
by Nicola Salvi

Notes

Select Bibliography

Index

Illustrations

Unless otherwise noted photographs were taken by the author. The abbreviation *GFN* stands for Gabinetto Fotografico Nazionale.

❋
Acknowledgments

Much as it did in the eighteenth century, Rome continues to provide a uniquely congenial setting for antiquarian and art historical research. One of the distinct pleasures of working on a Roman topic that cuts across history, as does the Fontana di Trevi, is the opportunity it affords to meet and exchange information with members of the international community of scholars that flourishes there, nourished by national academies and private research institutes. The specific contributions of my colleagues are recorded in the notes, but I would like to underscore the advice and support lent by the following individuals. Allan Ceen and Elisabeth Kieven both have been active collaborators in this project from its inception, and their constructive criticism has corrected and refined it in more ways than I could ever acknowledge. Among the many others who encouraged and aided my research I would like to single out the following: Barbara Bini, Joseph Connors, Michael Conforti, Mrs. Sophie Consagra, Karen Einaudi, Professor Robert Enggass, Architetto Maria Grazia Feretti, Dr. Jörg Garms, Dottoressa Anna Grelle, Professor Hellmut Hager, Roger Hoffmann, Nancy Hopkin, Cyril Humphris, Christopher Johns, Signora Inez Longobardi, Hellmut Lorenz, Elizabeth Hammond Llewellyn, Dr. Borje Magnusson, Tod Marder, Professor Jennifer Montagu, Mary Myers, Professor Valentino Pace, David Quint, Luigi Spezzaferro, Richard Tuttle, and John Varriano.

The administration of the American Academy in Rome, in particular its library staff headed by Lucilla Marini, provided valuable assistance and warm personal support over several years. Without the incomparable resources of the Biblioteca Hertziana and the opportunities for scholarly exchange it offers this book could not have been written. My ability to carry out research in Rome was greatly facilitated by a grant from the American Council of Learned Societies in 1981 and by sabbatical leaves approved by the President and Trustees of Smith College in 1981 and 1984. A fellowship from the Center for Advanced Study in the Visual Arts allowed me to prepare my manuscript for publication in a most stimulating environment. Thanks are due also to the College Art Association's Millard Meiss Publications Fund Committee, which generously awarded the book a subvention.

It seems appropriate here to acknowledge the profound and enduring debt I owe four scholars whose inspirational teaching and publications have directly influenced my approach to architectural history and to the urban fabric of Rome: James S. Ackerman, Richard Krautheimer, William L. MacDonald, and Henry A. Millon. I am also indebted to the late Anthony M. Clark for opening my eyes to the vitality of Roman settecento art and culture. As the dedication of this volume indicates, Meg Hopkin Pinto, both as editor and wife, has helped me more than I can possibly express.

The Trevi Fountain

Introduction

The Trevi Fountain is unquestionably the best known and most spectacular monument of eighteenth-century Rome. Since its completion in 1762, it has impressed successive generations of tourists and has inspired novelists, composers, and filmmakers. A survey of artists stimulated by the Trevi, from Piranesi and Chambers to Fellini and Charles Moore, attests to the range of its impact as well as to its enduring value as an artistic metaphor.

Perhaps because of its reputation as a tourist attraction, however, the Fontana di Trevi has been relatively neglected by art historians. While important contributions have been made by Hereward L. Cooke, Armando Schiavo, and Cesare D'Onofrio, among others, many questions regarding its history and design remain unanswered. In light of the Trevi's almost iconic character, it is not surprising that when it has been studied, scholars have tended to view it as an isolated monument detached from its urban context. This perspective, or rather lack of it, has meant that the prevailing view of the Trevi has a decidedly two-dimensional cast to it, rather resembling certain postcards sold on the site. I would like to suggest that by probing behind the Trevi's facade, in both historical and physical terms, we can arrive at a more balanced assessment of its design.

What confronts us as we stand in the piazza today is largely the work of the architect Nicola Salvi (1697–1751), whose design was executed over a thirty-year period between 1732 and 1762 (fig. 1). Salvi undertook the metamorphosis of a preexisting palace facade and simple basin into the most monumental fountain display in Rome, using the enormous scale of the Trevi dramatically to transform the modest square on which it fronts. The Trevi design successfully incorporates into a harmonious ensemble Salvi's elegant architectural veneer of the Palazzo Poli, his spirited grouping of sculpture and naturalistic rockwork, and the enveloping basin. Salvi brilliantly employs the element of water to fuse the component parts of the fountain, uniting facade, rockwork, and pool.

Salvi's facade, tied together by a colossal order of engaged columns and pilasters, functions as a grand scenic backdrop for the fountain proper. The central feature of the Trevi facade, a triumphal arch motif, concentrates our attention on the commanding figure of Oceanus, lord of water, as he appears to issue from a palatial residence accompanied by tritons and sea horses. To the sides and above Oceanus other allegorical statues amplify the theme of water, symbolizing its beneficial effects. Twin bas-reliefs below the cornice

1

Fig. 1. Trevi Fountain, general view with piazza

narrate the story of the Trevi's ancient origins. Dominating the attic is the escutcheon of Pope Clement XII Corsini (1730–40), who commissioned the fountain. The sculpture of the Trevi, while largely of Salvi's design, results from the collaboration of many artists; its execution dragged on long after Salvi's death.

The Fontana di Trevi, far from a two-dimensional wall fountain, aggressively moves out to occupy virtually all of the small piazza in which it is situated. The naturalistic rockwork, or *scogli*, forms imitation marine reefs over and around which the water rushes on its way to the enveloping basin. Petrified flora and fauna, appropriate to a wide range of geographical settings, are sculpted on the irregular surfaces of the *scogli*. The whole of this picturesque composition is animated by the sound and motion of water, which Salvi has orchestrated with consummate skill.

The steps that lead down from the street level allow easy access to those who would drink or fetch water from the basin. Much like the orchestra of a theater, they provide seating for observers inclined rather more to the allied pursuits of contemplation and relaxation. Around the edges of the fountain the traffic and commerce of the city go on unabated, as they have on this site for many centuries. Indeed, the pattern of streets in the neighborhood, together with the placement of many of the surrounding buildings, was largely determined by the site of the Trevi and the ancient aqueduct that feeds it. Salvi's fountain, therefore, is the result of a millennial process that began in the Augustan Age when Marcus Agrippa brought to Rome the water that still feeds the Trevi.

In order to illuminate both the form and the meaning of Salvi's eighteenth-century masterpiece it is necessary to trace its origins back to classical antiquity, for the Trevi, perhaps better than any other monument, embodies the full sweep of Rome's architectural history. My study of the Trevi is accordingly divided into two parts, the first treating the early history of the fountain and the second examining Nicola Salvi's executed design. The first chapter sets forth the archaeological and literary evidence bearing on the *Aqua Virgo*, the Roman aqueduct supplying the Trevi. The traditions associated with Agrippa's aqueduct, as well as the course it took through the city, directly influenced the iconography and siting of the present-day fountain. The next chapter explores the changing relationship between the Trevi and the developing city between 1453, when a modest forerunner of the Fontana di Trevi was inaugurated by Pope Nicholas V, and 1732, when work began on Salvi's fountain. This chapter places special emphasis on interpreting the changes in the position and proposed appearance of the Trevi as an expression of urban politics influenced by three interest groups: the papacy, the city government, and private families.

Chapters 3 and 4 focus on the numerous unexecuted projects for the Trevi, which constitute a miniature survey of fountain design in the seventeenth and early eighteenth centuries. The list of these projects includes designs by some of the most accomplished Late Baroque architects and sculptors, including Carlo Fontana, Filippo Juvarra, Ferdinando Fuga, Luigi Vanvitelli, and Edme Bouchardon. Many of these projects were entered in the competition Pope Clement XII sponsored in 1730 to select an architect for the Trevi, which two years later resulted in the appointment of Nicola Salvi.

The second part of my study begins with two chapters on the fountain as actually built, stressing Salvi's remarkable fusion of architecture, sculpture, and water. Careful study of the documentary evidence provides an account of its long construction history, spanning three decades. It also serves to underscore Salvi's role as the master designer and to define the specific contributions of the artists and artisans working under his direction.

In the concluding chapters I move from analysis to a synthetic interpretation of the Trevi. The seventh chapter treats the evolution of Salvi's design, based primarily on a new reading of prints and drawings representing the fountain, many of them unpublished. Salvi's controversy with the sculptor Giovanni Battista Maini provides a revealing example of the common practice of collaborative design in eighteenth-century Rome, while illustrating some of its attendant limitations and hazards. This is followed by an examination of Salvi's memorandum on the iconographical program of the Trevi, which surveys the literary and visual sources he drew upon and reveals the coherence and integrity of his original design.

The final chapter attempts to place the Trevi against a broad art historical background. A review of the *fortuna critica* of the Trevi introduces a discussion of the fountain's relationship to sources in the art and architecture of preceding epochs, an examination of artistic currents in the Rome of Clement XII, and a comparison with contemporary monuments in northern Europe.

My approach to the Fontana di Trevi is broadly historical and stresses considerations that all too often are neglected by art historians. While I have chosen to write a monograph on a single building, I have tried to avoid what might be termed monument fixation, a form of myopia that causes so many scholars to disassociate a work of art from its context. Indeed, the contextual relationships of a monument such as the Trevi reveal what the analysis of style alone cannot. First and foremost, the Fontana di Trevi functions as a civic monument, the design of which was shaped and periodically redefined to meet the changing needs and aspirations of the surrounding city. Salvi's executed design was a response to specific social and political interests as well as the embodiment of a tradition spanning many centuries. If I am successful, the Trevi Fountain will emerge more clearly both as a compelling symbol of Rome's classical heritage and as a concrete reality that posed specific design problems for architects, sculptors, and their patrons.

1

The Early History of
the Trevi: From the Aqua Virgo
to the Acqua Vergine

The millennial history of the Trevi Fountain, like that of the Christian era which it parallels, began during the reign of the emperor Augustus. In 19 B.C., on the ninth of June, the waters of the Aqua Virgo first gushed from the dark confines of their conduit to foam and eddy beneath the Roman sky.[1] June 9 was particularly appropriate because it was the feast day of Vesta, whose priestesses, fittingly, cared for the sacred water as well as the sacred fire. No doubt assisting at the inaugural display of the waters, and given special recognition, was the emperor's son-in-law Marcus Vipsanius Agrippa, who was responsible for building the aqueduct that brought the Aqua Virgo to Rome.[2] Agrippa's accomplishment must be seen against the background of the vast program of public works undertaken in the hitherto undeveloped quarter of the city known as the Campus Martius initiated by Augustus and ably executed by his adjutant.[3] Later, the popes, as inheritors of the imperial title of *Pontifex Maximus*—Bridge Builder (but by extension High Priest) responsible for the construction and maintenance of public buildings—consciously perpetuated the Augustan concern for Rome's embellishment. The Fontana di Trevi, from which the waters of the Aqua Virgo still issue, is perhaps the finest example of this centuries-long tradition.

The Campus Martius, occupying some six hundred acres of level ground, lies between the Tiber and the slopes of the Capitoline, Quirinal, and Pincian hills.[4] Set into a bend in the Tiber, this low-lying district is part of the flood plain of the river, and as such remained undeveloped long after Rome was established on top of the hills to the south and east. For the duration of the Republic it lay outside both the city's fortifications and its religious boundaries. Under the reign of Augustus, however, this quarter came to be developed on a large scale. Major monuments—including the emperor's mausoleum, a temple which was the forerunner of Hadrian's Pantheon, and a great sundial—were inserted into the Campus Martius as part of the ambitious Augustan program of urban development (fig. 2). Waterworks on a grand scale also figured prominently in this scheme. Among these the Baths of Agrippa (the

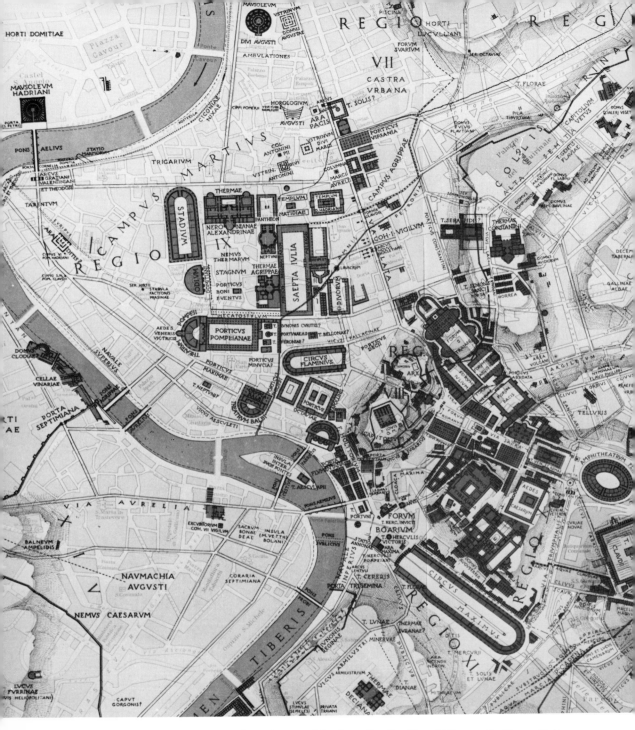

Fig. 2. Plan of the Campus Martius, after Lugli and Gismondi, *Forma Urbis*

first great public baths in Rome), an ornamental lake (or *Stagnum*), and a canal (or *Euripus*) are worthy of particular note.

Clearly, the water of the Aqua Virgo was essential to the development of the Campus Martius, for without it the baths, lake, and canal as well as numerous smaller fountains situated in the new quarter could not have been supplied. The Aqua Virgo was by no means the first of the great aqueducts to be built, nor even the first to be constructed by Agrippa, but it was nonetheless unusual in several important respects.[5] Not only was its source very close to Rome, but its conduit ran almost entirely underground and therefore was less subject to vandalism and easier to maintain; moreover, by entering the city from the north, it was capable of supplying the Campus Martius.[6]

Three classical authors comment on the purity of the Aqua Virgo. Pliny the Elder reports that it refused to mingle with the waters of a nearby stream sacred to Hercules, and therefore was named Virgin.[7] Cassiodorus clearly echoes this view when he writes, "Purest and most delightful of all streams glides along the Aqua Virgo, so named because no defilement ever stains it."[8] Only Frontinus relates the charming story of how the source of the Aqua Virgo came to be discovered; according to him a country maiden pointed out the springs to Agrippa's soldiers, and the water was henceforward called Virgo in her honor.[9] He adds that this picturesque legend was commemorated by a painting in a small temple situated near the spring.

The temple mentioned by Frontinus, of which no remains have yet been identified, may well have been a shrine sacred to the nymph of the springs. This conjecture is supported by an ancient gemstone which is known only from an eighteenth-century print (fig. 3).[10] While the obverse of the gem was engraved with the likeness of Agrippa, its reverse appears to have depicted two worshipers venerating the statue of a female deity set within a nymphaeum. Above the gem as it appears in the print is an illustration of Frontinus's story of the Roman soldiers and the rustic maiden. Published in the same year as the competition that led to the construction of the Trevi Fountain (1732), the printed scene strongly resembles a bas-relief of the same subject that is part of the present-day fountain's sculptural decoration (fig. 104). Agrippa's memory, too, is recalled in the Trevi by a second bas-relief set up as a pendant to that representing the Roman maiden (fig. 103). Not only do the origins of the Aqua Virgo figure in the decoration of the Trevi Fountain as we see it today, but they also influenced a number of unexecuted projects for the fountain prepared between 1600 and 1730. Both the figures and events associated with the construction of the Aqua Virgo in antiquity continued to play an active role in shaping the form and iconography of projects for the Trevi until its completion in 1762.

If the history and legend inspired by Agrippa influenced subsequent architects and sculptors of the fountain, his substantive accomplishment, in the form of the aqueduct itself, proved equally significant. For this reason a short description of the Aqua Virgo from its source to its ancient terminus within the city will shed light on important aspects of the Trevi Fountain's design and location.[11] The springs of the Aqua Virgo are situated at Salone, about

Fig. 3. Gemstone of Agrippa with nymphaeum on reverse, after Graevius,
Thesaurus

ten miles east of Rome's center, in a shady valley between the Via Collatina
and the river Aniene (fig. 4).[12] The site preserves to this day the cool and
verdant appearance that is captured in a delightful account of Pope Pius II,

an early and sensitive observer of landscape, who visited Salone on June 30, 1463:

> On the way [to Tivoli] he had the pleasure of visiting the springs of Salone. There are two bubbling springs near the Aniene ten miles from Rome so abundant that each alone could easily turn a mill with only a slight fall of water. The water is crystal clear and very cold, a circumstance which in summer causes the death of many rash persons. Nine cardinals accompanied the Pope and lunched with him under shelters which their attendants constructed of branches near one of the springs and the stream which flows from it.[13]

The refreshing coolness of the springs, especially during the hot summer months, was appreciated by other Renaissance prelates, one of whom, Cardinal Agostino Trivulzio, had a villa designed by Baldassare Peruzzi built at Salone

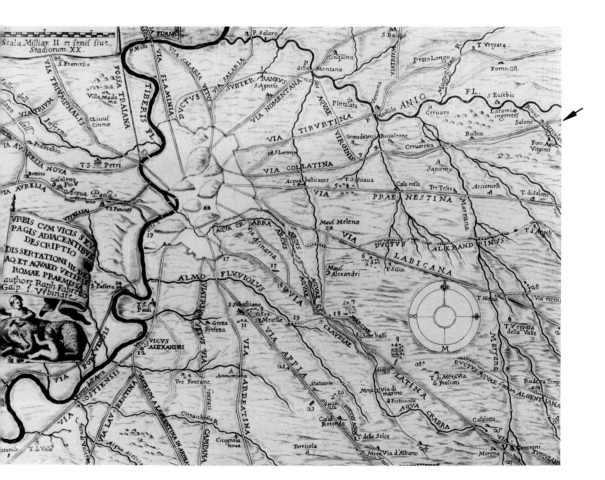

Fig. 4. Map showing the course of the Aqua Virgo after Fabretti, *De aquis*, 1680

in 1525.[14] In keeping with the classical associations of the site, Peruzzi's design was partially inspired by Pliny's well-known description of his Tuscan villa; moreover, the painted decoration, representing marine deities and *nau-machiae*, or staged naval battles, appropriately celebrated the element of water. The true genius of the place, the Nymph of Salone, was extolled in a poem by Angelo Colocci honoring his patron, Cardinal Trivulzio.[15]

In spite of frequent work in the area of the springs since the Renaissance, most recently in 1937 when a modern pumping station was built, remains still attest to the efforts of Agrippa's engineers. To the west of the pumping station traces of a small dam may be seen.[16] The dam was most likely intended to serve a threefold purpose: to collect the water as it issued from the ground, to prevent it from draining into the neighboring river Aniene, and to channel it into the conduit of the aqueduct itself. In spite of even more frequent repairs carried out on the fabric of the aqueduct, large sections of the Roman conduit, entirely underground, still survive intact (fig. 5). Clearly visible in the illustration are the essential characteristics of its construction: walls made of concrete faced with small, square blocks of tufa (a standard Roman masonry technique known as *opus reticulatum* from the netlike surface pattern which results) and a vault of concrete poured on top of wooden formwork, the marks of which are still visible on the exposed surface. The surviving Roman portions of the conduit are easily distinguished from subsequent restorations, as comparison with a view of the conduit immediately behind the Trevi, showing Nicola Salvi's eighteenth-century intervention, reveals (fig. 6). The stilted arches above the conduit proper are presumed to have allowed inspection by boat. Through channels of this kind the Aqua Virgo still makes its way to Rome, but by an unusually circuitous route.

The Aqua Virgo is a low-level aqueduct and was never intended to supply the more elevated quarters of the city on the hills. At its source the Aqua Virgo is only twenty-four meters above sea level, while ground level at the Trevi is barely six meters lower. The rate of fall, therefore, is very low, not exceeding thirteen centimeters to the kilometer.[17] At some points the conduit lies as much as forty meters below ground, a depth which attests to the remarkable abilities of Roman hydraulic engineers.

After running due west toward the city for some seven and a half kilometers, the aqueduct abruptly turns northward and by means of a nine-kilometer detour finally enters Rome from the north (fig. 4). There are two reasons for this detour. Agrippa's engineers obviously wanted to avoid crossing deep valleys, which would have necessitated the construction of arcades to carry the conduit and would have entailed considerable expense, preferring instead to follow the natural contours of the land. Also, as we have seen, a northern approach facilitated direct access to the developing Campus Martius.

Once having passed under the Aurelian Walls near the Muro Torto, the conduit continues underground, tunneling through the Pincian Hill beneath the gardens of what is now the Villa Medici (fig. 7). In antiquity the Aqua

Virgo does not appear to have supplied the gardens and monumental nymphaeum of the Pincio, which were most likely fed by a branch of the Anio Vetus. Only in the Renaissance were the waters of the Virgo brought up to the gardens of the Villa Medici, a vertical distance of nearly fifty meters.[18] It finally emerged from the ground near the modern Via Francesco Crispi to run along arches to its terminus in the Campus Martius.[19] The conduit was carried on top of some 139 arches, increasing in height to more than thirty feet as they moved from the slopes of the Pincio into the plain of the Tiber below.[20] Some idea of the appearance of this stretch of the Aqua Virgo in antiquity, in its measured march westward into the Campus Martius, is conveyed by the great model of ancient Rome in the Museo della Civiltà Romana (fig. 8), which clearly shows the serpentine line of the arcade exiting from the Pincian Hill (just below and to the left of center) and advancing to its terminus near the Pantheon (above and to the right of center). Relatively few traces of the impressive arcade of the Aqua Virgo survive today, but throughout the Middle Ages and well into the Renaissance it constituted an imposing landmark in this still-undeveloped portion of the city.[21]

At one point where the arcade carrying the conduit of the Aqua Virgo crossed a Roman street it was embellished by a monumental arch carrying an inscription commemorating its restoration under the emperor Claudius (A.D. 45–46). This arch, the so-called Arco del Nazareno, still survives in the modern Via del Nazareno, though it is mostly hidden from sight by the rise in ground level.[22] Two prints by Piranesi depict the Arco del Nazareno, one a reconstruction view stressing its expressive use of rusticated masonry, the other recording its actual appearance in the eighteenth century (figs. 9, 10). From the Arco del Nazareno the aqueduct continues as far as the Trevi Fountain, which straddles the conduit, as can be seen from a detail of Lanciani's map superimposing a plan of the modern city upon the remains of ancient Rome (fig. 11). Thus, the fountain's location within the city can be seen to have been largely determined by decisions made in antiquity by Agrippa's engineers.

In antiquity, however, the arcade of the Aqua Virgo proceeded farther than the Trevi, where it now stops. Just south of the fountain it turned west and crossed the Via Lata (the modern Via del Corso) at the level of the Palazzo Sciarra.[23] The conduits traversed the Via Lata by passing over another Claudian arch, erected between A.D. 51 and 52 to commemorate the conquest of Britain.[24] According to Frontinus, the Aqua Virgo continued into the Campus Martius, ending at the front of the Saepta Julia, a grand, porticoed enclosure situated just east of the Pantheon.[25] Imposing remains of both the arcade and conduit were found beneath the facade of Sant'Ignazio in the seventeenth century.[26]

From this point on, the substantive remains of the Aqua Virgo have practically disappeared, and it is difficult to trace its course through the Campus Martius with any degree of accuracy.[27] The Aqua Virgo undoubtedly supplied

Fig. 5. Conduit of the Aqua Virgo at Tor Sapienza

the Baths of Agrippa just south of the Pantheon.[28] The main block of this bath complex does not appear to have contained a swimming pool, which became a central feature of most large-scale thermal establishments in the following centuries. Robert B. Lloyd reasons that this function may have been performed by the ornamental canal (the *Euripus*) that was situated in the

Fig. 6. Conduit of the Acqua Vergine behind the Trevi

Gardens of Agrippa adjacent to the baths, and, together with an artificial lake (the *Stagnum*), was fed by the Aqua Virgo.[29] The *Stagnum* is thought to have been located to the west of the baths, between the present-day Corso Vittorio Emanuele and the Via degli Staderari. From literary references we learn that its shores were lined with quays and that it was large enough for boating; in

Fig. 7. Plan of the urban aqueducts, after Piranesi, *Antichità romane*, 1756

Fig. 8. Model of Rome in the reign of Constantine, showing the arcade of the
Aqua Virgo

Fig. 9. Arco del Nazareno, reconstruction, after Piranesi, *Antichità romane*, 1756

Fig. 10. Arco del Nazareno, view, after Piranesi, *Campus Martius*, 1762

Fig. 11. The Trevi superimposed on the remains of ancient Rome, after ► Lanciani, *forma Urbis*

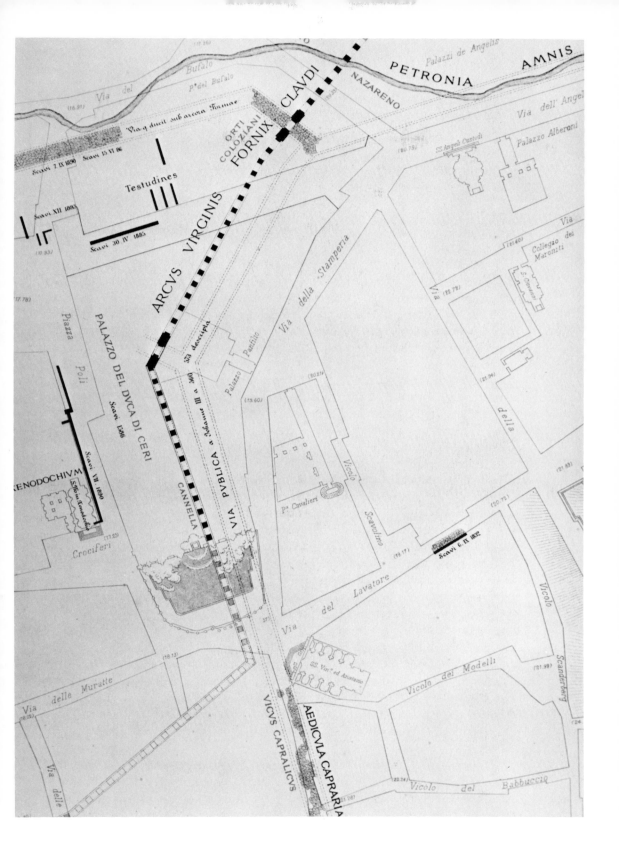

recounting the excesses of Nero's reign Tacitus describes a notorious barge banquet given on the *Stagnum*:

> The entertainment took place on a raft constructed on Marcus Agrippa's lake. It was towed about by other vessels, with gold and ivory fittings. Their rowers were degenerates, assorted according to age and vice. . . . On the quays were brothels stocked with high-ranking ladies.[30]

Significantly, there is no reference to swimming in the *Stagnum*, which leads Lloyd to conjecture that it may have been fed by the runoff waters of the baths.[31]

In contrast to the *Stagnum*, the *Euripus* was fed directly by the Aqua Virgo, drawing fully one-fifth of its capacity.[32] Repeated references in classical literature attest to the fact that the frigid running waters of the *Euripus* were used for swimming.[33] Seneca even remarks that as a youth he used to begin the new year with a plunge into the *Euripus* for good luck.[34] Traces of the *Euripus* have been identified running parallel to the northeast side of the Corso Vittorio Emanuele, and these archaeological remains, together with epigraphical evidence, strongly suggest that it ran all the way to the Tiber, debouching in the neighborhood of the Pons Agrippae.[35] While both classical literature and archaeology document Agrippa's lavish use of water in the Campus Martius, there is no evidence whatsoever that he built a monumental display involving architecture and sculpture comparable to the Trevi Fountain.[36] The effects seem rather to suggest an urban Versailles or Nymphenburg, with broad sheets of water extending to the horizon.

Though a great fountain structure does not appear to have marked the terminus of the Aqua Virgo in antiquity, such monumental nymphaea were not uncommon in Rome and the eastern Empire.[37] One such structure, the Castellum Aquae Juliae, or Nymphaeum of Alexander Severus, on the Esquiline Hill, was the object of repeated study from the Renaissance on and may well have influenced the design of the Trevi Fountain.[38] In A.D. 226 the emperor Alexander Severus issued a series of coins commemorating his construction or restoration of this nymphaeum which gives a general sense of its appearance in antiquity (fig. 12).[39] The coins clearly show the tripartite organization of the upper facade, which rises from an imposing basement. A central arch or niche flanked by two smaller arches appears to be occupied by sculpture; at the center, reclining on top of the basement is a figure which has been identified as Oceanus, the presiding deity of the Trevi today.[40] In front of the basement there appears to be an ample basin to collect the water that no doubt issued from the openings visible in the lower portion of the facade.

An engraving by Etienne Dupérac records the appearance of the Castellum Aquae Juliae in the late sixteenth century, which, with the exception of relatively modest losses, is substantially that of the ruins as we see them today (fig. 13). The central opening, clearly an apse originally crowned by a vault,

Fig. 12. The Castellum Aquae Juliae, coin of
Alexander Severus

is framed by two lateral arches in which are silhouetted large marble representations of Roman military trophies, the so-called Trophies of Marius, which in 1590 were removed to their present position on the balustrade of the Campidoglio. Dupérac's print and other Renaissance views as well as examination of the ruin itself show that the water originally exited from three main openings. Like the Trevi, the Nymphaeum of Alexander Severus was the terminus and grand urban display of a major Roman aqueduct also built by Agrippa, the Aqua Julia, and had at its rear extensive structures for the collection and distribution of this water. Such a well-known ancient fountain was likely studied by Nicola Salvi in the course of preparing his design for the Trevi and may have inspired the architect by its grandiose scale and general appearance. A revealing illustration of the compelling power of such grand images is provided by an extensive series of archaeological drawings attempting to reconstruct the Nymphaeum of Alexander Severus, some of which were obviously inspired by the Trevi Fountain.[41] One example dating from 1916 even takes as the source for the central niche the swirling diamond-shaped coffers of the vault framing Oceanus at the Trevi (fig. 14).

With the gradual disintegration of the Roman Empire and the fall of the imperial capital to successive invading armies in the course of the fifth and sixth centuries, the waters of the Aqua Virgo, which had flowed uninterruptedly for more than four hundred years, were repeatedly denied to Rome's dwindling population. Clear evidence of this disruption is provided by Procopius's account of the Byzantine reconquest of Italy during the third decade of the sixth

Fig. 13. The Castellum Aquae Juliae in a print by Dupérac, 1575

century. In the course of this campaign the emperor Justinian's general, Belisarius, found himself on the defensive, bottled up in Rome and besieged by the Ostrogoths. During the siege, which lasted for more than a year (February 537 to March 538), extensive and in some cases irreparable damage was done to the aqueducts in order to deny the defenders the city's water supply.

The aqueducts and the Aqua Virgo in particular played a significant part in the strategy of the Goths. The principal Gothic camp was situated three miles to the east of Rome, near the Tor Fiscale, where the massive arcades of the Claudian and Marcian aqueducts twice crossed one another, thus forming a large and easily protected enclosure.[42] The cutting of the aqueducts led naturally to another Gothic stratagem, from which we learn specifically about the state of the Aqua Virgo. Since water was no longer flowing through the conduits of the broken aqueducts, their channels were dry and, if left unprotected, could permit the enemy to infiltrate the city. Belisarius took the precaution of blocking these narrow channels with masonry plugs, but this did not prevent the Goths from attempting to force an entry through the conduit of the Aqua Virgo where it passes under the Aurelian Walls below the Pincian Hill.[43] Procopius describes the discovery of the Gothic sappers and the frustration of their attempt to effect a surprise entry into the city.[44]

While the Gothic siege resulted in extensive damage to many Roman monuments, Belisarius's Byzantine successors made efforts to repair the most essential structures—the walls, bridges, and aqueducts.[45] Nonetheless, following the siege Rome's population had shrunk drastically and the physical fabric of the city inexorably continued to deteriorate. There is evidence that some of the aqueducts were mended and continued to function fitfully for another two hundred years.[46] A written itinerary associated with a plan of Rome drawn up around the eighth century makes it clear that the arcades of the Aqua Virgo had already in large part fallen, and it appears that all subsequent restorations of the aqueduct were limited to the relatively short remaining stretch of arches that ran only as far as the modern Piazza di Trevi.[47] Major renovation work was carried out in the pontificate of Hadrian I (772–95) and continued to occur sporadically throughout the Middle Ages.[48] By 1363 the maintenance of the aqueduct and the fountain at its new terminus had been entrusted to officials of the secular branch of the city government.[49]

The retreat, as it were, of the Aqua Virgo from the Campus Martius effectively concludes the first phase in the history of the Fontana di Trevi. With the establishment of a modest fountain at the foot of the Quirinal Hill near the site of the present Fontana di Trevi the waters of the Aqua Virgo

Fig. 14. The Castellum Aquae Juliae, Gatteschi reconstruction, 1916

were diverted to serve new functions and to express different symbolic values. The form, the placement, and even the orientation of this fountain were determined in response to new needs rising from the changing aspect of Rome in the Middle Ages. The Aqua Virgo of the caesars gave way to the Acqua Vergine or Acqua di Trevi of the popes.

By the late fourteenth century, as a result of the barbarian incursions and the exile of the Papacy, Rome had shrunk to a population of only about 25,000, occupying a mere fraction of the area enclosed by the walls of the imperial capital.[50] The most densely populated part of the medieval city was the area of the Campus Martius, where narrow streets threaded their way around (and occasionally through) the shattered remains of antiquity, connecting the major churches and marketplace with the all-important bridgehead leading to the Vatican (fig. 15). While in antiquity the Campus Martius had been a new quarter of public monuments and parks set on the periphery of the city proper, in the course of the Middle Ages it had changed to become predominantly residential in character. Several reasons, most of them practical, explain this shift in Rome's center of gravity.

The political and religious heart of imperial Rome had been the Forum; the Rome of the Papacy, however, was more polycentric and focused upon fortified enclosures on the outskirts of the city, particularly the Vatican. It was natural, therefore, that the old Campus Martius, set into the bend of the Tiber and immediately adjacent to the sole surviving bridge leading to the Vatican, would provide a focus for the medieval city. The vicinity of the Tiber to this low-lying quarter also had another significance, for it ensured relatively easy access to a reliable source of water. Since the destruction of the ancient aqueducts which had served the elevated portions of the city, the hills remained for all practical purposes uninhabitable. From the tenth century onward Rome gradually expanded outward from its triangular core; hemmed in on two sides by the Tiber, the only direction in which it could expand was to the east across the ancient Via Lata, the main north–south axis of the city. The further one lived from the river, however, the more one relied upon the waters of the Trevi, conveniently situated on the eastern edge of the developing city. In commenting on the restoration of the Acqua Vergine, the biographer of Pope Hadrian I remarked that the water was "so abundant as to supply nearly the whole city," by which he certainly meant the densely populated Campus Martius.[51]

In antiquity, as we have seen, the Aqua Virgo had traversed the Campus Martius and eventually even crossed the Tiber, but following the fall of Rome and the resulting collapse of the arcades and canal system, the water could travel no farther west than the site of the present-day Fontana di Trevi. While the location of this medieval ancestor of the Trevi Fountain was in large part determined by the placement and ruined condition of the ancient aqueduct, this was not the only factor that exerted an influence on its siting. A second consideration was the network of streets that converged on the site. There is archaeological evidence that three of these, the modern Via delle Muratte, Via del Lavatore, and Via della Stamperia, closely follow the course of ancient Roman streets (fig. 11).[52] The intersection of these three streets, the *trivium* or *trivio*, ensured that it would be readily accessible from several directions.[53] Most of the traffic would have come from the populous Campo Marzio to the west, and that is why for nearly eight centuries, from its restoration under Hadrian I until its demolition under Urban VIII, the Trevi faced this direction.

The *trivium* of streets converging on the fountain most likely gave the Trevi its name.[54] Much ink has been spilled in an effort to clarify the etymology of the word *Trevi*, with no conclusive results.[55] The two most common alternate derivations for the name relate it to the three spouts of water issuing from the medieval fountain or to the *Rione Trevi*, the quarter in which the fountain is situated. In the seventeenth century an antiquarian went so far as to invent the name *Trivia* for the rustic maiden who led the Roman soldiers to the source of the Aqua Virgo, and then to identify her name with that of the fountain.[56] More recently, Cesare D'Onofrio has suggested that the name of the Trevi should be traced to a long-forgotten site, Castrum Trebani, situated in the general area of the source of the Acqua Vergine.[57] I am inclined, however, to favor the *trivium* of streets, or *tre vie*, as the source of the fountain's name, both because the Roman street pattern was a long-established fact and because it is a simpler, more straightforward explanation.

A suburb began to form around the Trevi Fountain quite early on, and by the middle of the tenth century several small churches had been established to serve the neighborhood. The area appears to have maintained a rustic character well into the thirteenth century, occupied predominantly by small, one-storied houses or cottages with gardens.[58] Most of the property between the Via del Corso and the slopes of the Quirinal was owned by the monasteries of S. Silvestro in Capite, S. Maria in Via Lata, and S. Ciriaco, all of which encouraged settlement of the area by the sale of small parcels of land. The clearest picture of the suburban development around the Trevi Fountain in the Middle Ages emerges from the records of these sales.[59] Two examples will suffice to convey the semirural character of the area: the first refers to a house sold in 1042, "with an apple orchard and access from the place called Trivio,"[60] the second to a lot at the north foot of the Quirinal described in 1217 as being located between two gardens and as containing vaults, perhaps ancient ones, on which there were several cottages and a garden.[61]

Another feature of the medieval quarter that grew up around the Trevi still survives. This is the portico standing opposite the present-day fountain, a characteristic example of structures that once were far more numerous (figs. 16, 17C). When the portico was built late in the thirteenth or early in the fourteenth century, it was open.[62] It continued to function as a sheltered extension of the piazza until it was filled in during the second half of the seventeenth century. This was a common fate of many porticoes, which were

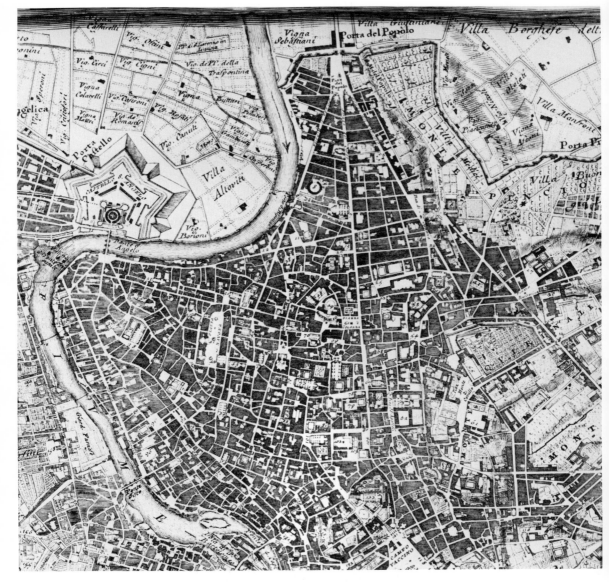

Fig. 15. Plan of the Campo Marzio, G. B. Nolli, 1748.
Piazza di Trevi: no. 54

systematically eliminated by successive popes because the dark recesses were thought to constitute a public nuisance.[63] Like other extant examples, this portico makes use of building materials despoiled from ancient monuments: granite columns and Ionic capitals of different sizes.[64] The abbreviated entablatures carried by the columns of the portico are set at different heights. This, together with the irregular spacing of the columns, produces a dissonant rhythm that is at odds with the symmetrical fenestration of the apartments above, the latter resulting from renovation work carried out in the first half of the seventeenth century. In the fourteenth century, just as today, the portico defined the southern boundary of the piazza, and an observer standing within it could have looked diagonally across to the east at the fountain, the principal attraction of the square (fig. 17).

The earliest representation of the Trevi Fountain, depicting its late medieval aspect, appears in a circular plan of Rome dating from 1414 and attributed to Taddeo di Bartolo.[65] The Trevi may be found below and to the left of center, just under the Dioscuri of the Quirinal (fig. 18, no. 48). This plan is typical of late medieval depictions of cities, which do not attempt to illustrate the precise topographical relationship of one feature to another but instead present the city iconically as a symbolic collection of marvels.[66] As a result of the conceptual attitude toward the representation of cities adopted in Taddeo di Bartolo's plan, which reflects a fourteenth-century prototype, it provides but scant information about the setting of the Trevi in its urban context. The fountain itself was evidently very simple in form, consisting of three polygonal basins set against a low wall from which the water issued in three separate streams. The wall, unrelieved by any ornament, appears to form one facet of a modest, four-square fountain house, or *castello*, which most

Fig. 16. Medieval portico on Piazza di Trevi

likely functioned as a final settling tank for the waters of the Acqua Vergine before they debouched into the basins of the medieval fountain. As depicted by Taddeo di Bartolo, the Trevi resembles a number of other late medieval and early Renaissance wall fountains in Italy and seems exceptional only in its apparent lack of ornament.[67] Little more than a generation after the me-

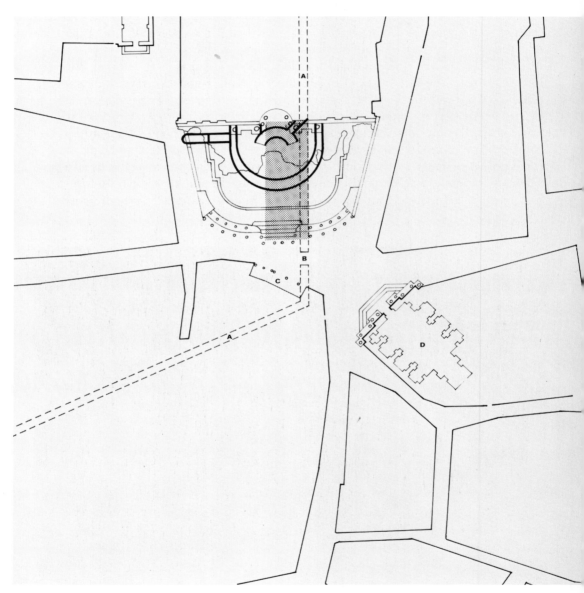

Fig. 17. Site plan of the Piazza di Trevi: (A) aqueduct of the Aqua Virgo; (B) arch of the Aqua Virgo; (C) medieval portico; (D) SS. Vincenzo e Anastasio. Trevi Fountain: stippled area: Alberti, 1453–1643; thick outline: Bernini, 1643–1732; thin outline: Salvi, 1732–1762.

Fig. 18. Depiction of Rome with representation of the Trevi, Taddeo di
Bartolo, 1414

dieval Trevi was painted by Taddeo di Bartolo, however, the fountain was
restored and embellished by Pope Nicholas V. This early Renaissance restoration constitutes the first of a long series of projects for the Trevi spanning
almost three centuries, and with it a new chapter in the history of the fountain
properly begins.

2

The Trevi from 1453 to 1730:
Urban Politics

The first of the Renaissance pontiffs to build on a large scale, Nicholas V (1447–55) initiated an ambitious program aimed at returning Rome to her former glory.[1] Advising the pope in planning for urban renewal, which included the laying out of new streets, the restoration of churches, and the erection of obelisks, was the great Renaissance humanist and architect Leon Battista Alberti. Part of the pope's program of public works, inspired by the accomplishments of the caesars, was the embellishment of the Trevi Fountain. As the terminus and principal urban display of the Acqua Vergine, the Trevi was renovated and adorned with inscriptions celebrating the restoration of the aqueduct by the pope in 1453.

Writing over a century later, the Florentine painter and biographer Giorgio Vasari recorded that Alberti, assisted by Bernardo Rossellino, was responsible for the alterations made to the Trevi:

> il pontefice col parere dell'uno di questi duoi, e coll' eseguire dell'altro, fece molte cose utili e degne di esser lodate: come furono il condotto dell'acqua Vergine, il quale essendo guasto, si racconciò; e si fece la fonte in sulla piazza de' Trievi, con quegli ornamenti di marmo che vi si veggiono, ne'quali sono l'arme di quel pontefice e del popolo romano.[2]

It is difficult to determine precisely the results of Alberti's intervention at the Trevi, for in clearing the piazza for a new fountain of his own design in 1643 Bernini demolished the Renaissance fountain. Unfortunately, the few surviving prints that depict Alberti's alterations to the Trevi are of only limited value. The earliest representation of the Trevi appears in Antonio Tempesta's plan of Rome, printed in 1593 (fig. 19). A comparison between the depictions of the Trevi by Taddeo di Bartolo and Tempesta suggests that Alberti's alterations were primarily cosmetic. An inscription and coat of arms have been applied to the formerly bare wall surface above the three openings through which the water streams, and where once there had been three separate basins, now there is a single large one. The relationship of the basin to the wall behind recalls Jacopo della Quercia's Fonte Gaia in Siena of 1409–19, perhaps the most important early Renaissance fountain design, and one which certainly was known to Alberti.[3]

Fig. 19. Detail of Antonio Tempesta's panoramic view of Rome, 1593,
showing the Trevi

A more detailed print representing the Trevi of Nicholas V dates from a
half century later than Tempesta's plan (fig. 20). This woodcut appears as a
small illustration accompanying a guidebook published by Giovanni Domenico
Franzini in 1643, the very year in which the Renaissance fountain was demolished by Gianlorenzo Bernini.[4] The inscription and escutcheons mentioned
by Vasari figure prominently in Franzini's print, but the wording of the
inscription differs substantially from an accurate transcription made while the
fountain still stood. Certainly very little in the fountain's appearance recalls
Alberti's architecture, for the classical orders are not employed and its pro-

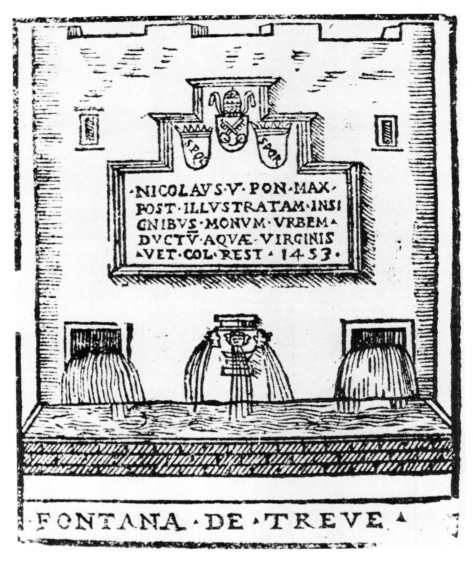

Fig. 20. The Trevi of Nicholas V, after Franzini, 1643

portions are far from harmonious. The Trevi's quattrocento aspect resides
principally in the bold Latin characters of the inscription, which may well
have constituted Alberti's primary concern.

Two different sources provide additional evidence regarding the arrangement of the inscription and heraldic devices which Alberti had placed on the
Trevi. The first of these is a fragmentary description of Rome written under
Pope Sixtus V (1585–90).[5] In addition to transcribing fully the inscription
of Nicholas V on the Trevi, the author observed that flanking the papal coat
of arms were two others, one of which bore the legend SPQR, presumably
to assert the role played by the city government in maintaining the fountain.[6]

The second source is an unexecuted project for the Trevi by an anonymous artist that was drawn during the pontificate of Clement VIII (1592–1605).[7] The draughtsman proposed incorporating the inscription and escutcheons of the old fountain in his new design, where they appear at the center (fig. 21). This arrangement confirms the general accuracy of Franzini's later rendering of these features and also establishes the continuity of the dual interest of the papal and secular branches of the city government in the fountain, a concern that was repeatedly expressed in designs for the Trevi. Other fountains in the Papal States display a similar arrangement and may reflect Alberti's design for the Trevi; one notable example is the Fonte Marcella in Assisi of 1556.[8]

As embellished by Nicholas V, the Fontana di Trevi conformed to a long tradition of architectural fountains set against mural backgrounds, as distinct from more sculptural, freestanding fountains. Ultimately this type of fountain design may be traced back to classical antiquity and to monumental examples like the Castellum Aquae Juliae (fig. 13). Not only the form of Alberti's Trevi, but its function as well may be related to the same tradition. Like the Castellum Aquae Juliae, the Trevi is the urban terminus of a long aqueduct, and as such it constitutes the main display, or *mostra*, of the water brought to Rome at great expense. With the addition of Alberti's inscription, the Trevi in effect became a celebration of Nicholas V's pastoral care for the city and an enduring memorial of his pontificate. Granted the expressive function of such fountains, it is no wonder that later elaborations of this particular fountain type came to allude to ancient triumphal arches in their designs. Prominent Roman examples are the Acqua Felice of Sixtus V (1587–88), the Acqua Paola of Paul V (1611–12), and, of course, the Fontana di Trevi as we see it today (figs. 22, 23).

While the effects of Nicholas V's renovation of the Fontana di Trevi endured for nearly two centuries, his restoration of the conduits supplying the fountain was shorter lived. Only twenty-two years later Pope Sixtus IV had the Acqua Vergine repaired again for the Holy Year of 1475, diverting funds from the city wine tax to help pay for the work.[9] The aqueduct continued to require attention throughout the sixteenth century, notably under Pius IV, but none of this maintenance affected the appearance of the fountain at its terminus.[10] The Acqua Vergine was the sole aqueduct supplying Rome throughout the Renaissance until Sixtus V conveyed the Acqua Felice to the city in 1587. During this period water from the Trevi was sold and transported all over the city.

In addition to the *trivium* of Roman origin, other streets converging on the fountain were laid out in the course of the fifteenth and sixteenth centuries, as can be seen in Bufalini's plan of 1551 and that by Dupérac and Lafréry dating to 1577 (figs. 24, 25). Both plans show the Trevi's location at the base of the Quirinal Hill on the periphery of the new houses occupying the eastern edge of the low-lying Campo Marzio. Indeed, in the sixteenth century one of the streets leading down to the fountain from the slopes of the Quirinal

Fig. 21. Unexecuted project for the Trevi drafted under Pope Clement VIII

Fig. 23. Fontana dell'Acqua Paola, 1611–12

Fig. 22. Fontana dell'Acqua Felice, 1587–88

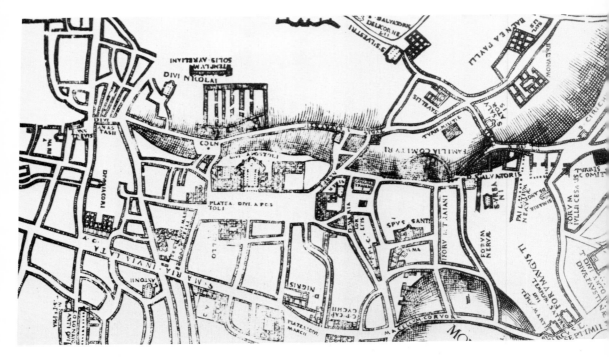

Fig. 24. Detail of Leonardo Bufalini's plan of Rome, 1551, showing the Trevi

was called "capo le case" (end of the houses), because at that time it marked the farthest extension of the city to the east. In Dupérac and Lafréry's plan this street is labeled and passes under an arch before entering the Piazza di Trevi. The arch, which was part of the arcade of the aqueduct of the Aqua Virgo, was demolished in 1617.

In the second half of the sixteenth century the pace of development around the Trevi Fountain quickened, partially in response to a new restoration of the Acqua Vergine undertaken between 1563 and 1570 by Giacomo della Porta.[11] As early as 1550 Baldovino del Monte, the brother of Pope Julius III, had begun to build his palace in the northwestern portion of the block stretching behind the present-day site of the Trevi (fig. 26A). Just a few years later, in 1566, his heirs sold this property to the city government, from whom it was acquired in the same year by Lelio dell' Anguillara, the duke of Ceri.[12] In 1573 Martino Longhi the Elder was hired by the duke to build a grand new palace incorporating that of Baldovino del Monte and extending to the south toward the Fontana di Trevi (fig. 26A, B, C). Construction proceeded slowly, and the long facade fronting on the Via di Poli was completed only after 1600 by Ottaviano Mascherino, who succeeded Longhi as architect following the latter's death around 1593.[13] The external appearance of the Palazzo Ceri is recorded by a seventeenth-century print which shows it to have been a characteristic example of late mannerist palace design.[14] Before its partial demolition in the nineteenth century, however, this palace would substantially affect Salvi's design for the Trevi Fountain, for its next owners, the dukes of Poli, extended it all the way to Piazza di Trevi.

At the same time the Palazzo Ceri was under construction, a second imposing family palace was erected on the eastern side of the same block, the two buildings being separated by the conduit of the Acqua Vergine, which divides the plot roughly in half (fig. 26F). This was the Palazzo Cornaro, the

Fig. 25. Detail of Dupérac–Lafréry plan of Rome, 1577, showing the Trevi

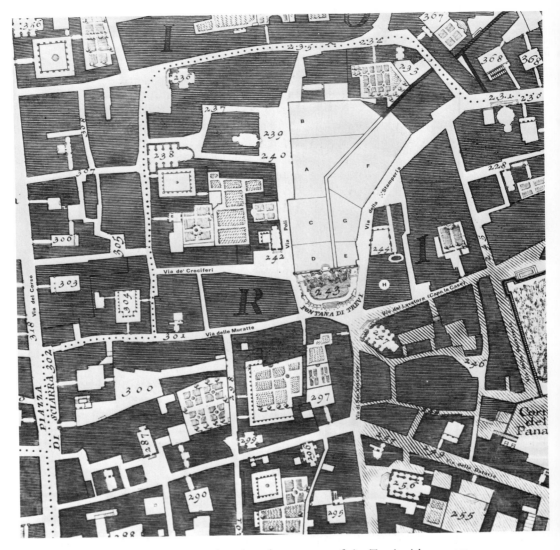

Fig. 26. Plan illustrating the urban context of the Trevi with property divisions, adapted from Nolli: (A) Palazzo Baldovino del Monte; (A,B,C) Palazzo Ceri; (A,B,C,D,E) Palazzo Poli; (D) Carpegna property; (E) Vitelleschi houses and Wool Guild; (F) Palazzo Cornaro; (F,G) Palazzo Pamphili/ Stamperia; (H) Palazzo Scavolini/Castellani.

present-day Palazzo della Stamperia, which was built in 1575 following the designs of Giacomo del Duca.[15] The same architect was also responsible for the renovation of a third building in the area, the church of S. Maria in Trivio, which fronts on the Piazza dei Crociferi and stands opposite the Palazzo Ceri–Poli (fig. 26, no. 242).[16] This modest church had been founded by Belisarius with the title of S. Maria in Xenodochio, but had come to be called S. Maria in Trivio, no doubt after the fountain and the region in which it is situated. By the sixteenth century it was badly in need of restoration. Work was carried out between 1570 and 1575 at the expense of the Cornaro family, for whom Giacomo del Duca was concurrently building a palace. Like the Ceri and Cornaro palaces, S. Maria in Trivio displays the characteristic late mannerist architectural forms derived from Michelangelo which prevailed in Rome during the last three decades of the sixteenth century. Together, these three buildings vitalized the neighborhood of the Piazza di Trevi and stimulated subsequent planning in the area.

The pattern of growth illustrated by this renewed building activity around the Trevi is also reflected in a ground plan of the area dating between 1561 and 1566 (fig. 27).[17] This drawing is probably the work of an anonymous draughtsman employed by the Maestri delle Strade, the city officials charged with maintaining the streets and approving new construction.[18] The plan seems motivated by two practical concerns: first, to make the Trevi more accessible through demolition work aimed at widening the piazza and adjacent streets, and second, to enlarge the fountain itself. Some of the clearing was accomplished, notably along the Via di Poli and the west side of the Piazza di Trevi, where the buildings to be removed are indicated on the plan by dotted lines. However, the more ambitious part of the proposal, which involved the expansion of the piazza to the north by knocking down the buildings on the site of the present-day Palazzo Poli, was not carried out. Neither was the thought of extending the fountain in this direction. Changes to the Trevi itself would have involved the construction of a disproportionately long and narrow basin set against the conduit of the Acqua Vergine and of a laundry basin to be set at a right angle to the fountain proper, neither of which would have enhanced the architectural distinction of the fountain. Here, as in many drawings made by the office of the Maestri delle Strade, practical concerns prevail over aesthetic ones.

Whatever may be said about the unsophisticated proposal for the Trevi set forth by the Maestri delle Strade, it did address the obvious need to embellish and bring up to date the fountain of Nicholas V, by then more than a century old. This desire is expressed in another anonymous project for the Trevi that dates from the pontificate of Clement VIII (1592–1605), a drawing that has already been discussed in relation to the escutcheon and inscription of Nicholas V, which it incorporates (fig. 21). Since it was first published by Egger in 1910, this project has been convincingly attributed to Giacomo Della Porta, who had been responsible for the restoration of the conduits of the Acqua Vergine in 1570 and who designed numerous other fountains in Rome.[19] While Della Porta's drawing depicts a wealth of late mannerist detail, much of it overwrought and fussy, the profusion of ornament does not obscure the fact that it was intended for the same site occupied by the old fountain. The back wall set against the conduit of the Acqua Vergine has been divided into seven bays of unequal dimensions, three of which project above the others to produce an animated silhouette. As with Alberti's fountain, the water rushes from three openings, corresponding to the larger bay units. Just as the spare, four-square simplicity of the old fountain elevation has been replaced in the

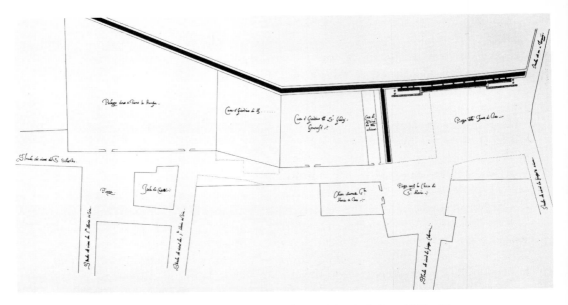

Fig. 27. Unexecuted project for the Trevi of circa 1561–66

drawing by more complex bay rhythms, so too has the simple rectangular basin of the Trevi been divided into a series of smaller linked basins of complex outline.

The principal sculptural figures in this design relate directly to the history of the Trevi and its associations with ancient Rome. Situated within the two outer end bays are identical reliefs of the Capitoline Wolf suckling Romulus and Remus. Within the two large bays flanking the center unicorns rest their heads on the lap of a seated maiden, clear references to the Acqua Vergine. In addition to the relics of the old fountain, the central bay contains a seated personification of Rome as well as an inscription and escutcheon honoring Pope Clement VIII. Set beneath the pediments of the two projecting bays to either side of center are other escutcheons, that of the city government on the left and that of Cardinal Pietro Aldobrandini on the right.[20] Other references to the Roman *comune*, the acronym SPQR, appear both on standards and isolated as inscriptions scattered throughout the fountain. This expression of civil authority is appropriate both for the Trevi, which was administered by the city, and for Giacomo Della Porta, who occupied the office of "architetto del popolo romano" until his death in 1602.[21]

Giacomo Della Porta's design for the Trevi was never realized, and this drawing stands as the first in a long series of unexecuted projects for the fountain which span more than a century. On the basis of style I am inclined to place the drawing late in Della Porta's career, and it may be that his death prevented the realization of his project.[22] In any event, the next important developments in the neighborhood of the Trevi were carried out under Pope Paul V Borghese (1605–21).

The pontificate of Paul V saw the construction of seventeen new fountains in Rome, not counting those erected within the Vatican.[23] The grandest of all was the monumental display of the Acqua Paola on the Janiculum, which celebrates the restoration of the ancient Aqua Traiana (fig. 23). Paul V was also concerned with improving access to the papal summer palace situated on the Quirinal Hill in a position overlooking the Fontana di Trevi. To this end he widened some of the existing streets in the neighborhood of the fountain and put through new ones as well. As part of this planning a project for embellishing the Trevi appears to have been drafted.

Both the fountain design and the new streets laid out under Paul V appear on the plan of Rome drawn by Giovanni Maggi and published in 1625 by Paolo Maupin (fig. 28).[24] No doubt in an effort to make his plan as up to date as possible, Maggi included features which were evidently in the planning stages when his wood blocks were being cut but which were never executed as they appear there.[25] The Trevi is one of these. To the right of the long facade of the recently completed Palazzo Ceri and situated on the site of the Trevi of Nicholas V is a large wall fountain of three bays crowned by an attic. As a type, it closely resembles the fountain of the Acqua Felice, which influenced the design of several fountains built under Paul V, most notably the Acqua Paola (fig. 22). Hints as to the possible authorship of this design emerge from an examination of the streets opened up under Paul V in the area of the Trevi.

In order to facilitate the passage of horse-drawn carriages between the Quirinal and the Vatican, as well as his family palace in the Campo Marzio, in 1610 Paul V began work on a long, straight street intended to connect the Quirinal Palace with the Piazza di Spagna (fig. 26).[26] Only the first stretch of this street, the modern Via della Panetteria, was actually put through; it appears clearly on the Maggi plan, aligned with the portal of the Cortile della Panetteria, just above and to the right of the Trevi. To provide access to the Quirinal from the Piazza Monte Cavallo the pope opened up the Via della Dataria, which also appears on the Maggi plan, aligned with the main portal of the palace. In order to allow traffic moving along these two new streets to pass smoothly through to the Via del Corso, between 1614 and 1617 Paul V widened the old street passing through the Piazza di Trevi, which today corresponds to the Via del Lavatore and Via delle Murtate. It was the demolition work involved in clearing this street that probably stimulated the project for the Trevi recorded on Maggi's plan.

The main bottleneck preventing smooth passage of traffic to and from the Via del Corso was the narrow arch of the Acqua Vergine that figures so prominently in the plans of Dupérac and Tempesta (figs. 25, 19). This arch sprang from the fountain of Nicholas V and its razing necessitated repairs on the Trevi (fig. 17B). A document of 1617 mentioning the Flemish architect Giovanni Vansanzio as supervising the repairs on the Trevi suggests that he was responsible for the design of the new fountain that appears in the Maggi plan.[27] This would not be surprising since Vansanzio specialized in the design of fountains and was particularly active under Paul V. However, like Giacomo Della Porta's earlier design, this project for the Trevi was not realized. The

Fig. 28. Detail of the Maggi-Maupin-Losi plan of Rome, 1625, showing the Trevi

new streets opened up by Paul V had a more lasting effect, however, for they established a direct relationship between the Trevi and the Quirinal, a relationship which was to be strengthened under the pontificate of Urban VIII Barberini (1623–44).

The first evidence of continued interest in the Trevi under Urban VIII is a drawing by an anonymous artist in the Albertina which obviously was designed for the site still occupied by the fountain of Nicholas V (fig. 29).[28] The iconography of the sculpture leaves no doubt that this is a project for the Trevi. Framed by the central arch is the maiden Trivia herself, who points out the water to which she led Agrippa's scouts. In the right-hand niche reclines a figure of Diana, whose virginity also alludes to the Acqua Vergine. Diana is balanced on the left by a figure of Hercules, very likely a reference to the Rivus Herculaneus that Pliny the Elder described as flowing near the source of the Acqua Vergine.[29] The principal display of water rushes forth from three openings, as in the fountain of Nicholas V, in this case from the mouths of three grotesque masks. A personification of Rome, accompanied by a group including the wolf suckling Romulus and Remus, crowns the central bay of the fountain.

The heraldic devices of the Barberini family are also scattered throughout the design. The arms of the pope figure prominently in a central pediment, which is flanked by the escutcheons of the two Barberini cardinals, Antonio and Francesco. In the frieze appear alternating metopes of bees and the solar disk as well as reliefs of laurel boughs, all three Barberini devices. Within the outer bays and set below the Barberini arms are escutcheons of the city authorities, repeating the theme first introduced in the fountain of Nicholas V.

On the basis of style Cesare D'Onofrio has related this drawing to the circle of Gianlorenzo Bernini.[30] While acknowledging Bernini's influence in certain details, notably the bee jetting water into a shell-shaped basin in the right foreground, I am inclined to attribute this drawing to an artist influenced by Pietro da Cortona. To my eye the treatment of the rustication and frieze is remarkably similar to Pietro da Cortona's portal of the Barberini gardens now set into the Quattro Fontane. In more general terms, the rustication and ornamental frames of the two lateral inscription plaques recall the work of mannerist architects working in Tuscany, particularly Ammannati and Buontalenti, both of whom influenced Pietro da Cortona. An artist associated with Cortona's studio and aware of Bernini's early fountain designs would be likely to produce such a drawing.

Bernini's direct involvement with the Trevi Fountain dates from 1629, when he was appointed architect of the Acqua Vergine.[31] As early as 1635 he appears to have drafted a plan to shift the fountain from its old site on the eastern side of the Piazza di Trevi to a new position on the northern side.[32] Only in 1640, however, did Bernini begin to intervene decisively in the history of the fountain. In a papal brief dated May 15 of that year, Urban VIII commanded that the Trevi be embellished with a new facade and authorized an initial expenditure of 6,000 scudi to this end.[33] In order to economize on the price of materials for the new fountain the pope also authorized the demolition of one of Rome's most celebrated antiquities, the

Fig. 29. Unexecuted project for the Trevi drafted under Pope Urban VIII

Tomb of Cecilia Metella on the Via Appia Antica. Urban VIII's willingness to despoil ancient monuments in order to use the material in constructing new edifices is consistent with his treatment of other antiquities. Fifteen years earlier Bernini had employed the bronze revetment from the portico of the Pantheon in casting the Baldacchino in Saint Peter's, an action that prompted the well-known epigram "Quod non fecerunt Barbari, fecerunt Barberini." (What the barbarians didn't do, the Barberini did). In the case of the Tomb of Cecilia Metella, however, those anxious to preserve the monument prevailed and Bernini's hand was stayed.[34]

Nothing, however, prevented Bernini from razing the fountain of Nicholas V, which had stood for almost two centuries. Moreover, between 1641 and 1643 many houses standing behind the site of the old fountain were razed so as to render Bernini's new monumental display visible from the Palazzo Quirinale.[35] Lieven Cruyl's print of 1667, made more than twenty-five years later, shows the effects of this demolition work (fig. 30). Bernini's semicircular basin at the left, occupying the site of the present-day Trevi, projects into the piazza, which has been substantially enlarged as a result of the removal of the old fountain (fig. 17). Between this basin and the imposing new facade of SS. Vincenzo e Anastasio is the vista opened up by Bernini's demolitions, linking the fountain in its new position to the Quirinal Palace, which projects above the church facade. While the pope's summer residence on the Quirinal would have enjoyed the best view of Bernini's fountain, Cruyl's *veduta* shows that it also would have been visible from the new Barberini family palace, silhouetted against the sky to the left of the Quirinal.

Bernini's reorientation of the Trevi was motivated by two related concerns. By demolishing the old fountain and shifting the new display to the north side of the square he not only enlarged the piazza but also obtained a much less restricted site on which to build a more monumental facade. In so doing he established a new relationship between the Trevi and its urban context, one which from this time onward shaped planning in the area. The Trevi no longer faced toward the growing Renaissance city but, as a result of Bernini's intervention, became linked to the most visible expression of papal authority in the area, the Quirinal Palace, which enjoyed a privileged view of the fountain (fig. 31). Unfortunately, in 1869 the vista created by Bernini was obstructed

Fig. 30. Lieven Cruyl, printed view of the Piazza di Trevi, 1667

Fig. 31. Detail of Giovanni Battista Falda's plan of Rome, 1676, showing the Trevi

when the Palazzo Castellani was erected on the site of the low shops defining the far side of the piazza as it appears in Cruyl's print (figs. 30, 26H).[36] However, from the *altana* of the Palazzo Quirinale it is still possible to see the attic of the Trevi projecting above the roofline of the Palazzo Castellani (fig. 32). Of course the view today is only partial, and we admire Salvi's fountain rather than Bernini's unexecuted design for the Trevi. Nonetheless, we see Bernini's intentions in the dynamic new relationship he established between these two monuments.

While Bernini's design for the Fontana di Trevi was never finished, as we have already seen he succeeded in shifting the fountain to the north side of the piazza and in laying the foundations for his monumental new display. The excavation of these foundations displaced a large amount of rubble that contributed to the existing slope of the piazza; a mound of earth is barely visible in early impressions of Giovanni Battista Falda's large plan of Rome. Between 1641 and 1643 Bernini approved numerous payments for work on the Trevi.[37] In 1645, following the death of Urban VIII, it was reported that in the last years of his pontificate the pope imposed a tax on those citizens owning property in the neighborhood of the Trevi in order to raise a sum of 30,000 scudi.[38] A tax on wine may also have provided funds for the Trevi, prompting the complaint expressed in another popular epigram: "Urban, poi che di tasse aggravò il vino, ricrea con l'acqua il popol di Quirino" (Urban taxes the wine and then seeks to amuse the Romans with water).[39] In any event, none of this considerable sum of money raised for completing the Trevi was actually spent on it, for the funds were diverted to military operations in the disastrous War of Castro undertaken in the last years of Urban's reign.[40]

What was the nature of Bernini's unexecuted project for the Trevi? Unfortunately, we can say very little about it, for none of Bernini's drawings for

Fig. 32. The Trevi viewed from the *altana* of the Quirinal Palace

the fountain has been identified, and the only written description of his design provides few specific details. However, Bernini's foundations for the Trevi survived until 1732, when they were destroyed by Nicola Salvi to make way for the present-day fountain, and they appear in a number of plans and views of the piazza.[41]

Lieven Cruyl's spirited *veduta* of 1667 representing the Piazza di Trevi clearly shows Bernini's concave foundation rising from the center of a semi-circular basin (fig. 30). A site plan of the piazza drawn by Carlo Fontana in 1706 shows the same feature as well as other important details (fig. 33). The water of the Acqua Vergine flowed directly from the aqueduct into the niche base, from which it exited in three streams, one at the center of the concavity and the other two symmetrically placed to either side. In the middle of the basin and below the water level was a circular base or platform. Behind the fountain proper a low wall separated the piazza from the undistinguished buildings belonging to the Carpegna family and the Wool Guild.[42]

On the basis of one document that refers to Bernini's project as a facade, it seems reasonable to speculate that he planned to construct a monumental wall fountain that would have covered the full extent of the northern side of the piazza.[43] The amount of money allocated for the construction of the fountain (36,000 scudi) also points toward a structure of monumental scale, for this figure far exceeds the entire sum expended on Bernini's Four Rivers Fountain during the reign of Urban's successor, Innocent X (29,760 scudi).[44] In very general terms, Bernini's design for the Trevi might be considered the forerunner of his second project for the east front of the Louvre, which, like it, would have been composed of a focal concavity flanked by two wings. From another source we also know that Bernini's design for the Trevi would have been embellished with sculpture. Federico Ubaldini, writing in 1653, relates that the sculptural ornament would have included a "statue of the Virgin and other beautiful friezes."[45] Ubaldini's passing reference to the sculptural component of Bernini's design does not make it clear whether it was the Virgin Mary or the Virgin Trivia who was represented, but granted the history and iconographical tradition of the fountain, the latter seems more likely.

A painting recently published by Cesare D'Onofrio sheds further light on the appearance of Bernini's project for the Fontana di Trevi (fig. 34).[46] Its provenance can be traced back to Bernini's first-born son, Pier Filippo, for in an inventory of his estate made in 1698 it appears as "un quadro rappresentante l'inventione della Fontana di Trevi."[47] The painting, attributed to Jan Miel, now hangs in the Rospigliosi Gallery.[48] The central sculptural group of the fountain depicted in the painting represents a seated virgin accompanied by a lamb, an obvious reference to the Acqua Vergine. The statue stands on top of a rustic base set within a curving niche, which is consistent with the foundations laid by Bernini for the Trevi. The escutcheon of Urban VIII in the tympanum that crowns the architectural enframement of the statue, as well as the bees scattered throughout the design, leaves no doubt that the

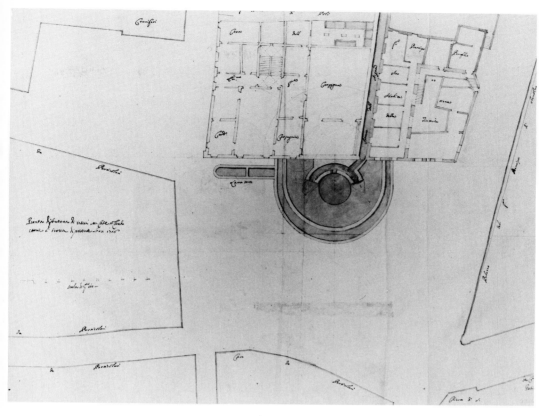

Fig. 33. Site plan of the Piazza di Trevi in 1706 by Carlo Fontana

fountain was commissioned by the Barberini pope, who appears in the foreground with the architect.

While it would be tempting to interpret the painting as an accurate copy
of Bernini's design for the Trevi, other elements suggest that at best it can
be considered only a distant reflection of it. In the first place, the style of both
the architecture and sculpture is static and altogether unlike Bernini's more
dynamic and sculptural approach to fountain design as manifested in contemporary works like the Fontana del Tritone. Indeed, the architectural enframement seems more appropriate for the stage than for the urban environment
of the Trevi. Moreover, the depiction of the fountain in a garden setting has
nothing to do with the realities of the site. While Jan Miel's painting brings
us closer to Bernini's design for the Trevi than does any other visual representation yet found, it seems clear that the artist took certain liberties in
interpreting the original project and as a result it is of only limited value in
reconstructing Bernini's intentions.

The death of Urban VIII and the failure of Bernini's project for the Trevi
meant that for almost a century the fountain remained unfinished, its undistinguished appearance stimulating the imaginations of successive popes and

Fig. 34. Jan Miel, painting of the Trevi incorporating aspects of Bernini's design

generations of artists, all of whom wanted to build a monumental display that would both be worthy of the site and would express the water's importance to Rome. While the appearance of the fountain did not change until 1732, shortly after Bernini's demolition work the Piazza di Trevi was embellished by the construction of an imposing new facade for SS. Vincenzo e Anastasio. In fact, it was the demolition work carried out by Bernini that made it possible for Cardinal Mazarin to move his titular church to a new site closer to the fountain.[49] As a result of Bernini's reorientation of the Trevi and his clearing away of the houses along the eastern side of the piazza to open up the vista to the Quirinal, it became possible to move the church to a position of greater prominence, one in which it would relate to the Fontana di Trevi.

The old church of SS. Vincenzo e Anastasio, which stood farther back from the Piazza di Trevi, had no visual connection with the fountain.[50] Urban VIII authorized the construction of the new church in 1640, the same year Bernini began work on the Trevi, which suggests that there may well have been a comprehensive plan for the development of the area.[51] The facade of SS. Vincenzo e Anastasio, which was built between 1646 and 1650 following the design of Martino Longhi the Younger, was certainly conceived as a visual foil to Bernini's Trevi.[52] Giovanni Battista Falda's print of 1665 clearly illustrates the way in which Longhi's spectacular Baroque facade faces diagonally across the piazza toward the fountain while also anchoring the vista up to the Quirinal (fig. 35).[53] Longhi's facade brilliantly places the escutcheon of Cardinal Mazarin, who became prime minister of France in 1643, in a direct visual relationship with the seat of papal power on the Quirinal as well as with the *stemma* of Urban VIII that in all likelihood constituted the crowning feature of the Trevi as projected by Bernini. The nonaxial relationship between church and fountain, which encourages more dynamic oblique viewpoints of both monuments, is a characteristic example of Baroque planning. So, too, is the way in which Longhi's facade relates to the street leading from the Via del Corso to the Quirinal, for its diagonal placement relative to traffic approaching the papal palace ensures its visibility. The facade projects beyond the property owned by the church to occupy part of the converging streets as well, emphasizing its prominence. A site plan accompanying the license of 1646 granting permission to build on two narrow strips of public land clearly illustrates Cardinal Mazarin's desire to secure the most favorable position possible for the new facade (fig. 36).[54] Today the dialogue between the facade of SS. Vincenzo e Anastasio and the Fontana di Trevi as built by Nicola Salvi constitutes one of the most eloquent examples of Baroque planning in Rome; the monuments appear to call and to answer one another, creating a visual counterpoint across the resonant space of the piazza that is metaphorically expressed by the pairs of trumpeting Fames perched atop the two facades (fig. 37).

While Bernini's intervention at the Trevi under Urban VIII had important long-term consequences for the history of the fountain, the short-term effects of his work there were decidedly negative. Bernini's next great fountain design, the Fontana dei Quattro Fiumi in Piazza Navona, commissioned by Urban's successor, Innocent X Pamfili, further detracted from the appearance and importance of the Trevi. The main reason for this concerns the water supplying the Four Rivers Fountain—the Acqua Vergine—which was taken from the Trevi. As a result, following its completion in 1651, the Four Rivers Fountain effectively replaced the Trevi as the principal display of the Acqua Vergine

Fig. 35. Print of the Piazza di Trevi with SS. Vincenzo e Anastasio, 1665, after Falda,
Il terzo libro

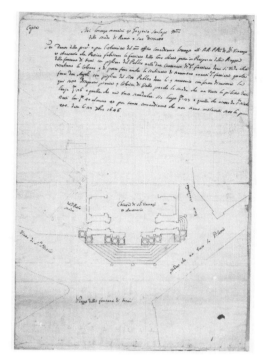

Fig. 36. Site plan of SS. Vincenzo e
Anastasio, 1646, illustrating its
encroachment on the public street

for close to a century. Innocent X, who at every opportunity endeavored to disassociate himself from the Barberini, did not content himself merely with neglecting their plans for the Trevi; he also substantially diminished the amount of water that issued from the Trevi, employing it instead for the aggrandizement of his own family name. Throughout history, and especially in Rome, water has repeatedly been used to express the munificence and power of rulers, both secular and spiritual. The long history of the Acqua Vergine, of all Rome's waters, provides the most vivid illustration of this practice.

If Innocent X's tapping of the Acqua Vergine to adorn his own dynastic monument had a negative impact on the history of the Trevi, Bernini's design for the Four Rivers Fountain exerted a powerful influence on subsequent projects for the Fontana di Trevi, including Nicola Salvi's executed design of 1732 (fig. 38). As is the case at the Trevi, the level of the Acqua Vergine at Piazza Navona is not very high above the ground. This meant that Bernini's fountain, if it were to provide a focal point for the piazza and the building surrounding it, had to attain a monumental scale through the use of large sculptural and architectural elements. This, of course, was brilliantly realized through the placement of a tall, projecting obelisk on top of an elevated rustic base. In the course of the next century many of the architects who drafted projects for the Trevi proposed to erect an ancient obelisk or column above the display of water.

Bernini's naturalistic treatment of the base of the Four Rivers Fountain is

Veduta della vasta Fontana di Trevi anticamente detta l'Acqua Vergine
Architettura di Nicola Salvi.

Fig. 37. Piranesi *veduta* illustrating the relationship between the Trevi and
SS. Vincenzo e Anastasio

also reflected in the Trevi as it appears today. Like Bernini, Salvi used quarried blocks of travertine for the base of the Trevi which then were finished in place in imitation of natural rock formations laid bare and shaped by the action of water. Both artists introduced effects of transparency together with countless details of flora and fauna. Indeed, if the rustic base of Bernini's freestanding Four Rivers Fountain were somehow to be unfolded and set up against a wall the relationship between the two designs would be even more apparent. Finally, the range of water effects employed by Bernini in the Four Rivers Fountain—from slender jets to broad sheets and conchlike sprays—was unsurpassed until the completion of Salvi's design for the Fontana di Trevi.

Innocent X's use of the Acqua Vergine at Piazza Navona to glorify his reign and family no doubt stimulated his successor, Alexander VII Chigi, to do likewise. The dynastic center of the Chigi family was located at the Piazza Colonna, not far from the Fontana di Trevi (fig. 15). The old Palazzo Aldobrandini occupying the north side of the piazza was acquired by the Chigi in 1659 and enlarged by Felice Della Greca between 1661 and 1665.[55] Following the removal of a block of houses separating the new family palace from

Fig. 38. Gianlorenzo Bernini's Fountain of the Four Rivers, 1648–51

the Column of Marcus Aurelius, the Palazzo Chigi dominated an ample piazza. The western side of the square facing the Via del Corso was occupied by a modest church and monastery belonging to the Barnabite Order. Around 1659, at the pope's request, Pietro da Cortona prepared designs for a monumental display of the Acqua Vergine to be situated on the western side of Piazza Colonna on the site of the property owned by the Barnabites.[56] Had Cortona's designs been executed, the site of the Trevi Fountain would have been moved from the Piazza di Trevi to the Piazza Colonna.

Of all the unexecuted projects for the Fontana di Trevi, Cortona's drawings, which are preserved among the Chigi papers in the Vatican Library, are unquestionably the most inspired and impressive (figs. 39, 40).[57] His design imaginatively fuses two forms which had never before been united: an imposing palace facade and a monumental fountain. In the grandest of Cortona's designs, the palace was to have been raised on top of a one-story-high rusticated basement. Rising from this level, a colossal order of engaged Tuscan columns would have bound together two additional stories. The considerable horizontal expanse of Cortona's facade was given a powerful central accent by the placement of a triumphal arch motif in the middle of its focal concavity, which would have framed a vista through to the Piazza Montecitorio behind. Set

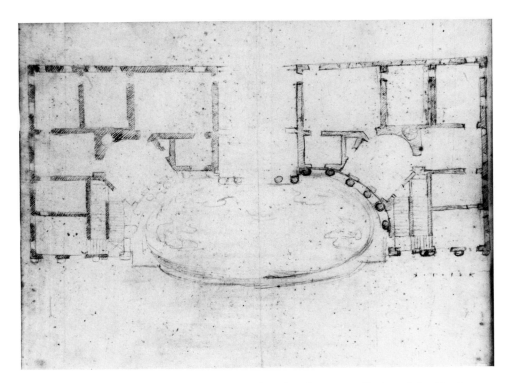

Fig. 39. Pietro da Cortona's unexecuted project for a new display of the Trevi at Piazza Colonna, plan

Fig. 40. Pietro da Cortona's unexecuted project for a new display of the Trevi
at Piazza Colonna, elevation

into this concavity at the level of the basement is the fountain proper, the
convex basin of which would have projected out into the piazza from the plane
of the flanking wings. Silhouetted against the embracing curve of the rustic
basement appears an abundance of statuary, including two reclining river
gods. Cortona's design for the Trevi recalls the crowning exedra in his reconstruction of the Sanctuary of Fortuna Primigenia at Palestrina, the ancient
monument that more than any other directed his approach to architecture.[58]

While Pietro da Cortona's ambitious project for the Trevi was never executed, I believe that it may have been known to Nicola Salvi and may possibly
have affected his design for the fountain. Cortona's fusion of palace and fountain
into a highly sculptural and monomorphic unity prefigures Salvi's solution of
seventy years later. So, too, does his use of a triadic composition and a colossal
order to unify the expansive facade. Even the sculpture above the naturalistic
rock masses set against the rusticated basement anticipates Salvi's design. Had
Cortona's project been executed, it would have replaced the old Fontana di
Trevi as the definitive display of the Acqua Vergine and inseparably linked
the name of Alexander VII and his family with the most grandiose fountain
design of the seventeenth century.

Throughout his pontificate, Alexander VII continued to experiment with different ways in which to embellish the Piazza Colonna with the waters of the Trevi. The pope kept a wooden model of Rome in his apartment in the Vatican, and many of his proposals for urban renewal appear to reflect his own personal approach to planning: the movement of major monuments from one point of the city to another as if they were small, detachable pieces on a model, with little regard for the feats of engineering involved.[59] Thus, in 1662 the pope considered moving the colossal statue of a river god known popularly as Marforio from the Campidoglio to Piazza Colonna and replacing it with the fountain by Giacomo Della Porta that stood in the piazza between the Column of Marcus Aurelius and the Via del Corso.[60] The statue of Marforio could have figured in the sculptural program of Pietro da Cortona's project for the Trevi, which, as we have seen, included two reclining river gods of enormous scale. Four years later, in 1666, Alexander VII wrote of moving Della Porta's fountain to Piazza Santi Apostoli,[61] and in 1667, the year of his death, he commented again on the possibility of moving the display of the Fontana di Trevi to the Piazza Colonna.[62]

The last of these remarks may well refer to a fantastic project by Bernini to move the Column of Trajan to Piazza Colonna. Not satisfied with this virtuoso feat of engineering, Bernini also proposed to place two fountains at the bases of the columns, the water of which would flood the entire square.[63] Bernini is known to have presented a drawing of his project for the Trevi to Alexander VII, who in turn gave it to Cardinal Jacopo Filippo Nini of Siena.[64] Unfortunately Bernini's drawing of this spectacular project has not been identified.[65]

With the death of Alexander VII in 1667 came the end of large-scale architectural patronage in Rome. The papal treasury was empty, trade stagnated, and in spite of sporadic efforts at fiscal reform the economy did not achieve a measure of stability until the pontificate of Clement XI Albani (1700–21). Largely as a result of these depressed economic conditions no work was carried out on the Trevi during the remaining years of the seventeenth century, although Pope Alexander VIII (1689–91) is known to have commissioned a design for the completion of the fountain.[66] In the course of the first three decades of the eighteenth century the Trevi continued to be neglected, and the piazza and fountain continued to appear much as they had in the mid-seventeenth-century views of Cruyl and Falda. This can be seen in a painted view of the Piazza di Trevi dating from around 1710 (fig. 41). The only visible change concerns the placement of the three streams of water issuing from Bernini's foundations, which were raised about three feet in the course of restoration work carried out on the aqueduct and fountain under Clement XI in 1708.[67]

While the situation on the site remained static until 1728, architects continued to make designs for embellishing the Trevi. Under the pontificate of Innocent XIII Conti (1721–24), however, important developments con-

Fig. 41. Painted view of the Piazza di Trevi of circa 1710 in the Museo di Roma

cerning the property immediately behind the site of the Trevi were set in motion. While these did not immediately alter the appearance of the fountain itself, they played a crucial role in the competition of 1730 and in Nicola Salvi's executed design. Moreover, the relationship between the Palazzo Poli and the Fontana di Trevi illustrates an important dimension of the Trevi's urban context and underscores the dynamic role played by conflicting public and private interests in its history.

In 1678 the powerful dukes of Poli, who were the secular lords of Innocent XIII's family, acquired the Palazzo Ceri, which, as we have seen, was set back a short distance behind the present site of the Trevi Fountain.[68] As early as 1721 the pope apparently initiated a project to add a new wing to the Palazzo Ceri, now rechristened the Palazzo Poli, which would front on the Piazza di Trevi.[69] Between 1722 and 1723, no doubt expedited by his brother the pope, Duke Stefano Conti purchased the properties separating the family palace from the fountain.[70] A survey drawing of 1728 clearly shows the situation on the site: between the Palazzo Poli and the Fontana di Trevi stand the houses and shops acquired from the Carpegna family, while on the other side of the conduit of the Acqua Vergine and also fronting on the Piazza di Trevi are the buildings purchased from the Wool Guild (figs. 42, 26D, E).

Once the Conti had acquired the land separating their palace from the Trevi Fountain both the conditions on the site and the family's interests favored a design that would allow the new palace facade to expand on both sides of the Trevi, while limiting the fountain proper to a restricted area at the center of the facade. The pope also contemplated demolishing all the old buildings fronting on the Piazza di Trevi and replacing them with apartments for the

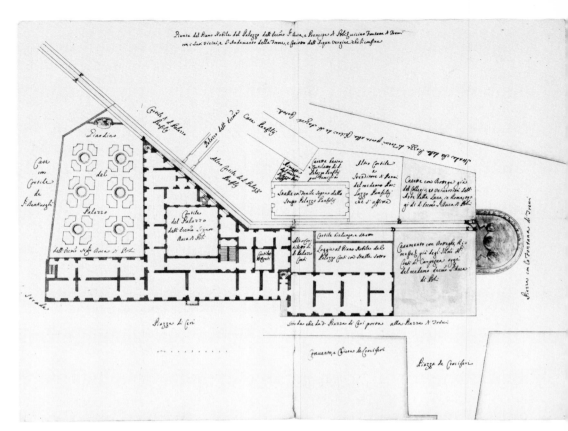

Fig. 42. Site plan of the area behind the Trevi in 1728

papal *famiglia*.[71] Neither of these projects was accomplished during the brief reign of Innocent XIII, however, and the family was unable to obtain authorization to begin construction on the new wing until 1728.[72]

Following the authorization granted by Pope Benedict XIII on July 9, 1728, work proceeded rapidly on the new facade of the Palazzo Poli. By 1730[73] it was virtually complete. Because of the unique character of the site and the restrictions stipulated in the building license, the design of the new facade departed from accepted Roman practice. Rather than a block of uniform height, it was composed of two symmetrical wings—corresponding to the newly acquired properties on either side of the conduit of the Acqua Vergine— which flanked a recessed center where the fountain was situated. Several unexecuted projects for the Trevi made in 1730 depict the facade of the Palazzo Poli before it was covered over by Nicola Salvi's fountain. One of these clearly shows the awkward proportions of the new facade (fig. 43), which justly merited the criticism of Edme Bouchardon, who described it as "d'une architecture qui est très médiocre."[74]

The two wings of the Palazzo Poli, each four bays wide, rise three stories and are crowned by a low attic. Set between the two wings is a recessed central element three bays wide, terminating in a balustrade. In place of the unexecuted project for the Trevi which occupies the center of the drawing, in actuality one would have seen only the foundations of Bernini's fountain set against a blank wall. Architectural ornament is used sparingly on this facade, which is not unified by a system of colossal columns and pilasters, as is the case today. The only notable ornamental features are the large triglyphs which appear to hang from the cornice; below the triglyphs are tapering, hermlike pilasters.

Not only was the facade of the Palazzo Poli actually built, but both in its structure and ornamental details it survives to this day, hidden behind the mass of Salvi's fountain. Before erecting the fountain in front of the palace facade, Salvi had the salvageable materials (the travertine used for the string courses and window frames, and the wrought iron balconies) removed.[75] Having no intrinsic value, however, the stucco ornament remained. Recent renovation work carried out in the Palazzo Poli has revealed some of these details, including the triglyphs, now visible in the narrow crawl spaces which, at intervals, separate Salvi's fountain facade from that of the palace (fig. 44).[76]

At the same time that construction began on the new facade of the Palazzo Poli, steps were taken to build a suitable display for the Fontana di Trevi that would form its centerpiece.[77] Work was begun on the Trevi under Innocent XIII's successor, Pope Benedict XIII (1724–30), following the designs of Paolo Benaglia. Construction had not proceeded very far, however, when

Fig. 43. Unexecuted project for the Trevi of circa 1730 showing the facade of
the Palazzo Poli

Benedict XIII died, with the result that Benaglia's design was subjected to review by the new pope, Clement XII Corsini, and found wanting. By this time, of course, the new facade of the Palazzo Poli dominated the Piazza di Trevi, accentuating the need to bring the fountain to completion. For the Conti the unfinished fountain undoubtedly constituted an acute embarrassment, since in place of a magnificent display crowned by the family's arms, there was an unseemly gap at the center of the new facade.

In halting work on Benaglia's project for the Trevi Clement XII appears to have been motivated by both aesthetic and political concerns. In general, the architectural projects undertaken by Benedict XIII and the artists he favored were criticized harshly by the Roman public, and this is particularly true of Benaglia's design for the Trevi. Moreover, in reaction to the emphasis placed on atectonic surface decoration by Filippo Raguzzini, Benedict XIII's favored architect, the Corsini pope preferred a form of monumental Baroque classicism stressing the sculptural play of large masses, as can readily be seen in the two great edifices built in his reign: the facade of the Lateran Basilica and the Fontana di Trevi. Much as Innocent X had disassociated himself from the policies and projects of Urban VIII, Clement XII desired to distance himself politically from his unpopular predecessor, whose reign was notoriously corrupt. It is no coincidence that Monsignor Jacopo Sardini, the official responsible for supervising Rome's water supply and work on the Trevi under Benedict XIII, was brought to trial and condemned to prison under Clement XII. The Corsini pope was also unwilling to have the escutcheon of the Conti family crown the Trevi, for although the fountain was set into the facade of their palace, its waters remained within the jurisdiction of the pope and his appointed city officials. The monumental display of the Trevi, it was thought, should express the munificence of the ruling pontiff and his care for the public good, rather than the private interests of a single noble family.

This conflict of public and private interests complicated the competition of 1730 organized by Clement XII for the purpose of obtaining a new design for the Trevi more to his liking and continued to inhibit Nicola Salvi in executing his winning design even after 1732. The architects participating in the competition all had to work within the considerable restrictions imposed by the facade of the Palazzo Poli. So long as the fountain was confined within the narrow space defined by the two ill-proportioned wings of the facade, it could not fail to appear like a chimera, an awkward and inorganic imposition of one form upon another. On the other hand, the Conti vigorously objected to any design which would do violence to the facade of their family palace. For a while a standoff resulted, and the projects submitted in the competition of 1730 came to naught. Then, with his directive of 1732 authorizing the fountain to occupy the entire breadth of the palace facade, the pope boldly cut the knot.[78] The result was Nicola Salvi's executed design for the Trevi, which adroitly fused palace and fountain (fig. 45).

Fig. 44. Triglyph on the facade of the Palazzo Poli visible
behind Salvi's fountain

In order to unify the two major components of his design, Salvi applied a
single colossal order of Corinthian columns and pilasters to both. He also
inverted the proportional relationship of the palace wings to the fountain,
giving predominance to the latter. Instead of taller palace pavilions four bays
wide flanking a narrow fountain only three bays in width, Salvi incorporated
one bay of each wing into the fountain and projected its crowning attic above
the twin pavilions. Naturally, this resulted in considerable nuisance to the
Conti family, who lost the light admitted by four windows, which Salvi's
expanded fountain blocked out. Moreover, so successful was Salvi in unifying
his design for the Trevi that few observers standing in the piazza ever realize
that they are looking at anything other than a monumental fountain. No
doubt most galling to the Conti was the fact that the new wing of their family

Fig. 45. Nicola Salvi's winning design for the Fontana di Trevi, Museo di Roma

palace, masked and for all practical purposes visually obliterated by Salvi's fountain, was crowned by the escutcheon of the Corsini pope, whose power had prevailed over their own. Clement XII, through his forceful will, and Salvi, through his bold, unifying project, together initiated the next phase in the long history of the Trevi, a story that admirably illustrates how the twin pressures of urban development and the desire to give concrete expression to political authority may combine to influence architectural design.

3

Unexecuted Projects for the Trevi Fountain, 1700–1730

Urban VIII's decision to abandon Bernini's project for the Trevi Fountain, coupled with his papal successors' disinterest in completing it, meant that for more than half a century the principal display of the Acqua Vergine languished, presenting a singularly undistinguished appearance to Romans and foreign visitors alike. Throughout this period, however, Bernini's massive foundations posed a tantalizing challenge to several generations of architects whose fondest dream would have been to construct a grand fountain worthy of the Acqua Vergine and its secular tradition. Not surprisingly, therefore, while relatively little transpired on the site, numerous projects for the embellishment of the Trevi were drafted in the first three decades of the eighteenth century. The vitality of the Trevi, its remarkable potential to stimulate the creative imaginations of artists and patrons, found graphic expression in an unparalleled series of unexecuted projects, including designs by some of the most accomplished Late Baroque architects and sculptors.

By far the most numerous and varied projects date from the first two decades of the eighteenth century, during the pontificate of Pope Clement XI Albani (1700–21). Other designs continued to be drafted during the reigns of Clement's successors Innocent XIII and Benedict XIII, until the election of Clement XII Corsini in 1730, when a competition was organized that ultimately resulted in the selection of Nicola Salvi's executed design. While none of these earlier proposals was actually built, they show that interest in the Trevi never died out and that architects continued to experiment with solutions to the complex problems posed by the site. These unexecuted projects, many of which exist only in fragmentary form and as two-dimensional graphic images, are nonetheless worthy of study in their own right, as much for what they reveal about the history of fountain design as for what they contribute to our understanding of the Trevi Fountain and its architectural evolution.

Clement XI was by nature inclined to be an active patron of the arts, which is perhaps best illustrated by his institution in 1702 of yearly artistic competitions, the *Concorsi Clementini*, for members of the Academy of Saint Luke.[1] Many new buildings and renovations were also undertaken by Clement XI. Prominent among these were utilitarian structures incorporating ancient monuments into their designs. The pope's desire to embellish Rome, his interest in rededicating Roman antiquities to Christian use, and his special concern for functional designs are all admirably illustrated by the projects for the Fontana di Trevi that were drafted during his reign.

Perhaps the first eighteenth-century project for the Trevi is an anonymous sheet in the Berlin Kunstbibliothek depicting a sculptural group of Neptune and Tritons set before a colonnade (fig. 46).[2] Paired Tuscan columns frame the central portion of the colonnade, which is set back and crowned by a blank papal escutcheon. An inscription in the frieze indicates that this project entails raising the water level of the Acqua Vergine twenty *palmi* (4.46 meters) and includes the date 1700 in Roman numerals.[3] The colonnade provides a link between two wings, which are elevated an extra story in height. The draughtsman appears to have included two different proposals for the design of these wings, for that on the left shows fenestration appropriate to a palace facade, while that on the right shows a continuation of the colonnade. A statue of a female figure stands before the right-hand wing, perhaps a representation of the Roman maiden Trivia, who figures in many of the unexecuted projects for the Trevi as well as on Salvi's fountain.

Worthy of special note is the way in which both the main sculptural group, placed on a miniature island rising out of the basin in the foreground, and the colonnade, set behind and above this group, relate to an extension of the fountain behind the open portico. A spectacular cascade plunges nearly fifteen feet to the level of the colonnade before falling again into the basin of the fountain proper. The architect's scale at the bottom of the sheet allows us to measure the precipitous drop of the first cascade to the rear of the colonnade: its height corresponds precisely to the twenty *palmi* given in the inscription above. The scenographic role of this colonnade, which frames an axial vista developing behind the statuary in the foreground, has been discussed by Hellmut Hager, who argues convincingly that the sources for this composition are to be sought in seventeenth-century architecture and especially in theater designs of the period.[4]

In order to realize the most important feature of this design, the cascade, it would have been necessary to raise the level of the Acqua Vergine quite substantially. Since the difference in level between the source of the Acqua Vergine at Salone and its outlet at the Trevi is very slight, the proposal to elevate the water level at the Trevi nearly four and a half meters could not have been undertaken without major engineering work on the conduits that supply the fountain. Such an endeavor would be costly and time-consuming and could not be undertaken casually. Thus any design for the Trevi incorporating a dramatic rise in level would most likely have been prepared only after it was known that the necessary hydraulic engineering was to occur.

In 1706, early in the pontificate of Clement XI, work began on a thorough restoration of the conduits supplying the Trevi.[5] When the project was completed in 1708 the level of the Acqua Vergine had been elevated four *palmi*

Fig. 46. Unexecuted project for the Trevi, circa 1706–08, here attributed to
Carlo Bizzacheri

(.89 meters), only a fifth of the height mentioned in the inscription on the anonymous project but nonetheless a substantial increment.[6] The inscription poses more questions than it answers, however. It is rather crudely rendered and may well be an addition by another hand. Moreover, the placement of the date is such that one must allow for the possibility that it is incomplete, with additional characters continuing around the corner of the projecting pylon entablature, as it breaks back to meet the colonnade.

Since neither the inscription nor the empty *stemma* furnishes information that securely dates this project, art historians have naturally employed the analysis of style in an effort to provide an attribution for it. Their conclusions have differed widely, however, ranging from the two artists responsible for the design of the present-day Fontana di Trevi, Nicola Salvi[7] and Giovanni Battista Maini,[8] to the direct heirs of Gianlorenzo Bernini's architectural studio, Carlo Fontana[9] and Mattia De Rossi.[10]

In my opinion the Berlin drawing is the work of a follower of Carlo Fontana, rather than of Bernini, and its author should be sought among a younger generation of architects trained in Fontana's studio. Of Fontana's numerous pupils, one in particular seems to be a likely candidate: Carlo Francesco Bizzacheri (1656–1721).[11] Bizzacheri's long, active career began in the last two decades of the seventeenth century and extended through the first two decades of the eighteenth century, coinciding exactly with the pontificate of Clement XI. His works include a fountain, that of the Tritons in front of S. Maria in Cosmedin, which was executed between 1717 and 1719.[12] The pyramidal base of this fountain, composed of rustic *scogli*, and the Tritons that rise from it are similar to their counterparts in the Berlin drawing. Like the sculptural component of the Berlin project, Bizzacheri's fountain is inspired by Berninesque precedents, in particular the Fontana del Tritone. However, Bizzacheri's executed fountain, as well as the Berlin project, is more loosely structured and appears to be a composite image, in sharp contrast to the organic unity of Bernini's composition.

While the evidence is not conclusive, I am inclined to date the Berlin drawing around 1706–08 and to associate it with the renovation of the Acqua Vergine carried out under Clement XI at this time. If I am correct and Bizzacheri is indeed responsible for the Trevi project, the sculptural component of his design may be seen as an anticipation of the Tritons Fountain he would build a decade later. In any event, the Berlin project itself anticipates several concerns that would continue to preoccupy architects seeking to adorn the Trevi until the completion of the actual fountain in 1762. Three issues in particular—the relationship between sculpture and architecture, the possibility of opening up a vista behind the fountain proper, and the need to raise the level of the water—were taken up repeatedly in the course of the next three decades.

The earliest securely dated eighteenth-century projects for the Trevi Fountain are by Bernardo Borromini (1647–1709),[13] the nephew of the great seventeenth-century architect Francesco Borromini.[14] The first of these, dated 1701, represents a rather bizarre three-story facade elevation with plans and molding profiles sketched in awkwardly both above and below (fig. 47). An inscription just above the roofline makes it clear that this proposal relates to the Trevi.[15] While Bernardo's draughtsmanship is awkward to say the least, and his inventiveness undistinguished to an extreme, this project displays a number of features that relate it both to earlier seventeenth-century designs and to later eighteenth-century projects for the Trevi.

Most interesting is the fusion of palace facade and fountain basin, and in particular the concave center of this fountain house, as it may truly be called.

Fig. 47. Bernardo Borromini, unexecuted project for
the Trevi, 1701

Fig. 48. Bernardo Borromini, unexecuted project for the Trevi, 1704

The placement of the fountain and its sculptural ornament at the center of this concavity, below a triumphal arch motif, may reflect Pietro da Cortona's project for a display of the Trevi in Piazza Colonna (figs. 39, 40). The fusion of palace facade and fountain, of course, also characterizes the Trevi Fountain as it was actually built by Nicola Salvi, and the use of a concave facade characterizes a number of other early eighteenth-century projects that we will shortly discuss.

The decorative program of Borromini's design is not particularly complex or sophisticated. At the center, framed by the triumphal arch motif, is a seated statue personifying Rome. To the left is a statue of Hercules, perhaps signifying *Roma Profana*, while to the right is a statue of a monk, possibly representing *Roma Sacra*. Below, we are in the realm of monstrous beasts, tritons with double fishtails, and a lion looking like an unhappy refugee from Bernini's Fountain of the Four Rivers. Above, Rome is alluded to a second time by the Capitoline Wolf with Romulus and Remus posed awkwardly below a martial trophy. The conscious parallel of classical and Christian themes in Borromini's project is significant, for it appears in a number of subsequent designs.

A second project by Bernardo Borromini, dated 1704, shares a number of features with the first (fig. 48). The concave facade is present, albeit in a

much restricted form, and recalls rather more Francesco Borromini's Sant'Agnese
than Pietro da Cortona's Trevi designs.[16] Gone, however, is the fusion of
palace and fountain; the function of the structure behind the fountain is entirely
subordinate to its role as an architectural setting for the display of water and
sculpture. In the sculpture of the fountain proper we see that the major
elements of Bernardo's first design—*Roma*, wolf, Hercules, tritons, etc.—
have been rearranged in a more logical if no more imaginative way. *Roma*
now holds the papal tiara and a cross familiar from the frontispieces of many
contemporary guidebooks, and the hierarchical distinction between *Roma Sacra*
and *Roma Profana* is made clearer by means of inscriptions and the placement
of the statues.

In 1706, two years after his second project for the Trevi, Bernardo Borromini
again turned his attention to the fountain and prepared a third design, this
time departing from his earlier plans for a monumental fountain house to
propose a more sculptural, freestanding composition (fig. 49). The stimulus
for this new project was twofold. In 1706, it will be recalled, Clement XI
undertook the restoration of the conduits of the Acqua Vergine, a project that
called attention to the undistinguished appearance of the aqueduct's principal
display, the Fontana di Trevi. Moreover, the discovery in 1703 of the Antonine
Column, a monolith of pink Egyptian granite nearly fifteen meters high that
had been found near the Via di Campo Marzio not very far from the site of
the Trevi, made available an impressive antiquity that could be used to
embellish the fountain.[17] In 1705 Francesco Fontana, assisted by Nicola Michetti, succeeded in the difficult task of raising the column from the deep
excavation that was required to expose it.[18] Following its excavation the
Antonine Column was moved to Piazza Montecitorio, where it lay unused
until, in 1764, the shed protecting it caught fire and irreparably damaged
the shaft. We know that between 1704 and 1706 the Trevi Fountain was
being considered as a possible site for the erection of the column, and two
sources mention Bernardo Borromini in this connection.[19]

Bernardo's 1706 design is a more refined and detailed elaboration of two
preparatory sketches in the Albertina.[20] Seated river gods adorn the rustic
basement as in Bernini's Four Rivers Fountain, and pairs of allegorical statues
lead the eye upward to the column. On the pedestal, the relief depicts not
the ancient scene of imperial apotheosis but what appears to be a Christian
subject. The most extravagant feature of the design is the spiral stair in
wrought iron that twists its way around the column, obscuring and disfiguring
its graceful proportions in the process. This stair was to provide access to a
viewing platform on top of the entablature carried by the column, but as is
evident from the plan that appears on the same sheet, no provision was made
for getting the stouthearted tourist or pilgrim interested in making the ascent
across the water in the lower basin; one simply cannot escape the conclusion
that he would have had to wade across.

In 1704 Clement XI appears to have invited architects to submit proposals

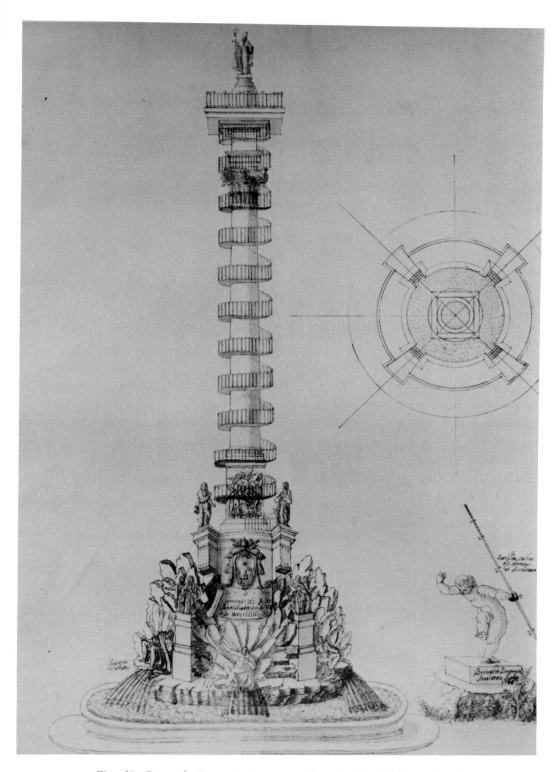

Fig. 49. Bernardo Borromini, unexecuted project for the Trevi, 1706

in an open competition for the Trevi.[21] In addition to Bernardo Borromini's projects there are four other proposals employing the Antonine Column that in all likelihood relate to this competition. Three projects are by architects trained in Carlo Fontana's studio, Romano Carapecchia, Nicola Michetti, and Filippo Juvarra, while the fourth is by an unidentified draughtsman. Unlike Bernardo Borromini's 1706 project, in which the Antonine Column was left freestanding and was not associated with an architectural backdrop, the designs in this group set off the column against an imposing facade. These facades and the structures to which they belong may have been stipulated as part of the competition program, which we are told included the opening of a spacious piazza. To this end measurements were made of the houses occupying the site immediately behind Bernini's fountain with a view toward demolishing them and building a new structure in line with the facade of S. Maria in Trivio.[22]

The first of these competition designs exists in two variants, one in London and the other in Stockholm (figs. 50, 51).[23] The sheet in London belongs to an album of drawings by Romano Carapecchia which contains dated drawings from the period between 1689 and 1704. Before I had studied the Carapecchia album I had thought, along with Braham and Hager, that the drawing in Stockholm was a copy after a design by Carlo Fontana.[24] I now believe that it may be attributed to Romano Carapecchia on the basis of style and technique, both of which closely resemble those of the autograph drawings in London. Carapecchia was active in Rome early in the pontificate of Clement XI, designing among other buildings the facade of S. Giovanni in Calabita (1711). Later in his career, between 1715 and 1736, he worked extensively in Malta.[25] The biographer Pascoli praised Carapecchia for his draughtsmanship, which, as Braham and Hager point out, closely resembles that of his master, Carlo Fontana.[26]

The Stockholm drawing places the column on top of a rustic base on which allegorical figures of Charity and Justice are seated. The freestanding monument and its trilobed basin are seen against the facade of an imposing palace that appears to be set back a considerable distance from the fountain proper. The U-shaped plan of this palace is unusual in Rome, though the lateral arcades and upper loggia recall aspects of the Quirinal and Barberini palaces and apparently result from an effort to accommodate existing conditions on the site. Carapecchia proposed three alterations to the site: (1) the demolition of the screening wall behind Bernini's fountain and of the other structures between it and the Palazzo Poli, (2) the regularization of the two flanking structures, and (3) the construction of a new facade in line with that of S. Maria in Trivio, all ideas mentioned in contemporary documents, as we have seen.

The London drawing lacks an architectural backdrop and appears to be a more detailed study of the fountain proper.[27] The allegorical figures are the same, though the attributes of Justice have been changed in part. Minor differences may also be detected in the capital and finial on top of the column, which represent the papal tiara and heraldic star of Clement XI.[28] The proportions of Carapecchia's design, like his draughtsmanship, reflect the balance and clear relationships so characteristic of his master, Carlo Fontana.

The next project relating to the 1704 competition is by another of Fontana's pupils, Nicola Michetti (ca. 1675–1758).[29] Three sheets in the Royal Library at Windsor comprise a plan, a section, and a facade elevation of Michetti's proposed design for the Trevi (fig. 52).[30] Michetti's plan makes it clear that he had no intention of altering the orientation of the fountain, which was to remain centered on the north side of the square. The addition of two curving stairs turning in at the center and emphasizing a focal concavity constituted the only real departure from the plan of the fountain as it existed in the seventeenth century. The critical factor determining the site and planimetric organization of the Trevi, both in actuality and in Michetti's project, was the extremely low level of the Acqua Vergine here at its main point of exit within the city.

Michetti's design sought to maximize the amount of movement and activity of the water by providing three separate changes in level within the limited vertical dimension available. Nonetheless, the effect, as much as it can be judged from the elevation, would have remained essentially that of a rather low fountain area set in front of and apart from an imposing architectural facade. This criticism, incidentally, also applies to the fountain as it appears today. Like the facade of the Palazzo Poli behind the Trevi Fountain as actually built, the backdrop of Michetti's project for the Trevi is essentially a thin architectural veneer.[31]

Michetti's elevation preserves intact the bas-relief on the pedestal of the Antonine Column, representing the apotheosis of Antoninus Pius and Faustina. On top of the column stands a statue of the Risen Christ, which would have served to celebrate the triumph of the Church over pagan antiquity. The central feature of Michetti's design for the fountain at the foot of the Antonine Column is an escutcheon bearing the arms of Clement XI placed directly below the pedestal. At either side, two personifications of rivers, recalling those on Bernini's Four Rivers Fountain both in scale and attitude, recline on boldly projecting, cushionlike scrolls. The play of water as it rushes in sheets from beneath these river gods and the papal *stemma* into smaller basins and then over the lip of a second, larger basin is effectively rendered in Michetti's drawing by the sensitive application of transparent blue washes.

A two-storied secular building with a central concavity was unusual in Rome at this time. Michetti's Trevi project appears to be an original design resulting directly from the need to provide an architectural setting that would emphasize the Antonine Column.[32] The architectural backdrop in Michetti's design of the building block, its anonymity achieved by the repetition of identical units, and the embracing concavity serve to throw the column into relief without distracting or overwhelming the observer by an excessively complicated background.

Fig. 50. Romano Carapecchia, unexecuted project for the Trevi, 1704–06,
Stockholm

Fig. 51. Romano Carapecchia, unexecuted project for the Trevi,
1704–06, London

Shortly after his arrival in Rome in 1704 yet another of Carlo Fontana's pupils, Filippo Juvarra, sketched a proposal for the Trevi Fountain (fig. 53). Unlike the other projects for the Trevi that we have examined thus far, Juvarra's is not a finished design but a quick *pensiero*, as he later labeled it when pasting it into a large volume of his drawings, now in the National Library in Turin.[33] A variation of this project appears in another sketch by Juvarra in the collection of the National Library in Madrid (fig. 54).[34] In spite of the rapidity with which they were obviously sketched, Juvarra's *pensieri* for the Trevi display a sureness of composition and an integration of architecture, column, and fountain that surpass those of the other projects we have examined and reflect his genius for scenographic design.

The summary plan at the upper right-hand corner of the sketch in Turin

Fig. 52. Nicola Michetti, unexecuted project for the Trevi, 1704–06, elevation

confirms that the Antonine Column would have been placed at the center of a circular basin set within a semicircular exedra. The exedra was to be articulated by niches containing statues, from beneath which water would flow into the basin; but the main display of water was reserved for the base of the column, from around which it was to rush out in concentric circles. Juvarra's sketch in Madrid moves the column back to the edge of the basin, allowing it to project only slightly from the embracing curve of the exedra. Juvarra gives the exedra a strong central emphasis by an arch breaking through the entablature and framing a recessed chamber set on axis, while two flanking oval windows also serve to make the architectural backdrop more transparent and open. Sheets of water fall into the basin from below the two oval apertures, reinforcing the triadic composition of Juvarra's design.

As in the other projects we have examined, sculpture was to ornament the base of the column as well as its summit, but the summary nature of Juvarra's sketches does not allow the identification of these figures; all one can say with certainty is that the eight-pointed star of the Albani *stemma* was evidently to have been the crowning feature of his design. This, together with the papal arms surmounting the twin pediments of the exedra and the statues that were to be set along the skyline, illustrates Juvarra's effective use of silhouette to animate his design. The *pensieri* may have been drawn preparatory to a finished drawing that was destroyed or remains unidentified, but Juvarra often recorded his ideas for competitions in which he had no intention of participating. The closest reflections of these early Roman sketches in Juvarra's later work may be found in the curving arcade depicted in an architectural fantasy of 1709 based on the Campidoglio[35] and in the fountain designs he made around 1714 for the Villa Orsucci in Lucca.[36]

The last of the designs for the 1704 competition, by an anonymous architect, is difficult to interpret because it survives only in part. A plan presently in the Gabinetto Nazionale delle Stampe,[37] like a lost perspective view published by Costanza Gradara in 1920, was once in the Bracci Archives (figs. 55, 56).[38] As in the other competition designs, the Antonine Column rises from a rustic basement similar to that of Bernini's Four Rivers Fountain. Water cascades from the basement into a circular basin. Unlike the other projects and Bernini's fountain, however, sculpture plays no part in this design. According to a rough sketch on the upper part of the perspective view, the column was to have been crowned by the heraldic device of Clement XI, which, as we have seen, also figures prominently in the other projects. Set back from the fountain proper and isolated from it stands a three-story building with a concave center.

A close comparison of plan and elevation reveals several minor inconsistencies, notably in the stairs leading down to the basin and in the fenestration of the lower story, but clearly both sheets pertain to the same project. Even allowing for the poor-quality reproduction of the elevation, one must admit that the design is repetitive and undistinguished. The author has manifestly failed to integrate the three major components of his design (fountain, column,

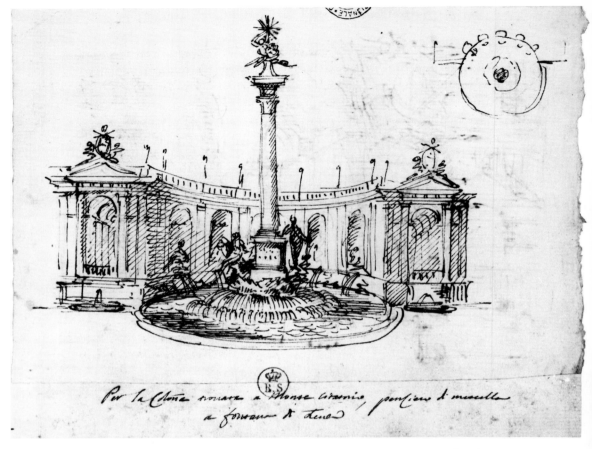

Fig. 53. Filippo Juvarra, unexecuted project for the Trevi, 1704–06, Turin

and architectural setting), which appear totally alien and unrelated to one another. Many of the graphic conventions employed in this project resemble those formulated by Carlo Fontana and used by his pupils and members of his studio; in my opinion its author is to be found among these. This anonymous project, as well as those of Bernardo Borromini, illustrates one pole of artistic quality in the Rome of Clement XI, which, it must be remembered, provided opportunities not only for architects of genius like Carlo Fontana and Filippo Juvarra, but for eclectic and unimaginative ones as well.

Carlo Fontana, whose international reputation had attracted Juvarra, Michetti, and others to his studio, also prepared designs for the Trevi. Among the thirteen volumes of drawings by Fontana in the Royal Library is one containing twenty-five sheets illustrating projects for the Trevi Fountain.[39] These drawings are well known, and I will limit myself here to a brief discussion of their general characteristics and to the analysis of a few select examples.[40] Six of the sheets are dated to the period between March and June of 1706 and are prefaced by a letter of June 16, 1706, addressed to the pope. The formality of this letter and the format of the designs strongly suggest that they were drafted as presentation drawings aimed at persuading Clement XI to award Fontana the commission to build the fountain; other indications suggest that they may also have been intended for publication. All of the drawings share a common presupposition: they propose different ways in which two antiquities, the obelisk of the Villa Ludovisi (now in front of the Trinità ai Monti) and the granite basin, or *tazza*, of the Campo Vaccino (now set below the obelisk of the Quirinal), could be used to adorn the Trevi Fountain. Fontana's explanatory letter stresses that one of the principal merits of his designs is that they would not require the demolition of the existing fountain. The date of 1706, Fontana's appeal to economy, and his proposal to employ other antiquities suggest that his projects were devised as alternatives to the use of the Antonine Column.

Among the Windsor drawings is a site plan that illustrates (in chalk) how Fontana's projects were to relate to Bernini's foundations as well as to the existing buildings on the site (fig. 33). The first of four more detailed plans

Fig. 54. Filippo Juvarra, unexecuted project for the Trevi, 1704–06, Madrid

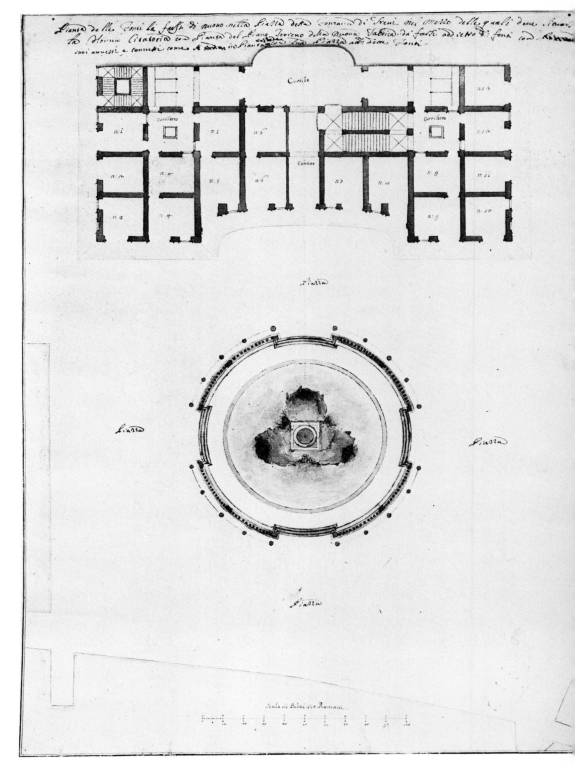

Fig. 55. Unexecuted project for the Trevi, 1704–06, plan

Fig. 56. Unexecuted project for the Trevi, 1704–06,
elevation, after Gradara, *Pietro Bracci*

of Fontana's projects shows this relationship even more clearly (fig. 57): a
pedestal with four concave sides (in dark wash) was to be set above the wider
arc of the concave foundations left by Bernini (in lighter wash), while the
tazza was to be placed on top of the circular base of Bernini's fountain visible
at the center of the basin. Behind, the conduit of the Acqua Vergine was to
enter on axis, instead of at an angle from the right, and the buildings belonging
to the Carpegna family and the Wool Guild were to be at least partially
demolished in order to make space for an ample, semicircular exedra embracing
the basin.[41] All of Fontana's drawings—plans and perspective views—are
variations on the same basic theme, and while several are numbered *primo
pensiero*, *secondo pensiero*, etc., there seems to be no logical progression from
one to the other.

The perspective view that Fontana identified as his first idea shows the
obelisk raised on its pedestal above the *tazza*, set just as we have already seen
in the plan, within the embracing concavity of Bernini's foundations (fig.
58). At the base of the obelisk allegorical figures of Justice and Benevolence
flank the papal escutcheon, while below, statues of Roman consuls (probably
Agrippa and Claudius Drusus, who are mentioned in Fontana's letter as the

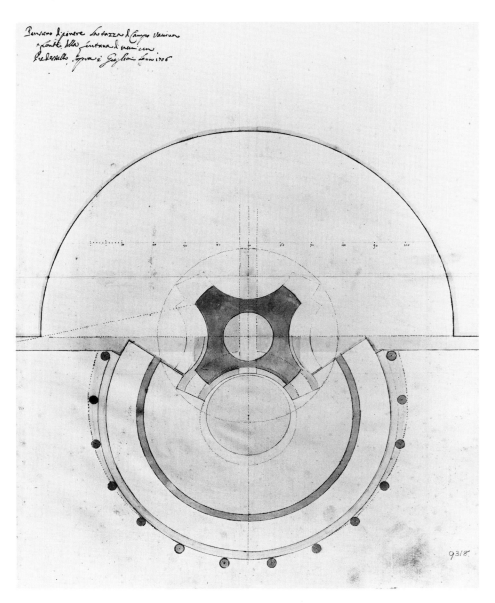

Fig. 57. Carlo Fontana, unexecuted project for the Trevi, 1706, plan

founders of the Acqua Vergine) frame an inscription. Beneath this inscription two putti support a circular bas-relief depicting the legend of the discovery of the Acqua Vergine, the waters of which rush out below from the three mouths of Bernini's fountain to fall into a polygonal basin. Behind the fountain proper a U-shaped building of modest proportions is visible. Fontana's second *pensiero* is virtually identical to the first, except that the fountain is set before a tall exedra like that which appears in the plans.[42]

Fontana's fourth *pensiero* (the third is either missing or unlabeled) introduces

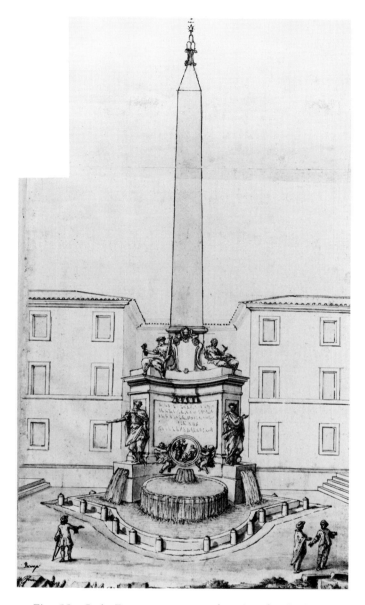

Fig. 58. Carlo Fontana, unexecuted project for the Trevi,
1706, *primo pensiero*

several variations not present in the first two, most significantly regarding
the placement of the obelisk, which is viewed along its diagonal axis, and its
illusionistic support by two colossal figures (fig. 59). One of these two giants
may be identified as Hercules on the basis of his attributes, the club and lion
skin. Perhaps this alludes to the Rivus Herculaneus, the stream with which
Pliny says the Aqua Virgo refused to mingle.

In addition to the numbered perspective views (five in all) there are four
other unnumbered perspectives at Windsor; with one exception, however,

Fig. 59. Carlo Fontana, unexecuted project for the Trevi, 1706, *quarto pensiero*

these introduce only minor variations on the basic themes already noted and can be passed over. The exception is Windsor 9331, which is unique among Fontana's projects in showing a remarkably naturalistic basin into which the waters of the Acqua Vergine flow from vases held by three nymphs (fig. 60). Here Fontana introduces a deliberate contrast between the sharp, refined edges of the obelisk and its pedestal and the apparently casual outline of the basin, which resembles the border of a natural spring. This particular solution appears rather tame and also strikes the eye as both inappropriate and impractical for

Fig. 60. Carlo Fontana, unexecuted project for the Trevi with naturalistic
basin, 1706

an urban fountain. Nonetheless, it does anticipate the spectacular rockwork that plays such an important role in the Trevi Fountain today.[43]

Considered as a group, Carlo Fontana's projects for the Trevi conform to a discernible pattern in the architectural patronage of Clement XI. Fontana's proposals combine the reuse of antiquities with the embellishment of structures intended for the public good, concerns that are closely reflected in contemporary works such as Filippo Barigioni's fountain in Piazza della Rotonda (1711) and Fontana's granary set into the Baths of Diocletian (1703–05).[44] His proposals also incorporate themes, such as the legends surrounding the fountain's early history, that continued to play a part in the iconography of the Trevi until its final execution. Moreover, Fontana's designs owe an obvious debt to his master, Gianlorenzo Bernini, whose influence on the Trevi continued to be felt until 1762. In an early study for the Four Rivers Fountain, for example, Bernini proposed aligning the obelisk along its diagonal axis.[45] In another instance, several drawings for Bernini's monument to Alexander VII in Piazza della Minerva depict giants struggling with the obelisk.[46] Carlo Fontana was familiar with Bernini's projects for the obelisk of the Piazza della Minerva, for signed drawings in the Chigi Archive show that he assisted his master in siting the monument.[47] Indeed, when one considers the Berninesque inspiration of the upper portion of Fontana's designs, along with the fact that Bernini had laid the very foundations from which they were to rise, one is struck by the weight of artistic tradition surrounding both the Trevi and the eighteenth-century architects who longed to work on it.

Another group of fountain designs also dates from 1706, the same year in which Carlo Fontana drafted his projects for the Trevi. In the *Concorso Clementino* of 1706 Francesco Fontana stipulated that the competing students in the second class of architecture at the Academy should "design in plan, elevation and prospect a public fountain . . . with three outlets for the water, and decorated with columns, statues, inscriptions, [and] coat of arms."[48] At first glance Francesco Fontana's program, like the drawings entered in the competition, is decidedly academic in character (figs. 61–64). It seems to be an abstract exercise having no reference to the Trevi apart from the prescribed three jets of water, which, after all, also characterize the displays of other monumental fountains like the Acqua Felice and the Acqua Paola. The context of the monumental fountain, in fact, was to be the square of an ideal city (which was the topic set for the first, or more advanced, class of architects), so it is unlikely that any of the competitors would have addressed the unique problems inherent in the situation of the Trevi.

Fig. 61. Giacomo Ciolli, *Concorso Clementino* project for a wall fountain, 1706, ▶
plan

Fig. 62. Giacomo Ciolli, *Concorso Clementino* project for a wall fountain, 1706, ▶
elevation

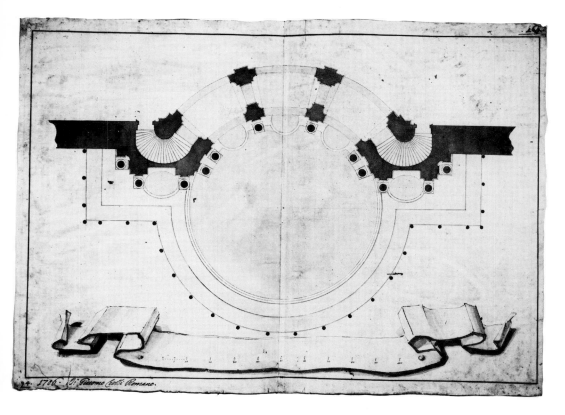

1706. Si Giacomo Colli Romano.

1706. Architectura Juondata de Jacombo Aromi. Giacomo Colli Romano.

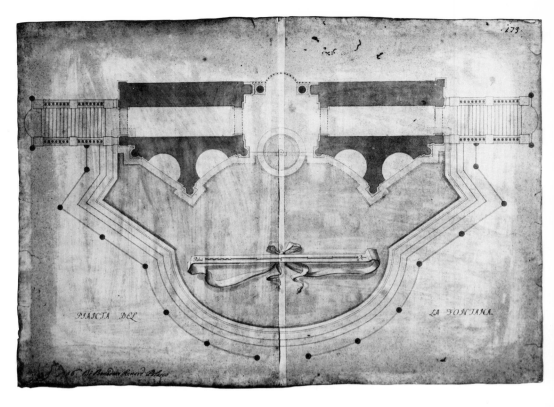

PIANTA DEL   LA FONTANA.

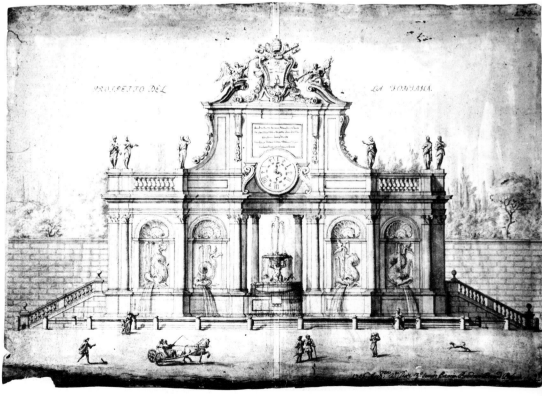

PROSPETTO DEL   LA FONTANA.

On the other hand, in 1706 the Fontana di Trevi was, as we have seen, the object of considerable study and discussion among practicing Roman architects and constituted a reality which, to my mind, exercised an influence on at least two of the five academic designs that received awards and survive in the archive of the Accademia di San Luca. The two projects in question, one by a Roman, Giacomo Ciolli, the other by a Polish architect named Benedykt Renard, share several significant characteristics. William Eisler has observed that unlike the other three projects, the designs of Ciolli and Renard are open at the center; that is, as at the Acqua Paola on the Janiculum, it would have been possible to look through these fountains to a view beyond, a vista to which the open space between the buildings behind the Trevi lent itself.[49] Moreover, unlike the other projects that vary in size, both are two hundred *palmi* long, a dimension that corresponds exactly to the frontage of the Fontana di Trevi and the disparate buildings behind it in 1706. The designs of Ciolli and Renard also have another dimension in common: the basins that collect the water rushing out from their monumental facades both project sixty *palmi* into the public square, which again corresponds precisely to the existing basin of the Fontana di Trevi as it had been left by Bernini. Finally, both of the projects by Ciolli and Renard were to be set in front of a low screening wall behind which there appears to be a garden; in Ciolli's plan and his preparatory elevation this wall is purposely left unfinished at its two ends, perhaps to allow for flexibility in accommodating the fountain to the existing buildings on the site.

Giacomo Ciolli's plan and elevation clearly illustrate the features that link his design to the site of the Trevi (figs. 61, 62). The element of transparency and the relation of the fountain proper to the garden behind are particularly evident in the elevation and section, which recall similar arrangements in the Berlin project, Juvarra's sketches, and Carlo Fontana's contemporary designs. The immediate impression made by Ciolli's elevation is decidedly theatrical, an effect enhanced by the vistas through the lower portico and behind the attic inscription, which in their openness resemble the contemporary stage sets of Filippo Juvarra.[50] The sculpture all too self-consciously imitates Bernini, especially the two lateral tritons and the river gods placed at the center. The statues of Roman consuls and generals in the attic, on the other hand, recall their counterparts in Carlo Fontana's designs.

Renard's project, while open at the center, is much less scenographic than Ciolli's and conforms more closely to wall fountains like Domenico Fontana's Acqua Felice (figs. 63, 64). Neither Ciolli nor Renard proposed to use an-

◄ Fig. 63. Benedykt Renard, *Concorso Clementino* project for a wall fountain, 1706, plan

◄ Fig. 64. Benedykt Renard, *Concorso Clementino* project for a wall fountain, 1706, elevation tiquities like the Antonine Column, which in any case were not mentioned in Francesco Fontana's program. That these academic projects appear more conservative than the other designs for the Trevi we have considered is in large part due to the nature of Francesco Fontana's program, which obliged young architects like Ciolli and Renard to refer to older precedents like the Acqua Felice and the Acqua Paola. In contrast, the architects striving to incorporate ancient obelisks and columns in their designs naturally turned to more recent precedents, like Bernini's Four Rivers Fountain, for inspiration.

After 1706 Clement XI apparently gave no further thought to the Fontana di Trevi. In any event, no projects relating to the Trevi date from the latter part of his reign. In all likelihood, the crisis posed by the War of Spanish Succession in 1708 caused the pope to cancel his ambitious plans for renovating the fountain. As a result, the next project for the Fontana di Trevi that may be securely dated was not made until the pontificate of Clement XI's successor, Innocent XIII Conti (1721–24). As we have seen in chapter 2, the brief pontificate of Innocent XIII proved to be crucial for the history of the Trevi Fountain. At this time the duke of Poli acquired the land separating the family palace from the Trevi with a view toward erecting a new wing incorporating the fountain and fronting on the Piazza di Trevi.

The ambitious plans of the Conti for the expansion of their family palace were not realized until 1728, four years after the death of Innocent XIII, but as early as 1723 the Conti commissioned Ferdinando Fuga (1699–1782) to draft a project unifying palace and fountain. The Berlin Kunstbibliothek has recently acquired the elevation of Fuga's project, signed and dated 1723 (fig. 65).[51] It corresponds in every detail to a ground plan in the Gabinetto Nazionale delle Stampe in Rome which has long been recognized as one of his early designs (fig. 66).[52] The discovery of Fuga's elevation allows us to analyze his project for the Trevi in detail.

As was true for other architects drafting projects for the Trevi, the relatively low level of the Acqua Vergine made it difficult for Fuga to produce a spectacular display of water, so naturally in his design the monumental character of the architecture dominates the sculpture and play of water. Fuga's project shows a modest basin of irregular outline, above which recline two statues representing personifications of the rivers Tiber and Erculaneo. The water of the Acqua Vergine flows from a vase set between these two figures and, after washing over the ornamental rockwork, falls into the basin below. Fuga's choice of the Tiber and Erculaneo as the central sculptural component of the fountain is unique among the numerous projects for the Trevi. The Tiber, of course, has obvious associations with Rome, while the Erculaneo, it will be recalled, ran near the springs of the Acqua Vergine in antiquity.

The upper portion of Fuga's design functions independently of the fountain at its base. Fuga's great *mostra*, or architectural display, of the Trevi is overtly scenographic in character, recalling contemporary festival designs. The high basement, angled staircases, and festive facade resemble designs for fireworks displays, such as those celebrating the *festa della Chinea*, as well as other ephemeral designs made by Fuga himself later in his career.[53] The central archway and projecting attic carrying an inscription also recall the temporary triumphal arches erected in the Campo Vaccino on the occasion of the papal *possessi*, two of which Fuga would design later in the century.[54] Finally, the vista framed by the central arch brings to mind the grandiose *macchine* that formed the architectural settings for sacred dramas like those staged in conjunction with the Devotion of the Forty Hours, called the *Quarant'ore*.[55] Even the staircase, with its sharp, angular turns, appears more festive than functional. These stairs reveal Fuga's awareness of the Spanish Steps (1723–26), perhaps the most spectacular example of scenographic urban design in eighteenth-century Rome, which were under construction at the same time Fuga's project for the Trevi was drafted.[56]

Four statues personifying the seasons (another iconographical theme that is unique among the projects for the Trevi) flank the central arch. Above, and placed between two allegorical statues of Fames, an inscription plaque records the date and patron of the commission.[57] Between the inscription and the split pediment of the arch rests the papal escutcheon of Innocent XIII.

The acquisition in 1723 of the land separating the main block of the Palazzo Poli from the Trevi meant that the Conti family could realize its ambition to expand their palace. They projected a new facade that would be centered on the display of the Trevi, rising behind the existing basin and extending to both sides of Bernini's foundations. In fact, this is what eventually occurred in 1728; but with the election of Pope Clement XII Corsini in 1730 events were set in motion that ultimately led to Nicola Salvi's executed design for the Trevi, incorporating the entire palace facade. Fuga's project for the Trevi, therefore, is the first of a series of unexecuted designs conditioned at least in part by the Conti family's desire to expand their palace and to incorporate the fountain into its new facade. Fuga's plan and elevation both make it clear that he intended the Trevi to be set at the center of the new palace facade, the first bays of which are visible to either side of the fountain proper. The central arch was to frame a view into the courtyard of the Palazzo Poli, and doorways opening off the loggia were to give access to the rooms of the new wing. In Fuga's elevation, the palace facade is only one story high and is crowned by a terrace, features that reflect the pope's desire to make use of the rather modest buildings already standing on the site. The pope's intentions are reported by Charles Poerson, director of the French Academy in Rome, in a letter of August 12, 1721:

> This water . . . is situated very near to the Conti Palace, where the Pope was born. His Holiness has resolved to demolish numerous unattractive houses that are nearby and to make a square and a terrace that will link together the [two wings of the] Conti Palace, all of which will constitute a considerable ornament for this city.[58]

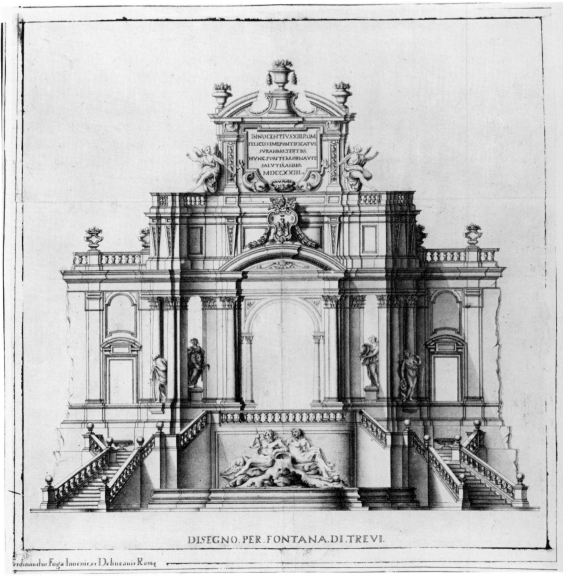

INNOCENTIVS.XIII.P.O.M.
FELICISSIMI.PONTIFICATVS.
SVB.ANNO.TERTIO.
HVNC.FONTEM.ORNAVIT
SALVTIS.ANNO.
MDCCXXIII.

DISEGNO. PER. FONTANA. DI. TREVI.

Ferdinandus Fuga Invenit, et Delineavit Romæ

Fig. 65. Ferdinando Fuga, unexecuted project for the Trevi, 1723, elevation

Fuga's drawing does not show the full extent of the facade, which suggests that a definitive design had not yet been settled upon.

Fuga's project for the Trevi is an important addition to the extraordinary series of unexecuted designs for the fountain. In certain respects it takes up themes that had been introduced earlier. But unlike many of the projects prepared during the pontificate of Clement XI, Fuga's design does not propose to employ specific classical antiquities like the Antonine Column or the obelisk of the Villa Ludovisi to embellish the Trevi. It does, however, resemble somewhat another series of fountain designs made under Clement XI, the drawings entered in the *Concorso Clementino* of the Academy of Saint Luke in 1706. A comparison of Fuga's design with those of the competitors underscores the academic character of Fuga's draughtsmanship, presentation, and conceptual process. However, the quality of Fuga's draughtsmanship as well as his powers of invention—especially evident at this early stage in his ornamental details—is far superior to those of the participants in the competition.

A drawing in Stockholm signed by Alessandro Rossini and dated 1727 records an extremely interesting, if somewhat problematic, project for the Trevi (fig. 67).[59] Relatively little is known about Rossini's career, but after successfully entering designs in three competitions of the Academy of Saint Luke (1677, 1679, and 1702) he appears to have left Rome to work in Germany, where his activity is documented between 1715 and 1736.[60] By 1727, then, Rossini had been away from Rome for more than a decade, and it is surprising that he would have been invited to submit a design for the Trevi. Moreover, this date is inconsistent with the papal escutcheon above

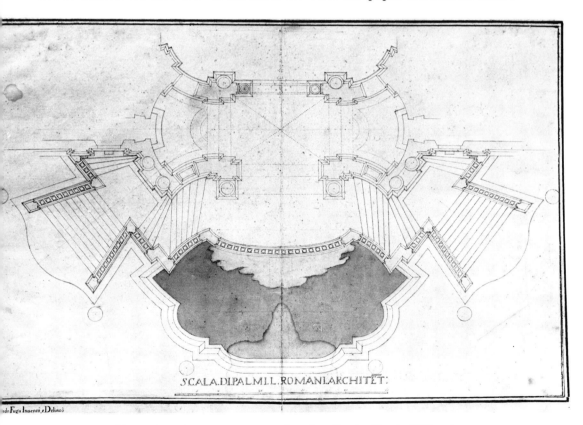

Fig. 66. Ferdinando Fuga, unexecuted project for the Trevi, 1723, plan

Fig. 67. Alessandro Rossini, unexecuted project for the
Trevi, 1727(?)

the central niche, for Clement XI, whose arms are clearly visible, died in 1721. This contradiction raises the possibility that Rossini may have drafted his project before leaving Rome, possibly as early as 1706, when so many other designs for the Trevi proposing to use ancient monuments were made.

Rossini's design is extremely ambitious—not to say a trifle bizarre—for he proposes to set three obelisks above a rustic fountain display three stories in height. Miniature obelisks, of course, had been employed to animate the skylines of fountains before—for example, Ammannati's design of 1552 for the public fountain at the intersection of the Via Flaminia and the approach to the Villa Guilia—but Rossini apparently proposed to use the real things, Egyptian monoliths of formidable size and weight. The history of the Roman obelisks lends further support to an early eighteenth-century date for Rossini's proposal. In 1706 Rossini could have chosen from among four available obelisks in Rome, two large and two small. The dimensions of the large central monolith correspond most closely to those of the Villa Ludovisi obelisk (the same appearing in Carlo Fontana's designs), but the obelisk dedicated to Antinoüs, then lying in fragments alongside the Palazzo Barberini, cannot altogether be discounted.[61] The most likely choices for the two smaller shafts would have been the obelisk of S. Macuto (which Barigioni set upon the fountain of Piazza della Rotonda in 1711) and its fragmented companion, which was given to Cardinal Annibale Albani in 1727 and reerected in Urbino in 1739.[62] Thus, by 1727 only one of the two smaller shafts required to implement Rossini's design was available.

Rossini's intentions should not be interpreted too literally, however. The project displays some of the characteristics of an architectural fantasy and may not have been prepared with a view toward using specific obelisks known to have been available at the time. Rather, as Werner Oechslin has observed, Rossini's design may reflect a general interest in obelisks as an architectural motif, an interest expressed in the designs of Juvarra, Fischer von Erlach, and Paolo Posi, among others.[63] The fact that Rossini's fountain was to be embraced by the Palazzo Poli, one wing of which is visible on the right of his design, argues strongly for a date after 1723, when the property separating the palace from the Trevi was acquired. Therefore I am inclined to accept provisionally Rossini's inscribed date of 1727, while acknowledging the unresolved questions posed by the anachronistic *stemma* and the obelisks.

Other features of Rossini's design, however, are also worthy of comment. A sphinx visible at the base of the central obelisk adds to the exotic flavor of Eastern antiquity in Rossini's design. The vigorous rustication of the central portion of the facade by the eighteenth century was considered appropriate for fountains associated with gardens. Never, however, had it been applied on such a monumental scale to an urban fountain display. Most remarkable is the way the base and lower shaft of the right-hand pilaster appear to be encrusted with rustication, an effect that occurs at a corresponding point of the Trevi Fountain as executed. The intended contrast between the naturalistic rustication and the refinement of the orders as well as that between the rockwork at the center of the basin and the flanking palace wings—so evident in Rossini's drawing—is also characteristic of the Trevi as built and prompts speculation that Salvi may have been familiar with Rossini's design.

Unfortunately, no drawings of the next unexecuted project for the Trevi, made under the pontificate of Benedict XIII Orsini (1724–30), survive to illustrate the detailed extant written description and documentary evidence. Writing in the summer of 1728, the diarist Francesco Valesio ridiculed a design apparently dreamed up by Monsignor Jacopo Sardini, who as *Presidente delle Acque* was the official charged with supervising Rome's water supply.[64] Sardini's ideas took three-dimensional form in a model by Paolo Benaglia, a Roman sculptor who later would carve some of the figures on the Trevi as actually built. Valesio, like many Romans, took a dim view of the artistic projects of Benedict XIII, who came from Benevento and favored southern Italian artists. Valesio remarked that Benaglia, whom he mistakenly believed to be Neapolitan, "has enthusiasm, but little or no knowledge of his art."[65] In spite of his Roman bias, Valesio's description of Benaglia's model for the Trevi is worth quoting for the light it sheds on Sardini's complex iconographical program, elements of which figure in other projects for the fountain for which drawings survive.

> In the highest position, is a seated statue of the Holy Virgin of the Rosary, which was requested by the Pope. Below, to the observer's left, is the Virgin Trivia, born from the head of this prelate [Sardini] like Athena from that of Jove. Trivia points with one hand to the Madonna and with her left to the water that issues from some rocks. To the right is a standing personification of Rome in armor, and next to her, without any justification, is a sow with several piglets, while to the side of Trivia is a unicorn. This beautiful work will be crowned by an inscription . . . by the same prelate. . . . I forgot to mention that there are two oak trees, one on each side, so that food for the sow will not be lacking.[66]

Monsignor Sardini's project for the Trevi was actually begun. On September 10, 1728, Benaglia signed a contract to provide the statuary and ornamental sculpture for the fountain "according to the design already sketched out,"[67] and between September 30, 1728, and February 9, 1730, he received 1,770 scudi for his services.[68] The work involved carving three statues, plus the papal escutcheon.[69] Benaglia's contract also makes it clear that he was not responsible either for the design or for the execution of the fountain's architectural component, which was entrusted to Maffeo Angelo Contini.[70] Benaglia's statue of the Virgin, intended as the crowning feature of Sardini's project, found its way to the sacristy of S. Maria Sopra Minerva, where it has recently been identified by Cesare D'Onofrio.[71] With the election of Clement XII Corsini in 1730 Sardini's design for the Trevi was scrapped. Like other corrupt officials surrounding Benedict XIII, Sardini was tried and condemned to prison. Benaglia fared much better; two of his statues, the Fames supporting the papal escutcheon, were placed on the fountain by his successor, Nicola Salvi, under whose direction he continued to work on the Trevi.

The next projects, drafted between 1730 and 1732 in response to the competition organized by Clement XII, differ from those of the preceding three decades in several important respects. Not only do they take into account the existence of the new facade for the Palazzo Poli, but they respond to consciously different expressive aspirations and aesthetic values projected by the Corsini pope. Moreover, as a group these projects may be said to document a transition between the early phase of the Trevi's history and the execution of the Fontana di Trevi as we know it today.

4

Nicola Salvi and the Competition of 1730

To understand the unexecuted projects for the Trevi made between 1730 and 1732, we must consider two important developments. With the first of these, the newly constructed facade of the Palazzo Poli, we are already acquainted. On July 9, 1728, only two days after Valesio's entry describing Monsignor Sardini's project for embellishing the Trevi, the Conti finally received the authorization to proceed with the construction of a new wing of their family palace fronting on the Piazza di Trevi. This facade was construced within two years, for in November 1730 Valesio remarked on its completion.[1] The new facade exerted a powerful influence on all subsequent designs for the Trevi Fountain, for every architect (including Salvi in his winning design) had to reckon with the imposing structure that rose behind the fountain.

But the primary factor motivating the next group of unexecuted designs was the election of Lorenzo Corsini as Pope Clement XII on July 12, 1730. Within one month of his election Clement discontinued the work begun under his predecessor by Sardini and Benaglia and ordered new designs to be made for the fountain.[2] Three months later Valesio noted that the first group of drawings and models was unsatisfactory to the pope and that four architects had been chosen to provide new designs.[3] The French sculptor Edme Bouchardon, in a letter from Rome dated September 3, 1731 (but describing events of at least five months earlier), also mentioned four "famous" architects and thirty different models exhibited in the Quirinal Palace.[4] Bouchardon's fellow *pensionnaire* at the French Academy in Rome, Lambert Sigisbert Adam, reported that at one point there were sixteen designs and models for the Trevi exhibited in the Quirinal Palace.[5] Francesco Valesio, commenting on the final stages of the competition, noted on August 6, 1732, that the pope had ordered many new designs made in addition to those furnished on previous occasions.[6] In this same entry Valesio reported that Luigi Vanvitelli's project had been selected by the pope as the winning design. Of course it was not Vanvitelli but Nicola Salvi who was named architect of the Trevi, a fact which Valesio correctly noted six weeks later[7] and which was officially confirmed in the papal *chirografo*, or directive, issued on October 2, 1732.[8]

Very little documentary information regarding the competition for the Trevi survives, and our understanding of the complex process that ultimately led to the selection of Nicola Salvi's design in the fall of 1732 is vague and incomplete. We know the names of five artists who competed (two of these—Bouchardon and Adam—entered unofficially), but we cannot be sure at what stage they were involved or how many designs they entered. Nor can all of the projects dating from this period be attributed to the three architects we know competed: Barigioni, Vanvitelli, and Salvi. The paucity of evidence probably relates to the problems that arose from the other great architectural *concorso* in Rome at this time, the competition for the Lateran facade, which was finally won by Alessandro Galilei in 1732. So acrimonious was the debate and so angry was the Roman architectural establishment at seeing the prize awarded to a Florentine that the pope may have appointed a *congregazione segreta* to handle the Trevi competition in a far less public fashion. Whether or not this was the case, Salvi's winning design for the Trevi was selected only after a complicated decision-making process that took more than two years and involved several different stages.

Granted the incomplete state of the available evidence, both documentary and visual, as well as the sporadic nature of the lengthy competition, I have divided the unexecuted projects dating from this period into three main groups which I feel probably correspond to the order in which they were made. The drawings in the first group, all anonymous, attempt to accommodate the fountain design to the newly erected facade of the Palazzo Poli. The second group, including the projects of Adam, Bouchardon, and Barigioni, while continuing to work within the limitations of the new facade, no longer appear so confined by them. The third group, comprising the designs of Vanvitelli and Salvi, certainly corresponds to the last phase of the competition in which the participants were encouraged to propose designs involving the entire facade of the Palazzo Poli.

The drawings in the first group of projects all represent the newly constructed facade of the Palazzo Poli in considerable detail, especially three anonymous drawings in Berlin (figs. 43, 68, 69).[9] The first of these bears a general similarity to Ferdinando Fuga's project of 1723 (fig. 43).[10] The fountain proper breaks forward from the palace facade, its central arch framing a scene representing the Roman maiden Trivia leading Agrippa's scouts to the source of the Aqua Virgo, which, to judge from the clouds, was evidently to have been rendered illusionistically in painting. From a source at the base of the painted scene where the Roman soldiers are drinking, the waters of the real Acqua Vergine were to rush forth, flowing over the three-dimensional forms of sculpted rockwork to be collected in the basin below. Above the level of the entablature appears an empty plaque, clearly intended for a dedicatory inscription, surmounted by a split segmental pediment framing a papal *stemma*, also blank. Statues of allegorical figures representing the four parts of the world (Europe, Africa, America, and Asia) also grace the upper portion of the fountain. Their presence recalls Gianlorenzo Bernini's use of represen-

Fig. 68. Unexecuted project for the Trevi with Neptune, circa 1730

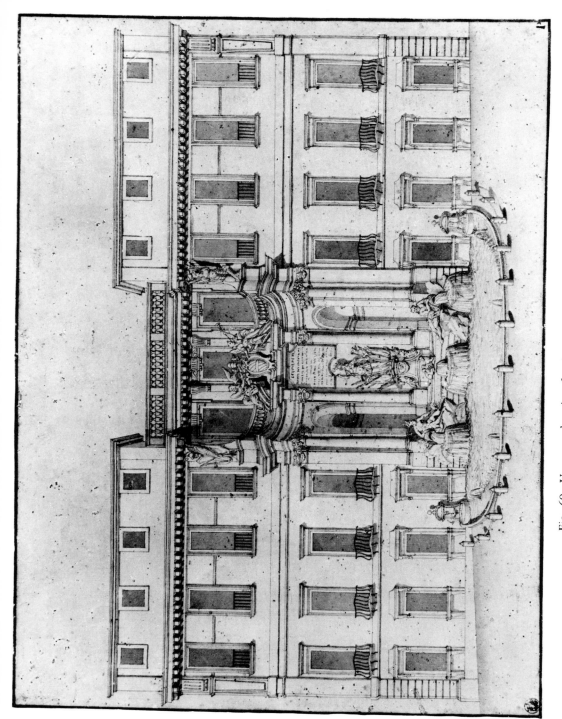

Fig. 69. Unexecuted project for the Trevi with *Roma*, circa 1730

tations of the Four Rivers to symbolize the universality of the Catholic faith, and, by implication, of papal rule.

A second project in Berlin is much more three-dimensional and sculptural in its effect (fig. 68).[11] The curvilinear architecture of the fountain clearly detaches itself from the planar facade of the palace and boldly projects into the piazza. Imitating numerous Baroque church facades, a central convex element is flanked by two concave bays. The arch of the central concavity frames a statue of Neptune with his trident standing on a shell chariot, urging on the four sea horses that pull him. This sculptural composition recalls Bernini's Neptune fountain in its original setting in the gardens of the Villa Montalto as well as aspects of the central sculptural group of the present-day Trevi Fountain. Figures of Agrippa and the maiden Trivia look down on the central sculptural group from pedestals set into the lateral concave bays. Above a central inscription is the papal escutcheon of Clement XII flanked by two trumpeting Fames, an arrangement that anticipates the *stemma* group on the Trevi as built. To the right and left of the *stemma* stand two pairs of allegorical statues whose attributes are difficult to discern; the figure on the left seems to carry a sword and a balance and therefore may represent Justice.

A third project depicting the full extent of the palace facade also records a peculiarity of the site: the sloping terrain that rises from west to east (fig. 69).[12] The architect clearly proposed to use the foundations of Bernini's *mostra* as well as his basin, both of which appear precisely as they were recorded in seventeenth-century *vedute*. Above and behind these foundations, from which the water issues in three jets, rises the concave facade of the fountain proper. A personification of Rome occupies the center, surrounded by martial trophies. At her feet appears the Capitoline Wolf nursing Romulus and Remus, flanked by two reclining river gods. Above the central figure of Rome is an inscription, which in turn is surmounted by the papal *stemma* of Clement XII set within a split pediment on which rest two trumpeting Fames. To the two sides appear other martial trophies linking the projecting ends of the fountain facade to that of the palace.

The drawings in the second group do not depict the new facade of the Palazzo Poli in its entirety but concentrate on proposals for the fountain at its center. These five projects are all by anonymous artists (figs. 70–74). The first proposes to open up the center of the palace facade by means of an arch which, like the proscenium arch of a theater, frames a group of figures set against an illusionistic background (fig. 70).[13] Statues of the goddess *Roma* and the maiden Trivia stand on the rough rocks of the foreground; the latter points out the source of the Trevi to three Roman soldiers shown in the act of drinking from their helmets. In the background is a view of the Roman Campagna, dominated by a ruined aqueduct (certainly a reference to the Aqua Virgo of Agrippa), which the popes (and particularly Clement XII, whose *stemma* appears above the arch) had restored. While this project may represent a view through the facade of the Palazzo Poli and into its courtyard, the

Fig. 70. Unexecuted project for the Trevi with a ruined aqueduct, circa 1730

shadow cast onto this background by the projecting elements of the palace facade makes it seem more likely that this scene was to be painted illusionistically onto a blind wall.

Of all the unexecuted projects for the Trevi, this one is the most overtly scenographic. Indeed, if it were cropped so as to eliminate the fountain basin at the bottom and those elements of the palace facade which appear above and to either side, the drawing might easily be mistaken for a set design. The use of sculpture against an illusionistic background recalls the eighteenth-century alterations of Bernini's designs for the Alaleona Chapel.[14] The role played by ruins in this design also deserves comment. Here, the broken arcade of the Aqua Virgo in its landscape setting functions not only as a picturesque *veduta*, but also as a testimony of the classical origins of the Trevi and the grandeur of ancient Rome, which Clement XII sought to revive. The anachronistic elements combined in the scene—the aqueduct in its ruined state, the legend of Trivia and Agrippa's scouts, and the modern setting with papal *stemma*—are reconciled by the presence of the goddess *Roma*, whose glory, both past and present, is celebrated in this design.

Three other drawings, all by the same hand, also represent projects for the Trevi placed at the center of the new facade of the Palazzo Poli (figs. 71–73). Each proposes to use the existing foundations of the Trevi left by Bernini, which appear virtually unaltered at the bottom of each sheet. Moreover, the projects have four features in common: (1) a statue of a unicorn placed within the concavity of Bernini's foundations, (2) two statues of reclining river gods set above the two projecting ends of the foundations, (3) a bas-relief representing the legend of Trivia adorning a convex pedestal which rises above the unicorn, and (4) the *stemma* of Clement XII as a crowning feature. The style of these three sheets is also identical; of the numerous conventions of draughtsmanship they share perhaps the most obvious is the rendering of water by means of successive registers of parallel lines executed in wash. Above the level of the sculpture embellishing Bernini's foundations, however, each of the projects differs substantially in architectural form as well as in iconography, and each drawing probably constitutes an alternate design by the same artist.

The first of these sheets, now in the collection of the Kunstbibliothek in Berlin, is concave in plan, recalling somewhat another project for a concave fountain display at the center of the Palazzo Poli facade, which we have already examined (fig. 71).[15] At the center a deep niche reaches back to the plane of the recessed central portion of the palace facade, in it a full-length statue personifying Rome. To the left what appears to be a pictorial bas-relief depicts the finding of Romulus and Remus, and to the right another panel represents the story of the Vestal Virgin Tuccia, who gave miraculous proof of her chastity by carrying water in a sieve from the Tiber to the Temple of Vesta.[16] The concave pictorial reliefs and the illusionistic receding perspective of cross vaults behind the statue of Rome recall the work of Ercole Ferrata and Antonio Raggi in Sant'Agnese in Agone, in particular the altarpieces of Saint Agnes

Fig. 71. Unexecuted project for the Trevi with the Vestal Tuccia, circa 1730

Fig. 72. Unexecuted project for the Trevi with *Roma*, circa 1730

Fig. 73. Unexecuted project for the Trevi with Atlas, circa 1730

and Saint Cecilia. Here the relationship between the sculptural reliefs and the architecture into which they are set is awkward. Particularly in the right-hand scene not only do the orthogonals within the relief conflict with the entablature of the fountain in which it is set, but the door through which the Vestal is entering is not aligned with the openings in the palace facade, thus causing an undesirable discordance between the architecture of the fountain and that of the palace.

The second sheet, one of two in the Lanciani Collection, resembles the Berlin drawing in its iconography (fig. 72).[17] A personification of Rome once again occupies the central position, but the architectural enframement of the fountain proper is more open and scenographic. In place of bas-reliefs to either side of center there appears an open enfilade of columns. Immediately behind the statue of *Roma* extends a vaulted space with an open oculus, recalling the atria of royal palaces as they appear in contemporary set designs.[18] In general, this project has a decided air of insubstantiality about it, as if it were a temporary festival structure rather than a design for a permanent fountain.

The Lanciani Collection includes a third project by the same anonymous draughtsman (fig. 73).[19] In this case the central sculptural feature is a kneeling figure of Atlas supporting a globe emblazoned with the arms of the Corsini family, which recalls the main group of the celebrated water theater of the Villa Aldobrandini in Frascati. Behind the statue of Atlas an open courtyard occupies the space separating the two wings of the Palazzo Poli. The architectural setting of this project appears more stable, if no less temporary and two-dimensional than that of its companion sheet in the Lanciani Collection.

A fifth drawing belonging to the second group of projects is in a private collection in Rome (fig. 74).[20] In this sheet a personification of Rome sits atop a pedestal decorated with a bas-relief of the Capitoline Wolf. *Roma* is silhouetted against an illusionistic background which represents the legend of the maiden Trivia and the discovery of the Aqua Virgo. Two pairs of seated female figures occupy the space below and to either side of center. While the summary quality of rendering makes positive identification of these figures difficult, one of the crowned figures on the left holding a globe may be a personification of Truth, and the figure nursing a child on the right probably represents Charity. Below these groups statues of tritons spout water into a basin and, on the central axis, a figure of Hercules subdues the Nemean Lion. Above the archway framing *Roma* an asymmetrical group composed of three putti and a trumpeting Fame sustains the escutcheon of Clement XII.

In contrast to the three preceding projects, the architecture of this design expresses the very essence of stability. Rusticated Tuscan pilasters support an entablature of sober simplicity. The anonymous draughtsman seems to be experimenting with two alternatives for the enframement: on the left a single engaged pilaster, on the right paired supports, possibly freestanding columns. The use of a rusticated order recalls the anonymous project drafted in the reign of Urban VIII, as well as that of Alessandro Rossini. The triangular

Fig. 74. Unexecuted project for the Trevi with *Roma*, circa 1730

composition of the sculpture and the spare treatment of the orders suggest an artist of a decidedly classical inclination.

The classical restraint of this project may reflect one of the designs prepared by two French sculptors, Lambert Sigisbert Adam (1700–59) and Edme Bouchardon (1698–1762), both of whom were *pensionnaires* of the French Academy in 1730. Like the other models entered in the competition of 1730, Adam's no longer survives, but its appearance is recorded in a detailed description written some twenty years later:

While Adam was in Rome among the other projects he designed for Clement XII was a model for the Trevi Fountain. This fountain was to be set against a wall, between the two wings of an imposing palace and in the middle of a large semicircular basin. There Adam designed a convex arrangement of rocks to suit the site, from which rushes a sheet of water measuring six feet, and to either side two other sheets of three feet each. On the rocks is a foundation around forty feet broad and fifteen feet deep where there is an architectural ornament of the Doric order. The center is adorned by two columns supporting the entablature, which are separated from one another by a space of twelve feet. Between them is a concave architectural background supported by fluted columns with *roseaux*[21] and ornamented with dentils and *glaçons*.[22]

To either side is a portal adorned with rustic architecture supporting an entablature. Above the projecting center, with its concavity, is an attic crowned by a cornice and a composite pediment, which rises exactly to the height of the two palace wings. Above the two portals are two windows in the attic that support a cornice running the full length of the attic and supporting a balustrade. On the projecting pediment is an allegorical figure of Fame with the arms of the Pope. In the middle of the attic, under the cornice, is an irregular cartouche in the shape of a banner to carry the inscription; this plaque is attached and supported by two terms or tritons, who also support the attic cornice.

On the rustic foundation between the two columns is [a statue personifying] Rome, represented by an armed woman seated on a pedestal adorned by an inscription. The pedestal is also ornamented with martial trophies on each side to illustrate the victory that Agrippa won over his enemies at the time the source of the waters supplying the fountain were discovered. On the bottom front of the pedestal, and above the central sheet of water, is a mask or shell accompanied by a console, on which is seated a young woman called Treve (after whom the water is named), who revealed the springs to a soldier, to whom she is [shown] offering a drink from a vase. The whole army benefitted from this discovery because it was dying of thirst, and Agrippa conveyed the waters of this fountain to Rome in this very place by means of an aqueduct he had built.

At the two sides are two urns from which rush the other two sheets of water, where one sees two reclining figures holding the urns, a male representing the Ocean and a female the Mediterranean. At one end of the basin is a triton leading a sea horse from which gushes water for public consumption; at the other side is a marine centaur who blows water from a conch shell he holds between his arms. The figures should be twelve feet in proportion when executed in marble; the architecture should be executed in local stone. This model was exhibited in the gallery of [the papal palace at] Monte Cavallo in competition with sixteen other models by different sculptors and architects: Adam's was chosen to be built.

The Romans, however, seeing that this work had been entrusted to a foreigner, convinced the Pope to build the facade of Saint John in Lateran rather than the Fountain, and this was done.[23]

While the architectural component of Adam's model was more elaborate and its sculptural oranament included certain figures—like Oceanus and the Mediterranean—not present in the drawing reproduced in figure 74, there

are other points of similarity. Principal among these is the central personification of Rome seated above a pedestal adorned with martial trophies. The
nervous calligraphy of the drawing is quite different from Adam's draughtsmanship with its sure, steady control of line. Nevertheless, the anonymous
artist may have studied Adam's model and incorporated parts of it into his
own design.

Like Adam's model, Boucharbon's project has also long been known from
a description contained in one of the sculptor's letters written from Rome to
his father, dated September 3, 1731:

> As you know, the Trevi Fountain is one of the most important undertakings
> in Rome at this time. This fountain had been entrusted to one of the worst
> sculptors who flourished under Benedict XIII. Since the death of the Pope there
> has been so much discontent over the work that the sculptor's hand has been
> stayed in spite of the large expenditures that have already been made. The
> reigning Pope has ordered four of the most famous architects to make models
> for the Fountain. Although I was not included I did not wish to miss an
> opportunity to show what I was capable of. The Pope wished to see [the model]
> and had it placed in the gallery of his palace at Monte Cavallo, along with
> about thirty other models for the Trevi made by different masters. I may say
> that my model was generally approved by all, and that if justice were done I
> would be given the commission over all the others, since none are composed
> so magnificently as is mine. I say this without pretension. There is no one,
> among all the connoisseurs, who does not favor me, and of all the models made
> for the Fountain, only mine, along with three others, was chosen by the Pope
> as the most beautiful.
>
> I left my model for five months in the Pope's gallery. One day, when I was
> walking in this gallery to study all the models, I observed that my own had
> been damaged, both sculpture and architecture. This made me so angry that
> I wanted to have my model returned to me that instant. However, they were
> unwilling to let me have it without the permission of the major domo, whom
> I twice sought out, and to whom I reported the damage done to my model.
> He told me that I should leave it there in spite of the fact that it was damaged;
> I explained that I had already spent two hundred and fifty *livres* on the archi-
> tecture alone, not counting the time and effort I had devoted to the figure and
> ornaments that embellish the model, and that since they still had come to no
> decision and were taking so long I would prefer to take back my model and
> keep it in my room, rather than see it perish, which he granted me.
>
> All those who follow this affair tell me that I did the right thing, that there
> is little likelihood they would spend such a large sum (at least 50,000 scudi)
> and that if they ever build the fountain they will only make something very
> mediocre with little expense because the palace to which the fountain is attached
> is already built and the architect who designed it did not pay attention to the
> fountain. The Fountain itself is the most beautiful ornament in the world with
> its three mouths from which the water, like rivers, rushes into the basin, which
> itself is of considerable grandeur. Prince Conti, who lives in the palace, will

never permit the palace to be covered over so as to decorate the fountain, which is why only a very poor design will ever be built.

I constructed my model in two different ways. The first: I conformed to the site and related the architecture and ornament to the palace, which has already been built according to a very mediocre design. The second: I followed my genius; I may say that it would be one of the most beautiful things of this type in Rome, but since half of the palace would have to be demolished to build it, the Prince would never consent. This is what leads me to believe that he who makes the worst model and has the most powerful supporters will prevail over all others; this is what one sees all the time in Rome judging from the poor works that are built in these days.[24]

While Bouchardon's model (like all the others) has been lost, a handsome red-chalk drawing by this master appears to record the simpler of his two designs (fig. 75).[25] Bouchardon's fountain, sculpture, and architectural back-drop are concentrated at the center of the new Conti Palace facade and are framed by its two projecting wings. The clarity and restraint of Bouchardon's design as well as its high quality distinguish it from the other projects we have studied and lend support to the artist's contention that his model was the most beautiful of those submitted to the pope. Bouchardon's use of a spare Tuscan colonnade erected on a concave plan to provide a setting for the fountain and to accentuate the recessed center of the palace facade is particularly successful. Charles De Brosses, who saw Bouchardon's model a decade later, considered it to be superior to Salvi's design.[26]

Bouchardon's design shares several features with that of Adam, notably the Tuscan colonnade and the central statue personifying Rome, and also anticipates the fountain on the Rue Grenelle in Paris that Bouchardon began in 1739 (fig. 76).[27] Common to both of Bouchardon's fountain designs are an embracing concavity and the governing role played by architecture in determining the placement and composition of the statuary. Specific details of Bouchardon's early design for the Trevi, such as the bas-reliefs set above the waterline and the reclining river gods with vases, have close counterparts in the fountain he later executed. Water, perforce, plays a minimal role in the Parisian fountain, only one of the many points of contrast distinguishing it from the Fontana di Trevi as executed by Nicola Salvi.

From a passing reference in a letter we know the name of another architect who participated in the competition for the Fontana di Trevi. This is Filippo Barigioni (1690-1753), a pupil of Carlo Fontana. Barigioni's numerous executed designs include two fountains: one in the Piazza della Rotonda, which he embellished for Clement XI in 1711, and the other in the cathedral square of Tarquinia, which dates ca. 1727.[28] Unfortunately, Barigioni's letter, dated March 20, 1731, and addressed to Marchese Alessandro Gregorio Capponi (1683–1746), fails to convey even the most general sense of his model's appearance: "I have made a clay model of the well-known Fontana di Trevi, which I am keeping at home while it dries so as to fire it in a kiln. Since this

Fig. 75. Edme Bouchardon, unexecuted project for the Trevi, circa 1730

Fig. 76. Edme Bouchardon, Fontaine de la Rue Grenelle, 1739–45

makes moving it both difficult and dangerous I make bold to entreat you to visit me to see it here."[29] The passage may, however, shed some light on the intrigue surrounding the competition for the Trevi Fountain. In all probability Barigioni hoped to win the support of the Marchese Capponi, Clement XII's private chamberlain, and through him perhaps to influence the outcome of the competition.

The architect responsible for the next project we shall consider figured prominently in the final stage of the competition and, according to Valesio, emerged as Nicola Salvi's closest rival.[30] This is Luigi Vanvitelli (1700–73), a lifelong friend of Salvi who, during Salvi's mortal illness, assisted him in the task of completing the Trevi. While Vanvitelli failed to win the competitions for the Trevi and the Lateran facade, Clement XII assigned him the task of enlarging the port of Ancona, far and away the largest architectural commission in the Papal States.[31] Today, however, Vanvitelli's fame rests on his design for the vast royal palace at Caserta, near Naples (1752–74). The garden at Caserta, which was also laid out by Vanvitelli, features extensive waterworks that in scale and iconographic complexity are among the closest rivals to Salvi's Fontana di Trevi.[32]

A plan and elevation of Vanvitelli's project for the Trevi, formerly in the Bracci Archives, are now in the collection of the Gabinetto Nazionale delle Stampe in Rome (figs. 77, 78).[33] The inscriptions on the facade elevation carry the date 1730, but the draughtsmanship of both sheets appears rather dry and mechanical, inclining me to consider them accurate copies of Vanvitelli's design rather than autograph originals. Relative to the other competition projects we have examined, Vanvitelli's design would have aggrandized the fountain at the expense of the Palazzo Poli facade. Comparison with one of the Berlin projects from the first phase of the competition shows how the central *mostra*, from being confined within the two projecting bays of the palace, has now expanded laterally to overlap the first bay of each wing (figs. 43, 77). However, Vanvitelli respects the fenestration and skyline of the existing facade. His respect results in several awkward compromises, the most obvious of which is the break in the entablature to the left and right of center so as not to interrupt the second-story windows.[34]

Vanvitelli proposed using engaged pilasters to articulate the architectural backdrop of the fountain, which curves gently at the center, taking advantage of the recessed space between the two wings to provide a shallow segmental concavity against which to set off the Antonine Column. The column itself would have been set at the center of the basin and well in front of the facade. The intervening space, in the form of an oval, would have provided an elevated viewing platform out over the fountain accessible from the interior of the palace. This terrace would also have allowed the close inspection of the celebrated reliefs on the sides of the pedestal of the Antonine Column. The main relief representing the apotheosis of the imperial couple, as in Michetti's earlier design, would have faced the square. The pavement of the piazza, composed of a concentric pattern radiating outward from Bernini's semicircular basin, would have focused attention on the fountain and compensated somewhat for the irregularity of the surrounding buildings.

The column itself was to have been crowned by a statue representing the Virgin and Child, recalling the sculptural programs of Bernini and Monsignor Sardini. One of the inscriptions on the facade records the dedication of the column to the Virgin, while the other commemorates its excavation under Clement XI.[35] The remaining sculpture is ranged around the base of the column, raised on rustic rocks. Two reclining river gods, probably representing the Tiber and the Nile, are accompanied by their respective attributes, the Wolf suckling Romulus and Remus, and a lion. Both sculpture and water play relatively modest parts in Vanvitelli's design, which is primarily architectural in character. In this respect Vanvitelli's project closely resembles Michetti's made more than a quarter century earlier, suggesting that the young architect may have studied the older master's drawings (figs. 52, 78).

The last unexecuted project of the series may be attributed to Nicola Salvi, the architect responsible for the construction of the fountain.[36] Two drawings that once formed part of the Bracci Archives, both of which have long been attributed to Vanvitelli, record Salvi's design.[37] A plan showing two variants (one with a stairway, the other without) is in the Gabinetto Nazionale delle Stampe in Rome (fig. 79),[38] while the corresponding elevation is in the collection of the Canadian Centre for Architecture in Montréal (fig. 80).[39] The elevation was generated from the right half of the plan, which shows a broad staircase curving out from the central fountain display, a feature that

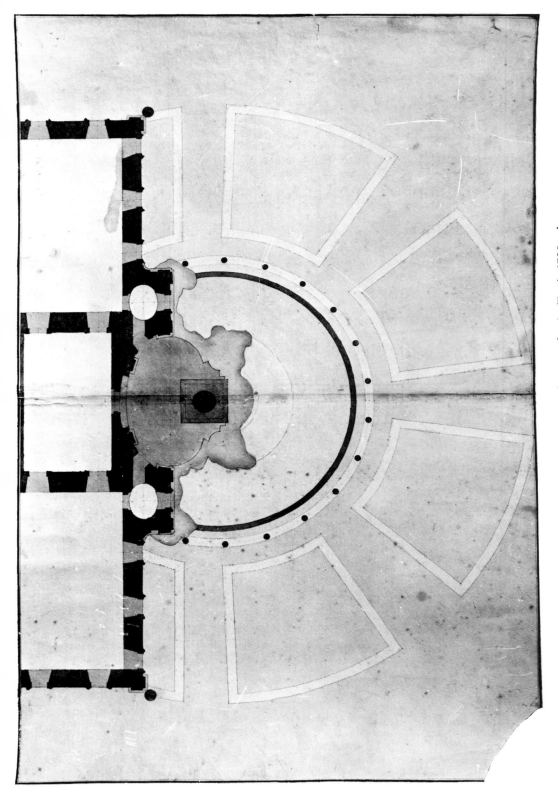

Fig. 77. Luigi Vanvitelli, unexecuted project for the Trevi, 1730, plan

Fig. 78. Luigi Vanvitelli, unexecuted project for the Trevi, 1730, elevation

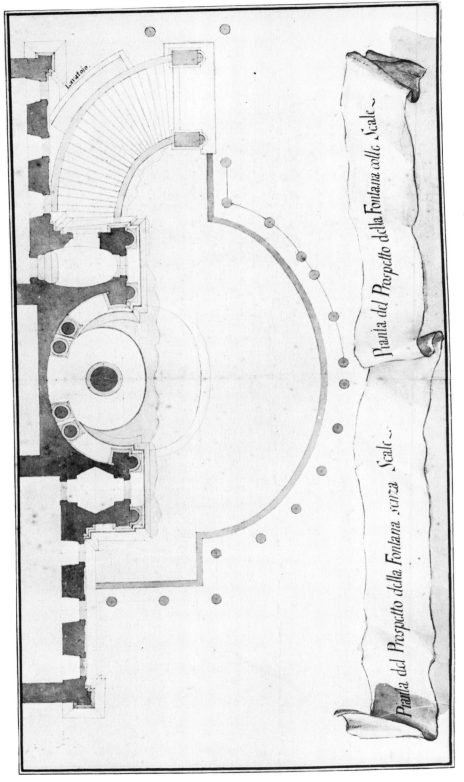

Lavatojo.

Pianta del Prospetto della Fontana colle Scale

Pianta del Prospetto della Fontana senza Scale

Fig. 79. Nicola Salvi, unexecuted project for the Trevi with *Roma*, plan

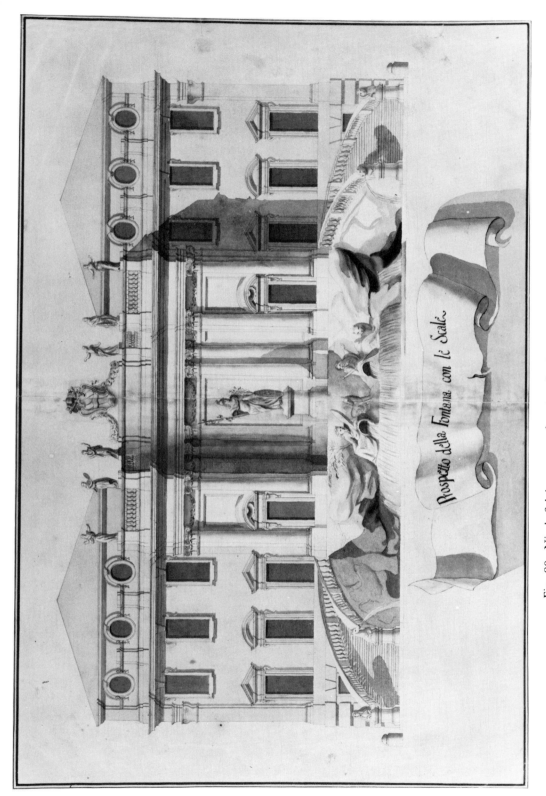

Prospetto della Fontana con le Scale.

Fig. 80. Nicola Salvi, unexecuted project for the Trevi with *Roma*, elevation once again recalls Michetti's project. Salvi's project focuses on a colossal statue personifying Rome, represented standing and holding two symbols: an olive sprig and the crossed keys of Saint Peter.

I owe the suggestion that this project is by Salvi rather than Vanvitelli to my colleague Elisabeth Kieven.[40] After studying the Montréal drawing I am convinced she is right, primarily because the design embodies Salvi's unique fusion of Baroque tradition and classical rigor. The inscribed banderoles present in both drawings, which recall a similar motif on another autograph Salvi drawing that was once part of the Bracci Collection, support the attribution to Salvi (fig. 129). Significantly, such banderoles do not appear in the two sheets recording Vanvitelli's project.

Like Vanvitelli's project, Salvi's design respects the existing fenestration of the Palazzo Poli facade while expanding the fountain laterally to overlap one bay of each wing. The sculpture set immediately above the basin, comprised of two river gods and their attributes, is virtually identical to its counterpart in Vanvitelli's design. Several explanations underlie the strong similarities between the two projects. Most important, the two sets of drawings are copies drawn by the same hand. Virginio Bracci (1737–1815), son of the sculptor responsible for the execution of the main group of statuary on the Trevi, may have recorded the projects of Vanvitelli and Salvi. The younger Bracci studied with Luigi Vanvitelli and in style his autograph drawings for the *Concorso Clementino* of 1758 resemble these sheets.[41] Moreover, both projects stress the central *mostra*, subordinating the facade of the Palazzo Poli. Finally, the personal styles of Vanvitelli and Salvi, like the men themselves, were very close in this period.

But the two projects differ also. Salvi's fountain pavilion projects far beyond the two wings of the palace so as to allow access to the curving staircase. The central concavity is correspondingly much deeper than its counterpart in Vanvitelli's project and is nearly semicircular in plan. This allows the colossal figure of *Roma* to be set within the resulting exedra, much like a smaller statue set within a niche.[42] Engaged columns as well as paired freestanding columns inside the exedra, rather than engaged pilasters, articulate the fountain proper. In the attic zone of the wings appear oval windows, while on the skyline of the fountain proper six statues of unidentifiable figures gesture toward the papal *stemma*, which provides a central vertical accent.

The far greater measure of sculptural relief visible in Salvi's design constitutes the most important distinction between the two projects. Not only does the central fountain pavilion detach itself more clearly from the palace facade, but its own internal structure has been strengthened. On the other hand, the proportions of the fountain relative to the palace wings tend to undercut the strength of the central *mostra*. In the absence of a broad attic projecting vertically, the fountain fails to dominate the composition. Salvi's decision not to continue the central entablature to the two wings exacerbates the sense of discontinuity present in his design. The lack of unity observed within the parts of the overall architectural composition also characterizes the relationships linking architecture, sculpture, and water; each appears to function separately and without compelling visual coordination. In this respect the projects of both Vanvitelli and Salvi mark a crucial juncture in the competition for the Trevi, for they point out the unavoidable necessity of covering and unifying the entire facade of the Palazzo Poli.

In his winning design for the Fontana di Trevi, Nicola Salvi succeeded precisely where his other project had failed (fig. 45). Salvi's design—and the fountain as executed—fuses the architecture with sculpture and water into a monomorphic unity. By simplifying the architecture of the central *mostra* into the form of a triumphal arch replete with a projecting attic level, he assures the dominance of the fountain. At the same time, by continuing the colossal order across the two wings Salvi effectively binds palace and fountain. The component parts of Salvi's executed design interpenetrate to an extent that makes it a difficult visual exercise to separate one from the other. Salvi's drawing brings to a close the remarkable series of unexecuted projects for the Trevi. A detailed examination of Salvi's design properly belongs to a later chapter. It now remains to examine Salvi's training and subsequent architectural career as they relate to the Fontana di Trevi.

In 1732, when Nicola Salvi won the competition for the Trevi Fountain, he was only thirty-five years old and had never received an important architectural commission.[43] Born in Rome in 1697, Salvi showed an early interest in philosophy and mathematics.[44] As a young man he devoted himself to the study of medicine and anatomy as well as to writing poetry. In 1717, at the age of twenty, he was admitted to the Accademia degli Arcadi, the prestigious literary society which had been founded in Rome by Queen Christina of Sweden. In reaction to the artificial and complex literary compositions of the High Baroque, the Arcadians self-consciously sought to return poetry and drama to simpler themes of a pastoral nature.[45] Salvi's contemporaries among the Arcadians included Pietro Metastasio, unquestionably the greatest Italian literary genius of the century, and the architect Luigi Vanvitelli.

Salvi's biographer Niccolò Gaburri records that he spent nine years deciding what career to pursue. During this time Salvi attended classes at the Roman Academy of Saint Luke offered by the painter Nicola Ricciolini, who directed his interest to architecture and introduced him to Antonio Canevari (c. 1681–1750), in whose studio Salvi trained. While studying with Canevari Salvi devoted special attention to Vitruvius, whose entire treatise he is said to have committed to memory.[46] Salvi also drew after ancient monuments as well as the acknowledged masterpieces of Renaissance and Baroque architecture in Rome, especially the works of Michelangelo and Bernini. In 1727, when Canevari left Rome to become court architect of King John V of Portugal, Salvi appears to have been charged with completing the Roman commissions his master had under way. These included the small baptistry of S. Paolo Fuori Le Mura (destroyed in 1823), the ciborium of the abbey church at Montecassino, and the choir of Sant'Eustachio.[47]

Salvi's first independent architectural commission was ephemeral in nature, a large fireworks apparatus celebrating a double wedding between the royal houses of Spain and Portugal, which was erected in the Piazza di Spagna in 1728. Salvi's grandiose *macchina pirotecnica* is depicted by two prints, one of which records its placement in the Piazza di Spagna (fig. 81).[48] The enormous scale of Salvi's festive structure is immediately apparent, for it stood more than a hundred and fifty feet tall, rising considerably higher than the Spanish Steps, the lower portions of which are just visible beneath the clouds to the right of the apparatus. Such large-scale, temporary architectural structures, made of wood, plaster, and painted canvas and designed to be blown up, were frequently employed to celebrate special occasions in eighteenth-century Rome.[49]

The imposing edifice rising illusionistically from a cushion of clouds represents the palace of Hymen, who appears enthroned within the central arch. The sources of this design provide a revealing indication of the comprehensive study Salvi devoted to historical monuments while in Canevari's studio. The first story is a free variation on Borromini's facade of Sant' Agnese in Agone and Pietro da Cortona's reconstruction of the Sanctuary of Fortuna Primigenia at Palestrina.[50] The first story also anticipates certain aspects of B. A. Vittone's design for a central-plan church submitted to the Accademia di San Luca in 1733.[51] The second story was most likely inspired by one of Fischer von Erlach's published designs for a garden pavilion.[52] The overall composition also betrays the influence of similar ephemeral designs published by Padre Andrea Pozzo in his influential treatise.[53] Salvi's design owes much to its seventeenth-century precursors, but it is nonetheless a creative synthesis of the sources, not a pastiche.

The relationship between the architecture and sculpture in Salvi's fireworks *macchina* anticipates his design for the Trevi Fountain of four years later. The central statue of Hymen set within a niche is paralleled by that of Oceanus at the Trevi.[54] The figures of Castor and Pollux with their rearing horses set diagonally below the center prefigure the tritons accompanied by sea horses at the Fontana di Trevi. The four statues crowning the attic of the *macchina* and the trumpeting Fame set within the central arch of the lantern also have their counterparts on the Trevi. Even the clouds that appear to support the palace of Hymen recall the rustic *scogli* at the base of the Fontana di Trevi. Significantly, in both of Salvi's designs sculpture is subordinated to architecture, its role and placement clearly defined by the system of classical orders.

The next important step in Salvi's career was the competition of 1732 for the facade of the Lateran Basilica, in which he entered three projects.[55] Two of Salvi's designs are known through reliable copies made by one of his pupils, while a handsome autograph drawing in the Accademia di San Luca represents

Veduta della Machina di fuoco artifiziato alta palmi 210, e larga 120 fatta innalzare in Piazza di Spagna dall'Em.o e Rm.o Sig.r Cardinal BENTIVO-GLIO d'Aragona in occasione de i reciprochi Matrimonij fra le Reali Corone di SPAGNA, e PORTOGALLO, e della ricuperata Salute di S. M. CATT.ca, e del Ser.mo PRINCIPE Spoſo

IMENEO nella ſua Reggia aſſiſo in Trono ſporge le faci nuziali a CASTORE, e POLLUCE, che rappreſentano i due Sereniſſimi Spoſi e ſiccome quelli inſieme la LUCE coſſi queſti le REALI SORELLE nel doppio Matrimonio ſi cambiano. Ambo ſono Coſtellazione benefiche, Numi tutelari della guerra, e ſimbolo dell'amicizia, che naſce da congiunzione di ſangue, e perciò alludono alla Pace e concordia, che paſſera fra queſti due Principi, e alla felicità de' loro Popoli. AMORE, che a pie d'Imeneo ſiede ſopra il Mondo, dinoſtra la ſua virtù di conſervarli in occaſione, e a reguardo anche di queſte feliciſſime Nozze, giache i due gran Principi cotanta parte ne poſſiedono APOLLO con tutte le MUSE, e colla FAMA, che fu la ſommità della Reggia feſteggiano l'univerſale applauſo ſignificano, con cui queſte glorioſiſſime Cambie viu-ne da tutte le Nazioni celebrato. Le altre Figure ſervono ad ornare, ed inſieme indicare le proprie particolari Inſegne, ed inclinazioni, che al Suggetto proposto ſi convengono.

A Machina di fuoco artifiziato   B Palcone teatrale di 2 ordini di Palchetti inalzato avanti il Regi   C Scala della Tenuta di Monti   D Fontana publica di Vino

Fig. 81. Nicola Salvi, fireworks *macchina* of 1728

a third (fig. 82).[56] In comparison with Salvi's fireworks *macchina* of 1728, his projects for the Lateran facade exhibit a more restrained classicism as well as greater unity and monumentality. Salvi's manipulation of the orders is at once more confident, bold, and sculptural; his composition builds to a powerful climax at the center of the Benediction Loggia, where pairs of free-standing columns frame a niche with a coffered vault recalling the central feature of the Fontana di Trevi, which was designed at most a few months later.

Unlike Alessandro Galilei in his winning design for the Lateran, Salvi did not propose to employ a colossal order to unify the two stories of the facade. Instead, he designed a double-tiered facade based on a creative reevaluation of fifteenth-century examples, especially Michelangelo's model for the facade of San Lorenzo in Florence. Salvi's rhythmic grouping of bay units and his extensive use of bas-reliefs attest to his close study of Michelangelo's design. So too does the way in which his central aedicular motif supported by paired Corinthian columns is framed by lateral bays. Another feature of Salvi's project is modeled on Michelangelo's design for the Campidoglio; the Ionic columns carrying flat lintels that frame the entrances to the narthex of the Lateran Basilica are juxtaposed to larger Composite columns carrying the main entablature in a way that deliberately recalls the portico of the Palazzo dei Conservatori. Nonetheless, he has used his Renaissance models creatively to generate original solutions specific to the problems posed by the Lateran commission, notably the monumental scale and four aisles of the basilica, which were different from those Michelangelo had to overcome in the more modest facade of San Lorenzo. In the clear definition of its component parts and the classical rigor governing its composition Salvi's facade is tempered by Renaissance precedent; at the same time, however, it possesses a unity and a dynamic tension that are characteristically Baroque.

The jury charged with evaluating the numerous designs submitted by the architects vying for the Lateran commission initially favored the projects of Nicola Salvi and Luigi Vanvitelli.[57] In the end, however, Alessandro Galilei was proclaimed winner of the competition in the summer of 1732. As we have seen, both Salvi and Vanvitelli also entered the competition for the Fontana di Trevi, which Salvi won in the fall of the same year. For the next two decades, until his death in 1751, the Trevi constituted Salvi's major preoccupation.[58] Salvi's biographers report that his dedication to the Trevi led him to decline several important positions, including offers from the courts of Turin and Naples and the *opera* of the Milan cathedral.[59] In the course of his unceasing labors on the Fontana di Trevi his health failed, perhaps, as one of his biographers suggests, because of the long hours he spent supervising work underground in the damp conduits of the Acqua Vergine.[60] A remarkable caricature by Pier Leone Ghezzi represents Salvi in 1744, when he was stricken with partial paralysis (fig. 83).

After 1744 Salvi's poor health severely limited his activity. In fact, he never executed another design approaching the scale and importance of the Trevi,

Fig. 82. Nicola Salvi, unexecuted project for the facade of S. Giovanni in Laterano, 1732

Fig. 83. Pier Leone Ghezzi, caricature of Nicola Salvi, 1744

but several of his smaller buildings attest to the range and quality of his work. Among the most important of these are his interior remodeling of S. Maria dei Gradi in Viterbo (1737) and the chapel dedicated to Saint John in the church of Saint Roch, Lisbon, which was executed in Rome in 1742 under Salvi's supervision and then shipped to Portugal. In 1745 Salvi undertook the expansion of Bernini's Palazzo Chigi-Odescalchi, a task in which he was assisted by his professional colleague and friend Luigi Vanvitelli.

As a result of Salvi's poor health and his preoccupation with the Fontana di Trevi, he was less productive than his better-known contemporaries Luigi Vanvitelli and Ferdinando Fuga. His command of architectural theory, his abilities as a teacher, and the outstanding quality of his design for the Trevi made him a figure of considerable stature, however. His accomplishments received official recognition in 1733, when he was elected a member of the Accademia di San Luca, and again in 1745, when he was admitted to the Congregazione dei Virtuosi del Pantheon.[61] More than is the case with most architects, Salvi's reputation is tied to a single work, his "unicogenita" as he often referred to it, and indeed, the Fontana di Trevi is the key to understanding Salvi's significance to the history of architecture.

5

The Trevi Fountain, 1732–1762:
Three Decades of
Artistic Collaboration

The architectural backdrop of the Fontana di Trevi occupies the full extent of the southern face of the Palazzo Poli, its monumental presence dominating the relatively small piazza onto which it looks (fig. 1). The fountain proper projects far into the square, which is largely taken up by its sculptured rockwork, ample basin, and the steps that provide the transition between street level and water level (fig. 84). So perfectly fused are the three component elements of Salvi's fountain—architecture, sculpture, and water—that they can never completely be separated. The smooth masonry and elegant decoration of the architecture are made to appear the logical refinement of the irregular *scogli* below; the eye moves from water and reefs to shell, niche, and pilaster in a progression of increasingly formal definition. The tension between the carefully elaborated upper portion of the fountain and the more naturalistic lower areas always exists but is tempered by Salvi's insistence on the organic unity and complementary affinity of his forms.

The architecture of the Fontana di Trevi appears to grow organically from the living rock (figs. 85, 86). A rusticated basement level articulated by drafted masonry is partially obscured by the rougher texture of the naturalistic *scogli* that rise from the fountain basin. The colossal order of Corinthian columns and pilasters tying the facade of the fountain together rises directly from the basement, which provides a transition between the polished sophistication required of an urban edifice and the rustic simplicity appropriate to a natural grotto. In several instances this transition is blurred by the intrusion of sculptural features—like the oak tree growing at the base of one of the columns—which visually bind the world of nature to the world of man (figs. 85, 87). At the far right of the fountain the stability of Salvi's architecture is illusionistically undermined by a pilaster base that appears to crumble and to fall away from the plane of the facade (figs. 85, 88). In an added touch, the lower portion of this pilaster shaft seems to revert to a state of nature; through a bizarre metamorphosis its crisp molding profiles become overgrown and distorted to resemble living, unquarried stone. In keeping with Salvi's

Fig. 84. Air view of the Trevi

creative use of ambiguity elsewhere in the fountain, this process may of course also be read in the reverse: the smooth planes and balanced architectural design of the facade grow organically from the jagged natural forms below.

Above the basement level rises the *mostra* of the Trevi, flanked by the twin pavilions of the Palazzo Poli (fig. 85). The separate parts of Salvi's triadic composition are unified by a Corinthian entablature carried by the colossal order as well as by an abbreviated Ionic entablature running between the first and second stories. The purpose of this second entablature is twofold. Since

Fig. 85. General view of the Trevi

it appears to run behind the pilasters and engaged columns of the colossal order and actually curves back into depth as it defines the central niche, it adds to the three-dimensional sculptural effect of the facade. Moreover, together with the attenuated shafts of the Corinthian order, it produces a rigorous grid system of interlocking verticals and horizontals that creates harmoniously proportioned compartments within which the window frames as well as the sculptural ornament are placed. Although Salvi's facade abounds with the very richest possible ornament, in every case it is subordinated to a governing system that is decidedly architectonic.

The central portion of the facade breaks forward, and, consciously recalling an ancient triumphal arch, supports an attic that projects above the roofline of the two wings (fig. 89). The three-dimensional relief of the facade builds toward the center, where engaged columns boldly project forward, casting deep shadows. Immediately behind the shafts of these columns is a Serlian motif, composed of an ample niche flanked by two smaller openings with flat lintels. The central niche is articulated by four Ionic columns and covered by

Fig. 86. Fontana di Trevi, detail of the southwest corner

an apsidal vault, the surface of which is richly decorated by a swirling pattern of coffering. All three niches are occupied by freestanding statues.

Sculpture also embellishes the upper portion of the fountain, notably in the two narrative base-reliefs placed above the lateral niches, the four allegorical statues in the attic, and the papal *stemma* supported by trumpeting Fames silhouetted against the sky. Underneath the escutcheon an inscription plaque, set in place in 1735, celebrates Clement XII's role in the construction of the fountain.[1] Two other inscriptions on the facade commemorate Clement's successors who completed the work he initiated on the Trevi. The first, occupying the frieze of the Corinthian order, is composed of elegant bronze characters designed by Pietro Marchesini that were set in place by Benedict XIV in 1744.[2] The second, celebrating Clement XIII, runs along the frieze of the lower Ionic order, the only remaining space available when it was affixed in 1762.[3]

The identical pavilions flanking the central portion of the Fontana di Trevi correspond to the two wings of the Palazzo Poli built in 1728–30 (fig. 85). Set between the pilaster strips of the colossal order are two registers of windows in front of which project balconies offering spectacular views out over the sculpture and fountain basin (figs. 90, 91). The windows of the first floor are framed by aedicules with triangular pediments, while those of the second floor are crowned by segmental tympana. The pediments of the second-floor windows break into the entablature of the colossal order, a violation of classical convention censured by Francesco Milizia.[4] Above the entablature square windows separated by rich bas-reliefs of cornucopiae and masks pierce a low attic (fig. 92).

The preexisting facade of the Palazzo Poli, which dictated the rhythm and placement of Salvi's fenestration, explains the unusually tight spacing of the windows on the facade of the Trevi and the license Salvi took in interrupting the entablature. Comparison between the fountain and an unexecuted project for the Trevi representing the facade of the Palazzo Poli in 1730, before it was covered over by Salvi, shows identical grids of windows, allowing for the fact that Salvi's *mostra* blocked the inside bays of each wing (figs. 43, 85). The narrow space between the windows of the second story and the attic was insufficient to accommodate a full entablature proportionate to the scale of a colossal order uniting both stories. As a result, Salvi had no choice but to interrupt the entablature with the pediments of the upper windows, a license sanctioned by at least one seventeenth-century treatise.[5] Salvi's fountain is a

◄ Fig. 87. Fontana di Trevi, detail of the oak tree

◄ Fig. 88. Fontana di Trevi, detail of the crumbling pilaster

Fig. 89. Fontana di Trevi, central pavilion ►

Fig. 90. Fontana di Trevi, sculpture and basin viewed from first-floor window
to the west

Fig. 91. Fontana di Trevi, sculpture and basin viewed from first-floor window
to the east

relatively thin veneer applied to the facade of the Palazzo Poli; when viewed frontally, the extreme two-dimensionality of the fountain facade is effectively masked, but when seen from either flank the disjuncture between fountain and palace immediately becomes evident (fig. 93). Granted the problems posed by the presence of the Palazzo Poli, Salvi's success in fusing fountain and palace facade is all the more remarkable, and doubtless explains why his design won the competition of 1732.

As we have already seen in examining the architecture of the Fontana di Trevi, Salvi lavished the sculptural ornament on the central *mostra* of the Acqua Vergine. For convenience the sculpture may be divided into three categories, the main group situated in the central niche and on the *scogli* in front of it, the allegorical statues and narrative bas-reliefs to either side, and the figures flanking the inscription and escutcheon in the attic. As executed, the sculpture of the Trevi is the work of nine different sculptors as well as numerous talented stonecutters; moreover, the statues were carved and set in place over a period of almost three decades. The following description will identify and date the contributions of the sculptors involved, but an extended analysis of their personal styles and the evolution of their designs will be deferred to a later chapter.

A gigantic marble statue of Oceanus, the personification of water in all of its many forms, dominates the fountain (fig. 94). Unlike Neptune, who presides only over the seas and who wields a trident, Oceanus holds a scepter

Fig. 92. Fontana di Trevi, detail of entablature and attic

Fig. 93. Fontana di Trevi, view from the west showing the disjuncture
between palace and fountain

as a symbol of his authority over all the waters. As he appears on the Trevi, Oceanus is wrapped in billowing drapery, the dark folds of which set off his forceful gesture of command. His long, flowing beard and full head of hair recall ancient Roman depictions of the deity in which the claws of a shellfish protrude from his locks.[6] Oceanus stands within an open oyster shell, the irregular convolutions of which gracefully make the transition from carved stone to water. A photograph of the statue with a human figure at its feet emphasizes its enormous scale (fig. 95); composed of several marble blocks and standing nearly nineteen feet tall, it surpasses even Michelangelo's *David* and the Dioscuri of the Quirinal in size.[7]

Oceanus is represented skimming over the water in a rocaille shell chariot pulled by a pair of winged sea horses accompanied by tritons (fig. 96). All the figures composing this central group were carved by Pietro Bracci (1700–73), who followed earlier models made by Giovanni Battista Maini (1690–1752). Bracci's statues were set in place on the fountain in 1762. The two groups of tritons and sea horses are represented in violent action, in contrast to the dignity and restraint shown by Oceanus. The bearded triton on the right of Oceanus leads one of the sea horses forward by its mane while blowing a conch shell to announce the imminent arrival of his master (fig. 97). The more youthful triton to the left is engaged in what appears to be an unequal struggle with a rearing sea horse, which he is attempting to control (fig. 98). Together with the action of the water that rushes out between them, these superb figures animate the vast composition of the Trevi with movement and vitality. Especially in the slanting rays of the setting sun, which dramatically spotlight their impetuous charge, the superb choreography of the Trevi comes to life (figs. 99, 100).

In comparison with the figures composing the central group, the allegorical statues occupying the two lateral niches appear relatively calm and detached (figs. 101, 102). Both statues were carved by Filippo Della Valle (1698–1768) and were set in place on the fountain in 1760. The right-hand figure, personifying Health, wears a laurel crown and holds a spear in her left hand. With her right hand she extends a libation cup from which a snake, sacred to Hygea and Aesclepios, drinks. The counterpart of Health in the other lateral niche is a representation of Fertility. This figure holds a cornucopia, from the mouth of which she extracts a cluster of grapes. Behind her an overturned urn spills water that causes plants to spring forth from the pedestal. Both of these allegorical figures express the beneficial effects of the Acqua Vergine.

Above the lateral niches two bas-reliefs illustrate the history of the Acqua Vergine in antiquity. These were set in place in 1762 (figs. 103, 104). The one on the right, by Giovanni Battista Grossi, depicts the story of the Roman maiden pointing out the source of the Acqua Virgo to Agrippa's soldiers. The figures are carved in full relief; some, like the kneeling scout at the lower

Fig. 95. Fontana di Trevi, Oceanus, with figures for scale

◀ Fig. 94. Fontana di Trevi, Oceanus

Fig. 96. Fontana di Trevi, Oceanus and triton group from above (B. Bini)

Fig. 97. Fontana di Trevi, right-hand triton from above

Fig. 98. Fontana di Trevi, left-hand triton from above

Fig. 99. Fontana di Trevi, right-hand triton

Fig. 100. Fontana di Trevi, left-hand triton

Fig. 101. Fontana di Trevi, Filippo Della Valle's statue of Fertility

Fig. 102. Fontana di Trevi, Filippo Della Valle's statue of Health

left, project outward and overlap the frame. The left-hand plaque, representing Agrippa supervising the construction of the Aqua Virgo, was carved by Andrea Bergondi. In this relief an architect kneels before Agrippa to show him his plans while the general points toward the arcades of the aqueduct, on which several masons are working. Together, these two reliefs effectively relate the Fontana di Trevi to its classical origins, both in legend (the part played by

Fig. 103. Fontana di Trevi, Andrea Bergondi's bas-relief of Agrippa supervising the construction of the Aqua Virgo

the maiden in its discovery) and in fact (Agrippa's construction of the Aqua Virgo).

In the attic four female allegorical figures, each carved by a different sculptor, symbolize the beneficial effects of water (fig. 105). On the far left a statue holds an overflowing cornucopia, representing the Abundance of Fruit, by Agostino Corsini. Immediately to the left of the inscription a second figure

Fig. 104. Fontana di Trevi, Giovanni Battista Grossi's bas-relief of Trivia pointing out the source of the Aqua Virgo

holds sheaves of grain, personifying the Fertility of the Fields, sculpted by Bernardo Ludovisi. To the right of the inscription a statue carries a cluster of grapes and raises a cup to drink. This figure, representing the Gifts of Autumn, was carved by Francesco Queirolo. The statue on the far right holding flowers in her upraised hand and in the folds of her garment is a personification of the Amenities of Meadows and Gardens, by Bartolomeo Pincellotti. Crowning the attic and silhouetted against the sky is the escutcheon of Clement XII, carved by the stonecutters Guiseppe Poddi and Francesco Pincellotti. Two winged Fames, sculpted by Paolo Benaglia, support the coat of arms. Unlike the sculpture below the level of the cornice, the finished marble versions of which were not completed until 1762, all of the statues in the attic were in place by 1735.

While the statues on the attic complete what might be termed the formal sculptural program of the Trevi, there remains an abundance of sculpture lavished on the irregular surfaces of the naturalistic rockwork that effects the transition between the facade of the fountain and the ample basin extending outward from it (fig. 106). Work on the *scogli* began late in 1735, after the completion of the facade, and continued for nearly a decade. During this period great quantities of rough-hewn travertine fresh from the quarries in Tivoli blocked the Piazza di Trevi and the neighboring streets as far away as the Piazza Santi Apostoli and the Piazza Barberini,[8] Salvi took infinite care in the design of the *scogli*, studying each detail by means of small models in wax and clay and repeatedly rearranging the travertine masses themselves.[9] Moreover, he often climbed out onto the *scogli* with charcoal stick in hand to sketch particular details onto the surface of the travertine for the stonecutters to follow.[10] Most of the representational sculpture on the *scogli* was executed between 1742 and 1744 by Giuseppe Poddi and Francesco Pincellotti, who had earlier carved the papal *stemma*.

Rather than seeming shaped by the hand of man, the *scogli* appear to have been deeply eroded by the action of the water, which courses through and over them, to create an extraordinarily expressive form of abstract sculpture (figs. 107, 108). Scattered over the surface of the *scogli*, and often situated in the most inaccessible crevices and grottoes, are naturalistic representations of some thirty species of flora.[11] Each is rendered with remarkable truth to nature and placed in a position appropriate to its natural habitat. The only liberties taken regard the scale of the plants, which in certain examples has been either enlarged or diminished so as best to suit the composition.[12]

At the left of the *scogli*, visible immediately below the head of the rearing sea horse in figure 107, flourishes a prickly pear, exposed to the sun and with some of its fruit fallen onto the ledge below. To the right an acanthus plant appears to have taken root beneath an overhanging shelf of rock. At the water's edge, just to the left of center where the water of the central cascade falls into the basin, grows a group of water plants: reeds and marsh marigolds, on one leaf of which a snail crawls (fig. 109). Behind and to the right of the young

CLEMENS·XII·PONT·MAX·
AQVAM·VIRGINEM
COPIA·ET·SALVBRITATE·COMMENDATAM
CVLTV·MAGNIFICO·ORNAVIT
ANNO·DOMINI·MDCCXXXV·PONTIF·VI·

Fig. 105. Fontana di Trevi, attic sculpture and inscription

Fig. 106. Fontana di Trevi, view down on the *scogli*

Fig. 107. Fontana di Trevi, detail of the *scogli* at left with a prickly pear
Fig. 108. Fontana di Trevi, detail of the *scogli* at right with the crumbling
pilaster and giant urn

triton blowing his conch shell is the oak tree we encountered earlier in discussing the rustic basement of the fountain, while further to the right a grapevine grows on an outcropping of rock (figs. 87, 110).

At the extreme right of the fountain, set between the basin and the retaining wall supporting the Via della Stamperia, the *scogli* envelope the observer to produce a total sculptural environment (fig. 108). In the upper right fore-ground, at the base of a colossal urn facing toward the street, flourishes a fig tree. From a fissure in the crumbling pilaster base grows a common house leek, the sculptural counterpart of many living examples of the same plant that have taken root on the fountain over the last two decades. Another weed sprouts in the shelter of an outcropping of rock beneath the pilaster, and further up along the same crevice there once emerged a lizard or salamander, only the hind parts of which still survive. This corner once contained the most extraordinary naturalistic feature of the Trevi, in the form of two snakes from whose mouths issued the twin jets of water that still fall into a trough beneath the colossal vase (fig. 111). The snake heads, visible in early depictions of the Trevi (fig. 157), were broken off sometime in the nineteenth century. A bill submitted by Giuseppe Poddi in 1744 specifically states that the snakes were studied from nature.[13] Facing opposite the colossal vase is one of the last details to be carved onto the surface of the *scogli*, the escutcheon of Monsignor Giovanni Costanzo Caracciolo di Santobono, the superintendent of aqueducts under Benedict XIV, which was added in 1744 (fig. 112).

The element of water, which of course constitutes the raison d'être of the Fontana di Trevi, provides the sound, movement, and vitality that animate the *scogli*. To sit on the rim of the basin at dawn when, suddenly, the waters of the Trevi rush forth, is to witness the great fountain coming to life. In the early morning, before the mechanized din of a sprawling modern city asserts itself, it is still possible to experience the way in which the Trevi announces itself to the ears long before it is visible to the eyes, a dimension of its charm which has enchanted generations of artists, from Madame De Stael, Hawthorne, and Respighi to Fellini.[14]

Because of the low level of the Acqua Vergine, Salvi could not produce towering jets of water commensurate with the vertical proportions of the fountain's architecture. Instead, in order visually to maximize the play of the water, he sank the collecting basin as far below the street level as possible and created the broad, horizontal shelves of the *scogli* out over which the water must run before plunging into the basin. Photographs taken with long ex-posure times reveal how the water plays over, around, and under the *scogli* (figs. 113, 114). The central cascade rushes from beneath Oceanus's shell chariot to fill three basins with segmental rims set on axis one below the other (fig. 115). These basins were cut into the *scogli* by Giuseppe Panini, Salvi's successor as architect of the Trevi, in 1760. From the smooth lip of the lowest basin the water falls in long, carefully controlled, curtainlike sheets (fig. 113).

Fig. 109. Fontana di Trevi, detail of the water plants to the left of the cascade

Fig. 110. Fontana di Trevi, detail of the *scogli* with grapevine

Fig. 111. Fontana di Trevi, detail of the
drinking fountain below the colossal urn

Fig. 112. Fontana di Trevi, detail of the escutcheon of Cardinal
Caracciolo di Santobono

Fig. 113. Fontana di Trevi, time exposure showing the fall of water, frontal

Fig. 114. Fontana di Trevi, time exposure showing the fall of water, oblique

Fig. 115. Fontana di Trevi, detail of the three central basins from above

Depending on the angle of the sun and the observer's position this water curtain may appear smooth and translucent or glittering, fragmented, and highly reflective before falling to produce a foamy spume at the base of the *scogli* (figs. 113, 116).

To the left of the central axis, aligned with the rearing sea horse, a secondary cascade illustrates Salvi's genius in creating rich and varied water effects (fig. 117). As a modest rivulet of water flows downward over the smooth and irregular contours of the travertine *scogli* it is interrupted at intervals by hidden jets that shoot upward into the air and even backwards, against the flow of water. At the feet of the sea horse is another set of nozzles from which rush broad, fanning arcs of water that suggest the splashing of frenzied hooves in the surface of the sea. At the lower left of figure 117 a trickle appears to emerge through a crevice from a spring deep in the natural rock. These and many other water effects—more than twenty-five different orifices and nozzles de-bouch water from the *scogli*—were all produced by means of the traditional technology employed by Renaissance and Baroque fountain designers, based on a gravity-fed system using pipes and jets of different dimensions.[15] While Salvi's design for the Trevi does not result from new developments in hydraulic

Fig. 116. Fontana di Trevi, detail of the water in the central cascade viewed from the side

mechanics, it represents a masterful display of the full range of effects possible using traditional technology.[16]

Extending outward from the *scogli* and occupying much of the piazza is the great basin, or *vascone*, the rim of which was carved between 1738 and 1742 (fig. 118). The view down from the attic emphasizes the relationship between the basin and the buildings defining the southern side of the piazza. This particular viewpoint also casts into relief another feature, which is usually

Fig. 118. Fontana di Trevi, detail of the basin viewed from above

◄ Fig. 117. Fontana di Trevi, detail of the secondary cascade below the rearing sea horse overlooked by visitors to the Trevi: the gently curving stairs protected by bollards and handsome wrought iron railings. The steps not only make the transition between street level and the *vascone* but double as seating for passing spectators who choose to pause a while and enjoy the aquatic spectacle.

Giovanni Battista Piranesi's magnificent *veduta* of 1773 depicts the basin, stairs, and retaining walls that separate the sunken area of the fountain from the street level (fig. 119). The retaining wall along the Via della Stamperia, constructed in 1742–43, merges with the arm of the *scogli* projecting from the right-hand corner of the fountain (figs. 119, 120). In the photograph, the boy reading on the parapet is sitting under the colossal travertine urn that emerges from a spur of the *scogli*; below the urn, under an overhanging crag, is the trough once fed by hissing snakes. The relationship between the urn as a reservoir of water and the snake fountain below can be appreciated only by an observer who has first passed along the outside of the parapet and makes the connection between the two (fig. 121). There appears to be no substance in fact to the amusing anecdote purporting to explain the location of the urn, according to which it was placed by Salvi on the parapet in order to block the view of the fountain from a barber's shop across the street where critics of his design were wont to gather.[17]

The relationship between the Fontana di Trevi and its urban context has largely been examined in chapter 2, which traced the history of the Trevi, piazza, and surrounding streets before 1732, when the actual fountain was begun. It remains to explore how Salvi's planning influences our experience of the Trevi today. A detail of Giovanni Battista Nolli's 1748 plan of Rome provides an accurate delineation of the way in which the fountain is set into the surrounding street pattern (fig. 26). While the fountain of Nicholas V was roughly aligned with the Via della Muratte, the main approach street from the city center, we have seen how Bernini's reorientation of the Trevi in 1643 established a new relationship between the fountain and its surroundings. After 1643 what mattered was not so much the immediate context as the vista linking the Trevi to a more distant monument, the Quirinal Palace (fig. 122). As a result of this radical shift the Trevi was no longer visually tied in to the main avenues of approach.

A glance at Nolli's plan shows that none of the streets leading into the piazza lines up on the Trevi (fig. 26). Only partial views of the fountain are revealed to the visitor, no matter which direction he comes from. A typical example is the vista framed by the Via di S. Vincenzo, which blocks off fully two-thirds of the Trevi from view (fig. 123). If instead one approaches from the Via de'Crociferi, the flank of the fountain itself screens all but a small corner of the basin from view. The visitor's sense of anticipation mounts, for the sound of the water is audible and the enraptured faces of the onlookers are visible before the object of their attention is revealed (fig. 124). The elements of surprise and anticipation often play an important part in Baroque urbanism, which relies so much on movement. In Bernini's designs for the

Veduta in prospettiva della gran Fontana dell' Acqua Vergine detta di Trevi. Architettura di Nicola Salvi

Fig. 119. Fontana di Trevi, frontal *veduta* of Piranesi, 1773

Fig. 120. Fontana di Trevi, detail of the *scogli* and parapet from above

Fig. 121. Fontana di Trevi, detail of the colossal urn and parapet

Fig. 122. The Quirinal Palace and SS. Vincenzo e Anastasio seen from the
attic of the Trevi

Piazza San Pietro the full experience of the basilica and square was to be
withheld until the very last moment by means of a screening element, the
so-called *terzo braccio*.[18] The preexisting street system was altered to open up
a long axial vista only in this century, thereby destroying the sense of revelation
intended by Bernini.

Pietro da Cortona's setting for S. Maria della Pace (1656–57) provides an
even more revealing comparison with the Fontana di Trevi. Like the Trevi,

it was inserted within the existing pattern of streets, none of which is axially aligned on the facade. Rather, the main approach gently curves, revealing only a portion of the church facade and piazza, the full extent and complexity of which can be appreciated only once the space has been entered. Moreover, pedestrians approaching the little piazza from either of the streets which flank the church have only a partial anticipation of the experience that awaits them. Like actors, they enter the piazza as if it were a stage with the church facade and its embracing arms composing the sets and scenery.

In the next century the scenographic quality of Cortona's design for S. Maria della Pace was carried further by Filippo Raguzzini in his Piazza Sant' Ignazio (1727–35).[19] In this piazza, however, the traditional relationship between a major architectural monument and its urban setting has been reversed. Raguzzini's square does not exist primarily to set off the church, which cannot in any case be viewed comfortably from within its confines; rather, it is from the ample stairs of the church, as from a stage, that the observer is invited to view the domestic structures that define the piazza and enjoy the ongoing spectacle of city life, which paradoxically takes place in the stalls and boxes that Raguzzini, with consummate skill, has carved out of the surrounding urban fabric. Raguzzini's inversion of the accepted relationships in Baroque planning and scenography gives the Piazza Sant'Ignazio its charm and compelling interest.

The Fontana di Trevi is perhaps the most overtly scenographic of all examples of Baroque city planning. Not only does its architecture function as

Fig. 123. The Trevi framed by the Via di S. Vincenzo

Fig. 124. The Trevi seen from Piazza dei Crociferi

a grand urban *scaenae frons*, but the stairs leading down to the fountain serve to accommodate an audience. From behind the set building the main group of sculpture appears to enter upon the rustic stage comprised of the *scogli*. The marble figures enact an event—the *adventus* of Oceanus—which has close parallels in contemporary dramatic compositions. One example is particularly worthy of note, for it was written by Salvi's fellow Arcadian and great contemporary, Pietro Metastasio. At the end of the third act of Metastasio's *Dido Abbandonata*, performed in Rome in 1724 and again in 1726 when Salvi might well have attended, there is a scene that may have influenced the design for the Trevi.[20] At the beginning of this scene a sea tempest extinguishes the fire which has destroyed Dido's palace. Following on this action Neptune's palatial abode, no doubt a large illusionistic *macchina* resembling Salvi's Palace of Hymen, rises from the waves. Neptune himself appears in a shell, pulled by sea monsters and surrounded by nereids, sirens, and tritons, to address the audience.

Metastasio's drama, expressing its heroic theme through the combined effects of music, lyrics, and illusionistic settings, is a characteristic example of late Baroque stagecraft. Salvi also conceived and executed the design for the Fontana di Trevi in consciously theatrical terms. The mythological figures of the main action aggressively move out from the plane of the facade toward the audience gathered to observe the continuing spectacle. The water over which Oceanus rides in his shell chariot is a sonorous and constantly moving reality which the spectator can directly experience, thus rendering him an active participant in the scene. The traditional barriers separating illusion and reality are blurred by Salvi's exquisite choreography uniting sculpture and architecture, which climaxes in the foamy crescendo of the central cascade.

The success of Salvi's grand theater is due in large part to the total environment he created. While the architectural backdrop, sculpture, and water naturally dominate, the observer's attention is further focused by the enveloping *scogli* and the embracing concavity of the stairs facing the main prospect. It is an important distinction that the Trevi is set off—but not cut off—from the piazza and the neighboring streets. The bollards and elegant railings provide a sense of security to observers below without presenting a visual barrier to passersby, many of whom are thus invited to pause and refresh themselves with a moment's peace or a cooling draught of the Acqua Vergine.

The enormous scale of the Trevi in relation to its urban environment constitutes another characteristically Baroque feature of its design. Like the facades of so many seventeenth-century churches, the sheer mass of the Trevi dominates the square, an effect compounded by the way in which the fountain proper moves out from the facade to occupy most of the area comprising the piazza (fig. 125). Moreover, the disparity in scale between the Trevi and the surrounding buildings is increased by their proximity to one another. The immediate visual impact of the fountain is in large part a function of its particular urban setting, which Salvi accepted, adapting his design to exploit the peculiarities of the site so that, in his own words, "this irregularity may serve in some way as an adornment of the whole work."[21] A revealing example of Salvi's sensitivity to the urban context of the Trevi is the way the axis of the Via della Stamperia, paralleled by the retaining wall, determines the right edge of the fountain's space and hence that of the basin itself (figs. 26, 125).

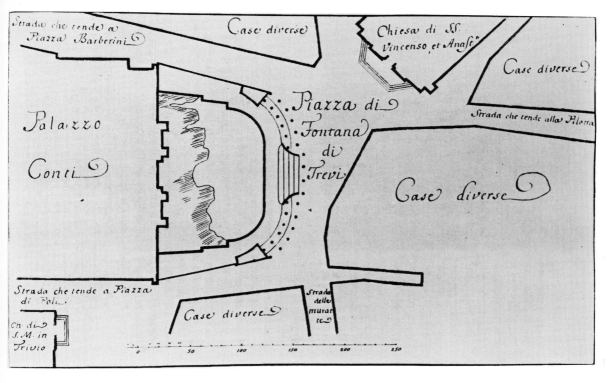

Fig. 125. Site plan of the Piazza di Trevi drawn by Filippo Barigioni, circa
1735

Later critics have repeatedly commented on the need for a piazza of larger
dimensions to enhance the Trevi.[22] In 1811, during the Napoleonic occu-
pation, the Neoclassical architect Giuseppe Valadier drafted a project that
would have created such a square by demolishing the block of houses defining
the south side of the existing piazza (fig. 126).[23] In 1925 the Fascist government considered a similar proposal to improve the area of the Trevi.[24] The
piazza, enlarged and framed by porticoes, was to become a traffic node. Both
designs would have allowed an axial view of the Fontana di Trevi from a
distance, thus altering the delicate balance between open space and architectural mass and destroying forever the sense of anticipation so essential to the
success of Salvi's urban scenography.

The cutting through of the Via del Tritone in the late nineteenth century
had a more positive and lasting effect on the Piazza di Trevi. By connecting
the Piazza Barberini with the Via del Corso the new street effectively bypassed
the Trevi, in the process creating an urban backwater frequented more by
pedestrians than by automobiles. While this has not kept the visual degra-
dation of modern commercialism away from the fountain, it has ensured that
the pattern of streets in the neighborhood of the Trevi has been preserved,
together with most of the buildings defining them. No one would deny that
our experience of the Trevi today, with its throngs of tourists, differs dra-

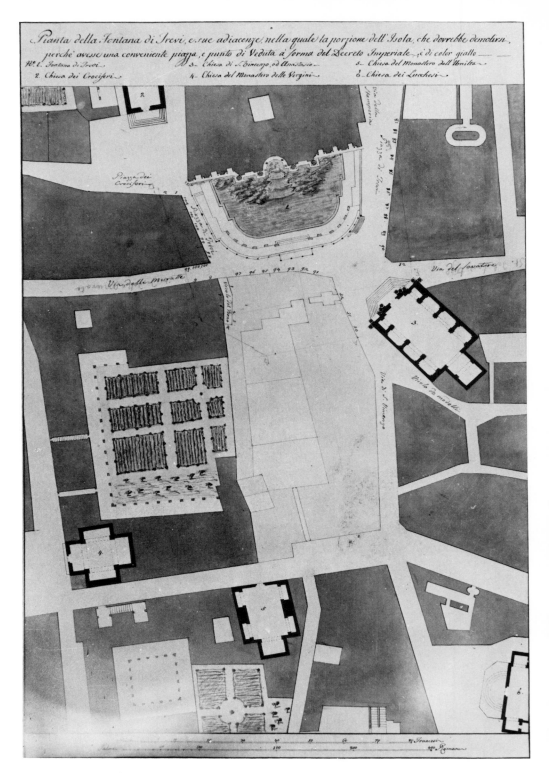

Fig. 126. Giuseppe Valadier, unexecuted project for enlarging the Piazza di
Trevi, 1811

matically from what it would have been in the eighteenth century. Still, the subtle relationship between the fountain and its urban context that makes it one of the great masterpieces of Baroque city planning has been preserved, and for this we may be grateful.

6

The Construction History
of the Trevi

The preceding description of the Fontana di Trevi has served to point out the component elements of the fountain as well as to identify the artists responsible for them and to indicate the dates of their execution. Since work on the Trevi continued sporadically for over three decades, however, it is necessary to account for its long and complex building history. For example, two sets of full-scale stucco models of the statuary, designed by another artist and differing in important respects from those presently on the fountain, were set in place on the Trevi only to be taken down and replaced by a third and final set of marble statues. An effort to reconstruct the evolution of Salvi's design and to define the nature of his collaboration with the sculptor Giovanni Battista Maini will be made in the next chapter. However, before attempting this analysis based on the interpretation of newly discovered drawings, it is essential to present the factual evidence for the construction history of the Trevi, based on the building accounts and on other contemporary documents.

There are two principal documentary sources for the building history of the Fontana di Trevi. The first consists of the financial records for work relating to the fountain, which survive largely intact in the Roman state archives. The major *fondo* in the Archivio di Stato is the *Presidenza degli Acquedotti urbani, Acqua Vergine,* the importance of which was first recognized in 1905 by E. Luzi.[1] These documents are mostly comprised of bills submitted by artists and other workmen involved in the construction of the Trevi, often itemized in extraordinary and revealing detail. They are called *giustificazioni* because they were intended to justify requests for payment. The *giustificazioni* are complemented by other financial records, shorter entries called *mandati* registering authorized payments, which often are accompanied by explanatory notes about the nature of the work being remunerated. Working from the *giustificazioni,* in some cases one can determine the precise date on which a piece of work was carried out, while in others the date on which the bill was submitted or approved for payment constitutes only an approximate *terminus ante quam.* A selection of these documents, arranged in chronological order, is presented in Appendix 1.

The second major source casting valuable light on the progress of construction on the Trevi is a diary kept by the Abate Francesco Valesio covering the period between 1700 and 1742.[2] After Valesio's death his diary was acquired by Pope Benedict XIV, who donated it to the Archivio del Popolo Romano, now part of the Archivio Capitolino, where it may still be consulted. A transcription of every entry in Valesio's diary referring to the Fontana di Trevi is also included in Appendix 1.

To an extent perhaps equaled only by Pier Leone Ghezzi's caricatures of Romans from all walks of life (figs. 83, 132), Valesio's diary entries are animated by a universal curiosity about contemporary figures and events in Rome as well as by an incisive yet compassionate wit. Valesio was especially interested in architectural projects undertaken in Rome and recorded their progress with great accuracy. Unfortunately, Valesio's death in 1742 anticipated the completion of the Trevi by two decades, but his diary nonetheless provides a valuable account of building activity at the Trevi and popular sentiment concerning it during a crucial period of its construction. Fortunately for the historian of the Trevi, the gap left by Valesio's death is partially filled by the *Diario Ordinario di Roma*, a printed resume of events occurring in Rome and abroad, extracts of which are also gathered in Appendix 1.[3]

On October 2, 1732, Clement XII issued a *chirografo*, or papal directive, authorizing Salvi to begin work on the Fontana di Trevi (App. 1.12). An initial sum of more than 17,000 scudi to finance construction was set aside from income raised by the lottery, which the Corsini pope had reinstituted in the preceding year as part of his comprehensive program to reorganize the economy of the Papal States.[4] In the decade between 1732 and 1742 more than 58,000 scudi from the lottery were spent on the Fontana di Trevi, roughly a third of the total expenditure on the Trevi during this period (App. 1.93). At the same time, even larger sums from the lottery were used to finance the construction of the Lateran facade and the Palazzo della Consulta, so the institution of the lottery played an important role in the building program of Clement XII.[5] Indeed, so closely was the progress of work on the Trevi thought to be a function of the proceeds of the lottery that in 1733, following a delay in paying the winners of the lottery, a satirical placard reading "Non plus ultra" was anonymously placed on the unfinished columns of the fountain (App. 1.19). The public drawing of the lottery was an event that continued to engage considerable interest, as is illustrated by a superb drawing made by Gian Paolo Panini in 1743 (fig. 127).[6]

On October 17, 1732, just two weeks after the *chirografo* authorizing work to begin on the Trevi was issued, Valesio observed that the demolition of the foundations laid by Bernini had begun (App. 1.13). The first bill for work on the fountain was submitted just one month later (App. 1.14).

Work on preparing the foundations for the Trevi was complicated by the poor quality of the foundation which had been laid—evidently in great haste—for the new facade of the Palazzo Poli, with the result that after only two

Fig. 127. G. P. Panini, view of the drawing of the lottery in Piazza
Montecitorio, 1743

years it already was leaning back, away from the piazza. From a report on
the solidity of Salvi's foundations for the Trevi we learn that to remedy this
situation he first excavated a wide trench parallel to the facade.[7] Piles were
then driven into the trench, which was subsequently filled with heavy stones.
The resulting foundation, constructed so as to slope down toward the palace,
provided a bed on top of which the large travertine masses composing the
scogli could then be laid. The *scogli* abutting the foundation of the palace were
set into it in a sawtooth fashion and bound together with wrought iron bars.
As a result the considerable weight of the *scogli* was transferred to the base of
the palace facade, stabilizing it. Salvi's design for the *scogli*, which rightly is
considered the most fanciful aspect of the Trevi, thus grew directly out of a
basic functional requirement for stability.

At the end of November 1732 the master mason and contractor Nicola
Giobbe (1705–48) received his first payment for work on the Trevi.[8] Giobbe
was a man of unusual learning for his profession; from his will we know that
he possessed a library of twelve thousand titles, including all the standard
architectural treatises, as well as a collection of some three hundred paintings
and prints.[9] When Giovanni Battista Piranesi first visited Rome in 1740
Giobbe served as his guide and introduced the young Venetian artist to Salvi,
Vanvitelli, and others. Piranesi's heartfelt dedication of the *Prima parte di*

architettura e prospettive, published in 1743, underscores the remarkable qualities of Salvi's principal contractor:

> But it is now time, revered sire, that, leaving my drawings aside, I come to the motives that induced me to ornament them with your honored name. And if I say first that I am persuaded to do this in order to give you, before my departure, clear evidence of the debt that I profess to you for having kept me most courteously in your house during all the time of my stay in Rome, and favored in various ways with those things that a foreigner in a strange city usually needs, [my offering] will be slight in comparison with the frequent and extraordinary help that I received from you in the practice of my profession. The rich and choice collection that you have of paintings, drawings, books, engravings, of which there is not a larger, or at least one formed with more exquisite taste or knowledge; this you have always left to my full disposition, allowing me to see at your house over and over whatever I wanted and to take wherever I needed. Most of all however I recognize what I owe to your teaching, since you not only showed me piece by piece all of the most singular beauties of this kind, ancient and modern that can be found in Rome; but you have shown with the example of your excellent drawings how one can make praiseworthy use of the discoveries of our great predecessors in new forms. [10]

In July of 1733 Salvi was reimbursed for his part in supervising the construction of a large wooden model of the Trevi representing his design for the facade at one-fifteenth the scale of the original (App. 1.18). The carpenter Carlo Camporese fashioned the model and, though badly damaged, it still survives in the collection of the Museo di Roma (fig. 128, App. 1.29). Renaissance and Baroque architects often made detailed models, both as aids in assessing the three-dimensional effect of a given design and as guides and consistent references for the workmen on the site engaged in executing the design. The documents record that trial *bozzetti* representing the sculpture and *scogli* were placed on and in front of the facade model, which was intended "for the convenience of the sculptors and stonecutters," much as can be seen in figure 128 (App. 1.34, 43, 56, 91). It should be noted, however, that the terra-cotta *bozzetti* of Oceanus and Fertility that appear in the photograph date from a nineteenth-century transformation of the wooden model into a miniature functioning fountain that played for many years within the Palazzo Albani del Drago. [11]

In conformity with Salvi's model, construction began on the central portion of the fountain, and by the fall of 1733 the shafts of the colossal order of Corinthian columns were far enough advanced to prompt the placement of the satirical placard alluding to the lottery mentioned by Valesio (App. 1.19). An autograph drawing by Salvi records the state of work around this time (fig. 129). [12] Construction continued throughout the following year at a rapid rate, to judge from the records. A large bill submitted by the *scarpellino* Francesco Tedeschi attests that the central portion of the facade was structurally complete up to the balustrade by the summer of 1735. [13] An entry in Valesio's

Fig. 128. Carlo Camporese's wooden model of the Trevi, 1733

diary confirms that the facade had already risen to a very great height and that Salvi had been ordered to finish it up to the cornice (App. 1.23).

As early as 1734 Salvi began to engage sculptors to provide the statuary for the Trevi. In August Giovanni Battista Maini received his first payment for a wax model of the Oceanus group, and in October of the same year Paolo Benaglia was reimbursed for the marble from which he fashioned the Fames supporting the papal *stemma* (App. 1.21, 22). In an entry dated May 17, 1735, Valesio reported that the pope had allocated additional funds for the completion of the escutcheon (App. 1.25). The sculptors responsible for the four allegorical statues in the attic received the first installment of their payments at the end of March 1735 (App. 1.24). Before the sculpture of the attic was actually installed, however, full-size gouache paintings of each statue were hoisted up on to the Trevi so that their effect could be judged. Antonio Bicchierari, the artist responsible, first made small drawings of the statues in each sculptor's studio and then, working from his sketches, proceeded to make full-scale cartoons, for which he was paid on the first of August 1735 (App.

1.31). Later in the summer, while the chiaroscuro mock-ups of the attic statuary were still in place, a painted version of the inscription was also put up, and corrections made in the size of the lettering and in the wording of the fourth verse (App. 1.33).

By June 1735 the central niche, including the finely detailed coffering of the vault, had been completed (App. 1.28). In the same month work began on the two lateral wings of the fountain, which until this time had remained unaffected by the ongoing construction at the center of the facade. On the first of June Nicola Giobbe's workmen began to remove the travertine string courses and wrought iron balconies from the new wing of the Palazzo Poli, which had stood for only five years, in order to prepare the wall for the new veneer of masonry with which Salvi obscured the last vestiges of the ill-fated palace facade (App. 1.27). Valesio noted that this demolition work was still in progress on the seventeenth of the month, adding that the pope had allocated an additional sum of 15,000 scudi to continue construction of the Trevi (App. 1.30). In September 1735 Carlo Camporese fashioned a detailed model of one

Fig. 129. Nicola Salvi, plan and elevation of the Trevi under construction, circa 1733

of the wings, most likely to be used as a guide for the masons (App. 1.32). At this time Camporese also made a table for the sculptors to use in modeling the *scogli*, on which work was shortly to begin (App. 1.32).

Valesio, writing in September 1735, reported that the pope had authorized the expenditure of another 10,000 scudi on the fountain, noting that work had almost ceased, presumably due to lack of funds. Another possible reason for the near suspension of building activity may be that the stonemasons were waiting for new models to be made (App. 1.34). No doubt as a result of the additional funds allocated by the pope, work began again with renewed vigor; in October 1735 Valesio reported that a "prodigious quantity" of travertine was being employed in forming the *scogli*, and again the next month he referred to the "infinite number" of travertine blocks being set into place (App. 1.36, 37).

In the course of 1736 the lateral wings were finished, and the imposing facade of the Trevi stood structurally complete. Moreover, Antonio Bicchierari's gouache paintings of the attic sculpture were replaced by the finished statues themselves, justifying the Annual Medal that was struck in this year to celebrate the completion of the facade (fig. 130).[14] The sculpture that is depicted below the attic level of the fountain in the medal, of course, had not yet been installed and must have been studied from drawings furnished the die engravers by Salvi and Maini. A large bill submitted by the mason Francesco Tedeschi documents the completion of the two lateral wings by the end of July (App. 1.39). In September the bronze features of the four allegorical statues in place on the attic were given a coat of paint "color di travertino" (App. 1.42). In the same month the stonecutters Giuseppe Poddi and Francesco Pincellotti were paid for their work on the papal *stemma* (App. 1.41). Late in September the ironsmith Simone Moretti began to secure the *stemma*, together with Paolo Benaglia's Fames, by means of pins and an impressive armature of wrought iron (App. 1.40).

Toward the end of 1736 work on the Trevi once again came to a halt, this time for more than a year. Writing in December, Valesio observed that following the placement of the papal *stemma* Salvi had been ordered to draw up a summary of accounts, which Valesio interpreted as a sign that the pope did not intend to spend any more money on the fountain (App. 1.44). Work was suspended through the next year, in spite of printed epigrams urging the pope to complete the fountain and to allow the Acqua Vergine once again to flow from it (App. 1.45, 46). Early in 1738 the pope paid a settlement to the Conti for damages to the family palace incurred during the construction of the fountain, and work began again (App. 1.47).

In March 1738 Valesio reported that the pope had allocated an additional sum of 10,000 scudi to enable work on the Trevi to resume and noted that the stonecutters were busy carving the lip of the *vascone* (App. 1.48). Early in June a large scaffold was built to allow the full-scale models of the statues composing the Oceanus group to be installed on the fountain (App. 1.71).

Fig. 130. Annual Medal of 1736, reverse

In a letter of August 19 the sculptor Giovanni Battista Maini wrote that since "the pope has decided to finish the Fontana di Trevi immediately" he was sending one of his assistants to the quarries at Carrara to select the marble and arrange for its speedy delivery.[16] The next month Maini was paid a first installment "for executing the large statue at the center, the tritons, and two sea horses" (App. 1.49). Also at this time efforts were made to increase the amount of water feeding the Trevi by adding to the tributary springs near the source of the Acqua Vergine at Salone (App. 1.50). In order to raise the funds necessary for completing the Trevi, Valesio reported, the pope late in 1738 floated a new bond issue (App. 1.51).

Early in 1739 Clement XII allocated another 10,000 scudi for work on the fountain, prompting Valesio to comment that the Trevi was a "work in which much was spent but little accomplished" (App. 1.52). Contributing to the delay was another lawsuit, this one brought by the Canons of S. Maria Maggiore, who owned the land on whith the tributary springs of the Acqua Virgine were located and who were demanding recompense for the loss of this water (App. 1.57).[17] Throughout the year work continued on the *scogli*, which, according to Valesio, Salvi was constantly rearranging, with no end in sight (App. 1.58). Several models of the *scogli* were made in this period, one of which was based on a drawing furnished by Salvi and Maini (App. 1.56). Early in April the large wooden model of the fountain was taken to Maini's studio, no doubt to assist him in designing the full-scale models of the figures composing the central group of sculpture (App. 1.56).

Other documents attest that Maini was hard at work on the Oceanus group in this period. Late in February and again early in March Valesio noted that marble for the statues and bas-reliefs had arrived, presumably by sea from the quarries at Carrara (App. 1.53, 54). This is confirmed by a payment in date of March 19, 1739, of "800 scudi . . . for the price of the marble blocks from Massa di Carrara for the *ornato* of the Trevi . . . of which 200 scudi are for the transport of these blocks, as well as for moving another large block from the studio of the deceased Benaglia to that of G. B. Maini" (App. 1.55). The large marble block moved from the studio of Benaglia, who had died in 1738, almost certainly corresponds to one that was acquired in 1730 before the election of Clement XII, when the unfortunate Benaglia was in charge of work on the fountain under Monsignor Sardini and Benedict XIII (App. 1.7). Late in 1739 Maini was paid for the "model of the large statue and the group that he is executing for the *ornato* of the Trevi" (App. 1.59).

In order to allow Maini and his assistants to install the first set of full-scale stucco models of the statues undisturbed, a wooden barrier was erected around the *scogli* in the middle of April 1739.[18] This hoarding is visible in a print etched by Giuseppe Vasi in the same year, which shows the Trevi under construction (fig. 131). Vasi's etching is one of a collection of thirty prints by Domenico Campiglia illustrating buildings constructed under Clement XII, and, unlike the Annual Medal of 1736, accurately depicts the empty niches and vacant frames awaiting Maini's statues and bas-reliefs.[19] The fountain still appeared this way on February 2, 1740, when Pope Clement XII died, for in his personal copy of Campiglia's publication in the Biblioteca Corsiniana, Cardinal Neri Corsini wrote, "This is how Clement XII left the fountain, along with 40,000 scudi to finish it."

Clement XII, who had spent so much to complete the monumental display of the Acqua Vergine, did not live to hear the water issue from Salvi's magnificent facade.[20] Work on the site did not cease immediately upon the pope's death, however, as the funds allocated for the Trevi could still be spent during the *Sede Vacante*, until Clement's successor was elected. In March 1740 Valesio recorded that the imposing armature of Maini's model of Oceanus was transported to the fountain, and by the end of the summer Maini was paid a final installment for his model, now described as "set in place," in return for

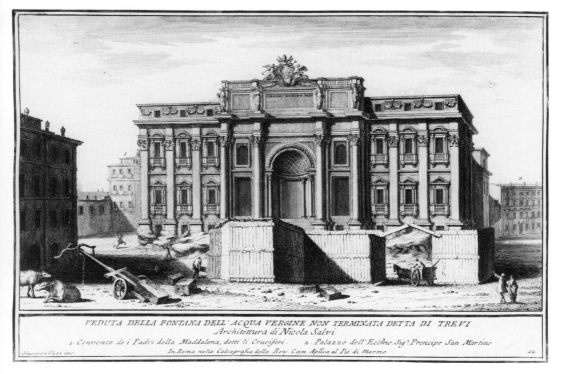

VEDUTA DELLA FONTANA DELL'ACQUA VERGINE NON TERMINATA DETTA DI TREVI
Architettura di Nicola Salvi
1. Convento de i Padri della Maddalena, detti li Cruciferi.   2. Palazzo dell'Eccmo Sigr Prencipe San Martino
In Roma nella Calcografia della Rev Cam Aplica al Piè di Marmo

Fig. 131. Giuseppe Vasi, view of the Trevi under construction, 1739

which he agreed to make any corrections deemed necessary without payment (App. 1.61, 64). Following closely on the death of the pope, three disasters occurred that directly affected the progress of work on the Trevi. On February 10, only four days after Clement's death, Valesio reported that a Genoese ship transporting marble for the sculpture of the Trevi was captured and sunk by Turkish pirates (App. 1.60). In the middle of May the low-lying area of the work site was accidentally flooded,[21] and a month later one of Maini's assistants, a Portuguese youth, fell to his death from the fountain (App. 1.62).

After a *Sede Vacante* of more than six months, Benedict XIV, Clement's successor, was elected on August 17, 1740. Only two days later, Valesio reported that Cardinal Neri Corsini accompanied Cardinal Silvio Valenti Gonzaga, the newly appointed secretary of state, to inspect the Fontana di Trevi (App. 1.63). Cardinal Valenti appears to have advised the new pope to proceed cautiously because in September Valesio reported that work on the Trevi had been suspended owing to lack of funds, noting also that a controversy had broken out between Salvi and Maini (App. 1.65). In a letter of September 16, 1740, addressed to Cardinal Corsini (then residing in Tivoli), Cardinal Felice Passerini, who as Presidente delle Acque was responsible for the work on the Trevi, complained of his inability to pay outstanding bills. His letter also touched on the state of the work:

> Here [in Rome] work on the *scogli* is being finished, but due to the disagreement that has arisen between Salvi and the sculptor Maini over the central

group, its execution in marble still has not begun. Maini is obliged to make a new model in reduced scale quite different from the large one, since Salvi says that Maini made many mistakes in its composition.[22]

In Cardinal Corsini's reply, dated the following day, he expressed doubts that the fountain could be completed unless Benedict XIV assigned new funds to the project. This prospect he deemed very unlikely, however, remarking bitterly on the horror provoked by the enormous estimate for completing the work drawn up by Salvi, "who with 100,000 scudi didn't know how to make a fountain."[23]

At some point late in 1740 or early in 1741 the disagreement between Salvi and Maini over the design of the large models was resolved through outside arbitration. Maini, writing on April 1, 1741, about his work on the "Fontana Eterna," as he bitterly called it, noted that he was currently engaged in altering the models on the site and would be finished by the end of the month, following which he hoped to proceed directly to carving the model, a task he declared himself able to complete within one year.[24] A memorandum drawn up in the summer of 1741 by the respected painter Agostino Masucci explains how he was appointed by Cardinal Corsini to effect a compromise between architect and sculptor, and that he had recommended certain changes which ought to satisfy all parties concerned (App. 1.69). Masucci's compromise solution allowed work to begin again; on March 15, 1741, Valesio reported that Maini's large-scale stucco models were being altered, and two weeks later the pope stopped on his way from the Vatican to the Quirinal in order to observe the changes being made (App. 1.66, 67). In August Maini was paid "in recognition of his renewed efforts in revising the stucco model set up in the Piazza della Fontana di Trevi according to the new idea of the painter Agostino Masucci" (App. 1.69).

Unlike his predecessor Clement XII, Benedict XIV did not initiate an ambitious building program; neither did he welcome the heritage of unfinished monuments left to him. A letter written in 1743 captures his attitude: he refers to the large sums expended on building by his predecessor as "two million [scudi] won from the lottery and employed in stones."[25] Benedict's one desire as far as the Fontana di Trevi was concerned seems to have been to finish the work as fast as possible while keeping expenses at a minimum. Writing in May 1741 Valesio noted that

> His Holiness, desiring to bring the Fontana di Trevi to completion, ordered the architect to submit an estimate of the costs necessary to finish it, and authorized the expenditure of 14,000 *scudi*. The statues and bas-reliefs will not be executed in marble, but will be left as they presently are, of stucco. This most expensive project was displeasing [to the pope] from the beginning. (App. 1.68)

In another entry written four months later, Valesio observed that although work proceeded, it did so very slowly (App. 1.70).

By the end of 1741 activity at the Trevi must have yet again ceased, if, early in February of the following year, Valesio could write that work had begun anew following the pope's allocation of additional funds (App. 1.72). The pope's intention was to finish the construction once and for all and to allow the Acqua Vergine, which for nearly a decade had been diverted from the fountain, to flow from it once again. In Valesio's last diary entry mentioning the Trevi, dated February 7, 1742, he was understandably skeptical about the possibility of work on the Trevi ever ending, observing that Salvi had changed his mind yet another time about the *scogli* and ironically remarking that "one waits to see what will result" (App. 1.72). Pier Leone Ghezzi, another acute observer of the Roman scene, also expressed doubts whether Salvi could ever finish the Trevi. In April 1742 he drew one of his celebrated caricatures of Giovanni Battista Maini, noting in the caption that the sculptor "is supposed to carve the Oceanus and tritons for the Fontana di Trevi, but God only knows when they will be done since the architect finds himself in a real mess" (fig. 132).[26]

During the second half of 1742 work continued on increasing the supply of water feeding the Trevi, which involved not only the restoration of the existing aqueduct but also the construction of a new conduit to convey the additional water from the tributary springs to the old line at Tenuta di Bocca di Leone, four kilometers from the source. In the course of this work Salvi discovered and purged the conduit of the ancient Aqua Virgo.[27] In March of the same year Pier Leone Ghezzi accompanied Nicola Giobbe in inspecting the springs at Salone and recorded his impressions in a sketch and a lengthy memorandum (fig. 133).[28] Ghezzi's charming view of the site shows the line of the aqueduct in the foreground, while the background is dominated by a picturesque medieval tower erroneously identified as the "House of the Virgin Trivia." Ghezzi's accompanying memorandum praises Nicola Giobbe for his ingenuity in solving the difficult problems of engineering posed by the site.

At the fountain, according to a notice in the *Diario Ordinario* of June 16, the basin was completed and the foundations of the stairs were being laid (App. 1.74). A payment dating from the same period indicates that workmen were still engaged in dismantling Maini's first set of stucco models representing the tritons and sea horses (App. 1.78). Another bill documents the execution of the sculptural ornament of the *scogli* by the stone carvers Giuseppe Poddi and Bartolomeo Pincellotti at this time (App. 1.73). The account makes specific reference to the shell chariot of stucco and numerous plants (all of which are identified), which were executed following models provided by Salvi, as well as the two serpents, for which Maini provided the models.

In the following year Maini labored to perfect the second set of full-scale stucco models of the central group of the fountain. In February and again in April of 1743 he was paid for "the new model on which he is working in the basin of the fountain" (App. 1.76, 77). Workmen set up a large canvas awning

Fig. 132. Pier Leone Ghezzi, caricature of the sculptor Giovanni Battista
Maini, 1742

at this time to protect the sculptor and the stucco models from the elements, and, one suspects, from the derisive comments of onlookers (App. 1.75). Although the new branch aqueduct was not yet finished, it was decided to allow the Acqua Vergine to flow into the recently completed basin. On August 24 the pope visited the Trevi, "enriched by its precious water," where he was attended by Salvi, other dignitaries, and a large crowd of onlookers (App. 1.78). After more than a decade the Trevi once again was functioning, and, for a moment at least, the gathered throng must have overlooked the provisional state of the sculpture in its enthusiasm for the return of the water.

Bills dating from the following year offer a more detailed picture of the ornament in place on the fountain. An extensive description of Oceanus's ornate shell chariot confirms that by 1744 the provisional shell formed of stucco by Francesco Ruggieri (App. 1.73), which was in place by 1742, had been replaced by the final version of cut stone by Poddi and Pincellotti (App. 1.86). Antonio Bicchierari furnished oil paintings of the statues representing Agrippa and the maiden Trivia occupying the lateral niches, as well as chiaroscuro paintings, "color di travertino," of the two bas-reliefs (App. 1.87). On July 4 the inscription of Benedict XIV occupying the frieze of the colossal

Fig. 133. Pier Leone Ghezzi, view of the springs of the Acqua Vergine at Salone, 1744

order was unveiled (App. 1.83). The antiquarian Ridolfino Venuti composed the inscription; as in the attic inscription of Clement XII, its elegant letters were designed by Pietro Marchesini (App. 1.80, 81, 85). The following week the pope paid a second visit to the Trevi, where he was once again attended by Salvi and other dignitaries. Gian Paolo Panini commemorated this visit in a painting in which he depicts the pope descending the stairs on the central axis of the fountain (fig. 134).[29]

With the inauguration of the now functioning fountain and the placement of the temporary statues and paintings on the facade in 1743, for all practical purposes the Trevi was complete, and after this date the pace of work subsided. The escutcheon of Cardinal Caracciolo, the Presidente delle Acque under Benedict XIV, was carved out of the *scogli* by Poddi and Pincellotti in 1744. In 1745 an inscription commemorating the restoration of the aqueduct and the additions made to the flow of the Acqua Vergine under Benedict XIV was placed above the portal on the Via della Stamperia that gives access to the reservoir behind the fountain (App. 1.88–90, 95).[30] In fact, work on the new aqueduct dragged on until 1747, and minor payments concerning the fountain itself continued to be made through 1748 (App. 1.92).[31]

Salvi's paralysis, which had manifested itself as early as 1744, showed no

Fig. 134. G. P. Panini, painting recording the inauguration of the Trevi in 1744

sign of improvement, and in 1748 the signature of his friend and colleague Luigi Vanvitelli begins to appear in the accounts as Salvi's assistant, bearing the title "Pro Architetto dell 'Acqua Vergine" (App. 1.96). Early in 1751 Salvi died after a protracted and painful illness; the announcement of his death prompted Vanvitelli to remark that "his life was a slow death, and he experienced purgatory in this world."[32] Giovanni Battista Maini survived Salvi by only one year, and the deaths of the principal artists concerned with the design of the Trevi, who naturally were the most anxious to complete its sculptural ornament, meant that there was no longer any immediate pressure to do so.[33] Between 1751 and 1758 another long hiatus in the building history of the fountain occurred. The aqueduct had to be maintained, of course, and Salvi's death left the position of architect of the Acqua Vergine vacant. Vanvitelli's hopes of obtaining this job rested on the service he had rendered gratis during the last years of Salvi's illness, but much to his disgust Giuseppe Panini, the son of the famous view painter Gian Paolo, was appointed Salvi's successor in 1751.[34]

The year 1758 brought the death of Benedict XIV and saw the election of his successor, Clement XIII Rezzonico, who provided the impetus for the definitive completion of the Fontana di Trevi. In a *chirografo* of March 14, 1759, the pope allocated sufficient funds to enable work to begin on replacing Maini's stucco models as well as the painted statues and bas-reliefs of the Trevi with permanent marble sculpture (App. 1.98). Over the next three years a total of 24,447 scudi would be spent on this project (App. 1.101). A superb sanguine sketch by Hubert Robert, who was living in Rome at this time, depicts the appearance of the Trevi during this last phase of work (fig. 135).[35] Twin scaffolds provide access to the bas-reliefs, a canvas awning and a wooden hoarding atop the *scogli* protect the sculptors working on the monumental figures below, and a temporary wooden bridge facilitates the transport of materials over the sunken basin. Robert's picturesque placement of a creeper in the right foreground recalls his abiding interest in the organic growth and decay of great architectural monuments and the civilizations that created them, a theme which is expressed in many of his paintings as well as in the Trevi itself.

Several artists were engaged in completing the work on the fountain; Pietro Bracci was responsible for the central sculptural group, Filippo Della Valle carved the allegorical statues occupying the lateral niches, and two sculptors, Giovanni Battista Grossi and Andrea Bergondi, executed the bas-reliefs. A diary kept by Bracci records the progress of his work on the main sculptural component of the Trevi.[36] During the four months between April and July 1759 small clay models just under three feet high were made after Maini's full-scale stucco models, which were subsequently dismantled and removed from the site. Over the next eleven months, between August 1759 and July 1760, Bracci was engaged in roughing out the marble blocks in his studio.

Fig. 135. Hubert Robert, view of the Trevi under construction, circa 1760

Seven months, between July 1760 and January 1761, were spent in assembling the blocks composing the Oceanus figure in place within its niche on the Trevi and finishing it there. A final period of ten months, from July 1761 to May 1762, was spent in placing and finishing the two groups of tritons and sea horses.

Filippo Della Valle's statues representing Fertility and Health (not Agrippa and Trivia, as had been planned by Salvi and Maini) had been erected on the fountain by 1760.[37] Andrea Bergondi's bas-relief representing Agrippa inspecting the Aqua Virgo and Giovanni Battista Grossi's scene depicting Trivia leading Agrippa's soldiers to the source of the Trevi were both in place by 1762 (App. 1.100). Giulio Cigni's inscription celebrating the completion of the Trevi and the placement of the statues and bas-reliefs under Clement XIII was unveiled at the final inauguration of the Trevi on May 22, 1762 (App. 1.100). One last change dating from this period should be noted: in the course of installing Bracci's statues of the tritons and sea horses considerable damage was done to the *scogli* and in particular to Salvi's central cascade. In order to replace the damaged surfaces, a series of three segmental basins designed by Giuseppe Panini was carved into the *scogli* on axis with the statue of Oceanus.[38]

In the more than two centuries since the completion of the Fontana di Trevi it has undergone no major changes affecting its appearance. At some time in the nineteenth century the snakes carved beneath the large urn were vandalized. Toward the end of the last century the elaborate cast iron gas lamps were installed and the small watering trough at the top of the steps leading down to the basin was removed. The most notable development of the present century, though not visible to the eye, substantially altered the way in which the water supplying the Trevi is brought from the source. In 1937 a new pumping station and pressure tower were built close to the springs, enabling the Acqua Vergine to serve the more elevated portions of the city.[39] Behind the Trevi itself, another set of pumps was installed to recycle the water flowing through the fountain. As a result the water issuing from the Trevi no longer plays by the force of gravity, as it did in Salvi's day, but is pumped through the fountain under pressure.[40] However, examination of photographs of the Trevi taken before 1937 reveals no visible differences in the appearance of the water. A thorough restoration of the Trevi, preceded by a comprehensive photogrammetric survey, is scheduled to begin within a few years.

7

Salvi's Design for the Trevi:
Evolution, Conflict,
and Compromise

The long and complex building history of the Fontana di Trevi underscores the value of documentary evidence in resolving questions of attribution and dating. For all of their presumed accuracy and usefulness, however, such written accounts cannot provide a complete picture of how the design of the Trevi evolved. In order to bring such a picture into sharper focus another, complementary body of evidence must be examined: the visual representations of the Trevi, mostly prints and drawings, which date from the period when it was under construction. It is one thing to be aware, from written documents, that Maini was obliged to change his full-scale stucco models of the principal statues in 1740, but quite another to visualize and understand the nature of the changes he made. The relevant graphic evidence sheds light on three main points: (1) the evolution of Salvi's design for the Trevi, including architecture and sculpture; (2) the nature of Salvi's controversy with Maini and the compromise brought about by Masucci; (3) the extent and effect of the transformations to the fountain introduced by Bracci and Panini.

Nicola Salvi's winning entry in the competition of 1732 for the design of the Fontana di Trevi appears to have embodied all of the essential characteristics of the fountain as executed. If not the winning presentation sheet itself, an autograph drawing by Salvi in the collection of the Museo di Roma is certainly the earliest and closest reflection of his design (fig. 45).[1] With the exception of the pilaster base at the right corner, which is not shown to be crumbling, Salvi's rendering of the architectural component of the fountain corresponds in every detail to the Trevi as it appears today. The basin and the *scogli*, however, differ substantially from the fountain as executed. Salvi's depiction of the statuary, too, contrasts with what we see today, but these important differences will be examined in a later portion of this chapter devoted to Salvi's design for the sculpture.

The basin is smaller than at present, meeting the facade at the midpoints of the lateral *casini*, while as built it embraces all but the outermost bay of each wing. Since Salvi's rendering is an orthogonal projection, representing every feature of the fountain as if viewed frontally, it is difficult to judge accurately the three-dimensional development of the *scogli* without a plan corresponding to his elevation. As depicted in the drawing, the *scogli* differ in many respects from their counterparts on the fountain today, for Salvi repeatedly altered his design as work progressed. The drawing shows several plants sketched on the surface of the *scogli* and against the rusticated basement of the fountain, demonstrating that Salvi planned the flora eventually carved by Poddi and Pincellotti from the outset. The most prominent feature of the *scogli* as they appear in Salvi's drawing is the central cascade, the surface of which is covered with scalelike facets, dropping directly into the basin from beneath the shell chariot of Oceanus.

Salvi's drawing in the Museo di Roma corresponds to the large wooden model in the same collection in every particular, including the absence of the crumbling corner pilaster (figs. 45, 128). Its close resemblance to the model, which was finished by 1733, supports an early dating for the drawing. As a three-dimensional representation of the Trevi, however, the model illustrates one important aspect of Salvi's design that his two-dimensional facade elevation could not: the continuation of the fountain's facade around the corners of the lateral wings, where it extends back two bays in depth (fig. 136). The main facade of the Trevi, of course, was never allowed to envelope the recently constructed wings of the Palazzo Poli and remains a two-dimensional veneer. Salvi's model, however, shows how concerned he was as an architect to establish a more logical and coherent three-dimensional relationship between fountain and palace facade, and if his intentions had been followed, the appearance of the Trevi would have been considerably enhanced. This wraparound extension of the main facade resembles Michelangelo's Palazzo dei Conservatori, especially in the way it was intended to convey an illusion of three-dimensional depth and continuity, while in reality being nothing more than a thin veneer applied to a preexisting palace. The two-bay extension of the facade toward the rear appears in many early prints representing the Trevi that were drawn after the model and not the monument itself.

Probably dating from 1735 or 1736, when the wings of the Trevi facade were under construction, is a handsome rendering of one of the second-story window frames of the facade, a signed drawing by Salvi that has been brutally cut into two parts (figs. 137, 138). The bottom portion of Salvi's sheet is in the Lanciani Collection and has been published by Valerio Cianfarani and Armando Schiavo.[2] The upper portion in the Museo di Roma has never been related to its companion sheet and remains unpublished.[3] Salvi's working drawing, in all likelihood intended as a guide for the stonemasons, is subtly modeled and displays his characteristic use of transparent washes to clarify the three-dimensional forms that they depict. Over the course of two decades Salvi must have drafted many such working drawings for the Trevi, of which only a precious few survive.

The Annual Medal, which was struck in 1736 to celebrate the completion of the facade of the Trevi, clarifies the development of Salvi's design, partic-

Fig. 136. Carlo Camporese's wooden model of the Trevi, 1733 +, oblique view

Fig. 137. Nicola Salvi, drawing of the second-story windows of the Trevi, ▶ upper half, Museo di Roma

Fig. 138. Nicola Salvi, drawing of the second-story windows of the Trevi, ▶ bottom half, Lanciani Collection

ularly regarding the *scogli* and the relationship of the basin to the piazza (fig. 130). As we would expect of an image of this date, the facade is represented precisely as executed, including the crumbling corner pilaster. However, as we have already noted, the medal also depicts the sculpture of the lower part of the facade, which was not actually raised into place until 1740. Neither had the *scogli* nor the *vascone* been completed by 1736, so evidently the die cutters worked from a drawing recording Salvi's intentions. Such a drawing would represent a second stage in the evolution of Salvi's design for the architecture and planning of the Trevi.

While autograph Salvi drawings representing his ideas for the fountain around 1736 have not been identified, accurate copies of Salvi's design made by one of his pupils have recently been discovered in Czechoslovakia.[4] The Moravian architect Franz Anton Grimm (1710–84),[5] who studied with Salvi between 1739 and 1740, copied many of his master's drawings.[6] Among Grimm's drawings, which are currently divided between the libraries of the Moravian Gallery in Brno and the State Castle at Rájec nad Svitavou, are seven sheets depicting the Trevi, including a plan and elevation of the fountain (figs. 139, 140).

Grimm's reliability as a copyist may be determined by comparing his drawings representing the Trevi with Salvi's originals. Grimm distinguished between his drawings made as copies, which he designated with the notation "Grimm delineavit," and his own free inventions, which he signed "Grimm fecit."[7] He designates all seven of his Trevi drawings as copies. The first represents one of the second-story window frames on the facade of the fountain (fig. 141). A lateral elevation and a section of the same window appear to the left and right. Grimm almost certainly drew this study, like the others probably a studio exercise, after the original, mutilated drawing by Salvi (figs. 137, 138). While Grimm's drawing appears cold and flat by comparison with Salvi's, it is faithful to the original in every detail. Another drawing by Grimm, for which no corresponding original drawing by Salvi survives, represents one of the first-story window frames of the Trevi (fig. 142).

A third drawing by Grimm depicts the great *stemma* of Clement XII, the crowning feature of the fountain as executed (fig. 143). The escutcheon, as it is depicted in Grimm's drawing, is blank; moreover, there are differences between the poses of the two personifications of Fame as they figure in his representation and as actually executed on the fountain. Since the *stemma* (carved by Giuseppe Poddi and Bartolomeo Pincellotti) and the Fames (sculpted by Paolo Benaglia) were unveiled in 1736, it follows that Grimm's drawings must reproduce an earlier design by Salvi. As executed by Benaglia, the right-hand figure of Fame is closer to Grimm's drawing than is the left; only the position of her legs has been altered (fig. 144). The left-hand Fame points her trumpet upward to the sky in the drawing, while her counterpart on the fountain looks downward, playing to a terrestrial rather than to a heavenly

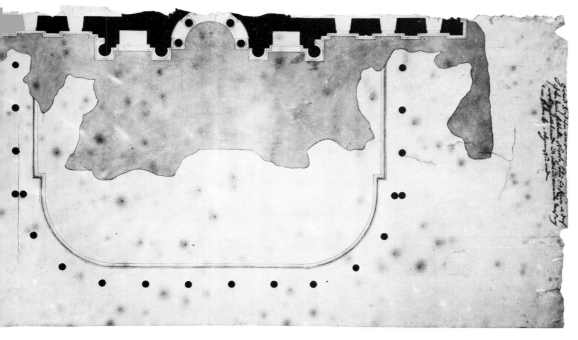

Fig. 139. F. A. Grimm, plan of the Trevi, 1739–40

Fig. 140. F. A. Grimm, elevation of the Trevi, 1739–40

Fig. 141. F. A. Grimm, second-story window of the Trevi, 1739–40

audience. The same details appear in the escutcheon as depicted in Salvi's early design for the fountain in the Museo di Roma (fig. 45). Not only are the positions of the two figures identical in these two drawings, but so are the boldly flaring trumpet mouths and blank *stemma*.

Fig. 142. F. A. Grimm, first-story window of the Trevi, 1739–40

Grimm may have copied another, more detailed study of the escutcheon by Salvi, but in any case his drawing unquestionably records Salvi's ideas for the sculpture. We know that Salvi, as architect of the fountain, provided designs for the sculpture, a procedure which eventually led to controversy.

Fig. 143. F. A. Grimm, escutcheon of Clement XII crowning the Trevi,
1739–40

In the case of the *stemma* and the Fames, however, the differences between
Salvi's design and the sculpture as executed are hardly significant; Benaglia
succeeded brilliantly in realizing the spirit, if not the letter, of Salvi's intentions. The minor changes that were made were probably responses to the
appearance of the full-scale model of the *stemma* group painted in chiaroscuro,
which we know from documents was hoisted into place in the summer of
1735.

The fourth of Grimm's drawings also depicts the *stemma,* this time viewed
from the rear (fig. 145). This drawing shows the elaborate system of wrought-
iron clamps that binds the gigantic escutcheon to the attic of the fountain,
above which it appears to hover. Most of this ironwork is no longer visible,
having been hidden beneath a great mass of reinforced concrete at some point
in the twentieth century (fig. 146). Like a view from behind a stage set out
toward the audience, Grimm's drawing reveals the mechanical means and
physical realities—ordinarily hidden from the eye—which work to sustain the

Fig. 144. Fontana di Trevi, detail of the escutcheon of Clement XII

extraordinary illusionistic effects of Baroque spectacle, both theatrical and architectural.

A fifth drawing by Grimm represents a plan and elevation of the Trevi in the course of construction (fig. 147). As is immediately evident upon comparison, it too is a copy of a surviving drawing by Salvi, this one the sheet in the Gabinetto Nazionale delle Stampe (fig. 129). While the drawing in the Farnesina was tentatively attributed by Cooke to Salvi, it is still erroneously catalogued under the name of Vanvitelli. The discovery of Grimm's copy now confirms Cooke's attribution and provides another opportunity for us to check Grimm's reliability and accuracy. Grimm has inverted the relative positions of the plan and elevation as they appear on Salvi's sheet and omitted the illusionistic scroll carrying the captions, but in all other essentials the two correspond completely.

Grimm's plan and elevation of the Trevi provide a wealth of information concerning the evolution of Salvi's design for the fountain. An inscription in

Fig. 145. F. A. Grimm, escutcheon of Clement XII viewed from the rear,
1739–40

Fig. 146. Fontana di Trevi, detail of the escutcheon of Clement XII seen
from behind

Grimm's hand, though partially damaged, identifies the plan as the Fontana
di Trevi, by "my Roman master, Nicola Salvi."[8] Grimm's plan records the
situation on the site before 1739 and (together with the elevation) shows
Salvi's decidedly rustic treatment of the central cascade. The outline of the
basin in Grimm's plan differs slightly from its appearance today; when executed
during the summer of 1742 it was broadened somewhat, and the two sides
were made to converge slightly toward the piazza. Most interesting is the
great mass of travertine *scogli* that projects into the piazza from the northeastern
corner of the Palazzo Poli. This feature exists today, but because it is set off
from the Via della Stamperia by a retaining wall, it figures less prominently.
At an early stage Salvi apparently proposed to integrate fully piazza and
fountain; in any case, the steps, which provide an element of transition as
well as a more intimate *teatro* for viewing the fountain, were built in 1742,
two years after Grimm's Roman sojourn. Grimm's elevation shows that the
two most characteristic features of the projecting *scogli*, the colossal vase and
small drinking fountain beneath, were planned before 1739, even though
they were not executed until 1744. Grimm's drawing clearly shows the giant
snakes, now lost, from whose mouths the water originally issued.

As rendered in Grimm's elevation, the architecture of the Trevi corresponds
in every respect to the building as executed, including such details as the

Fig. 147. F. A. Grimm, plan and elevation of the Trevi under construction, 1739–40

broken pilaster base at the extreme right. Both the papal *stemma* and the inscription plaque are blank, which may indicate that Salvi's drawing was made before 1736, when the sculpture of the attic was unveiled. Grimm's perspective rendering of the basin (as opposed to the strict orthogonal projection of Salvi's earlier drawing) reveals more about Salvi's intentions regarding the *scogli* and the relationship of the fountain to the piazza. This added detail suggests that early in the planning process Salvi was primarily concerned with the architectural backdrop of the Trevi and had not yet settled on a definitive solution for the fountain proper.

If Grimm's drawing differs from Salvi's earlier elevation of the Trevi in significant details, it agrees in every particular with the representation of the fountain on the Annual Medal of 1736 (fig. 130). While the small size of the medal (39 mm in diameter) would not seem to allow a detailed image to be realized, the redoubtable skills of the Hamerani as die engravers overcame this limitation. Several important features are quite clear, most notably the relationship of the basin and *scogli* to the piazza, which appears almost identical to the situation as shown in Grimm's elevation. Such details as the bollards, the smaller basin (relative to the fountain today), the crumbling corner pilaster, and even the snake fountain are common to both. The medal, then, offers further evidence that the Salvi drawing Grimm copied in 1739–40 may have been made as early as 1736.

Grimm's drawing also clarifies Salvi's intentions for the sculpture of the Trevi (fig. 148). His elevation shows the two bas-reliefs on either side of the central niche, which were not depicted in Salvi's earlier drawing. The bas-reliefs had not yet been executed when Grimm was in Rome, and the spaces they occupy would have appeared blank, as in Vasi's print of 1739 (fig. 131). Grimm's study shows that while Salvi's choice of subjects for these reliefs was respected, their appearance was altered when they were executed long after his death. In the relief representing Agrippa supervising the construction of the Aqua Virgo, Bergondi had the felicitous idea of introducing the architect, who shows his plans to the general. In Grossi's relief depicting the Roman maiden Trivia indicating to Agrippa's scouts the springs that supply the Trevi, only the relative positions of the figures have changed. Grimm's drawing also shows two over-life-size statues situated in the lateral niches, one representing Agrippa and the other the maiden Trivia, each placed beneath the narrative bas-relief in which his part in the history of the Acqua Vergine is recounted. These niches, too, were empty when Grimm came to Rome and, like the relief panels, would have been blank, just as they appear in Vasi's print. Grimm's copy of Salvi's lost drawing shows his master's preferred design for these statues, which was altered by Filippo Della Valle, whose allegories of Fertility and Health were installed in 1760.

If Grimm's elevation reproduces an original design by Salvi made between 1736 and 1740, it very likely records Salvi's mature ideas for the principal sculptural group. From documentary evidence we know that the controversy that arose between Salvi and the sculptor Giovanni Battista Maini led to alterations in the composition and placement of the full-scale stucco models of the statues comprising the central group. This dispute came to a head in 1740, when work on the statues was halted because of the differences between Salvi and Maini. A memorandum of August 1741 by Agostino Masucci, respected painter and former *Principe* of the Roman Academy of Saint Luke, records that he was asked to arbitrate the difference between Salvi and Maini and to effect a compromise that would permit work on the fountain to resume. What precisely was the nature of this disagreement and how was it resolved?

If we accept Grimm's drawing as faithfully recording Salvi's mature design for the central sculptural group of circa 1736–40, we can use it first to characterize Salvi's style and then to compare it with Maini's. While making allowances for the fact that we are dealing with a copy, and not the original of Salvi's design, I believe that Grimm accurately records the essentials of Salvi's scheme, in particular the placement and relationship of the fountain's sculpture to its architecture. The figures are placed with rigorous regard for symmetry, and their positioning is also determined by the architectural backdrop. The tritons' heads, for example, coincide with the strong vertical elements of the colossal columns framing the central niche, while the sea horses disport directly beneath the lateral niches. Similarly, the figure of Oceanus stands frontally on axis, and his head fits perfectly within the horizontal register

Fig. 148. F. A. Grimm, elevation of the Trevi, detail showing sculpture

of the Ionic captitals crowning the smaller niche columns. Each figure is clearly defined, separate, within a place of its own, scaled to the architectural setting. The overall effect is rather flat and relieflike, lacking a strong volumetric dimension; the figures, rather than projecting from the facade, seem spread out along it, occupying a shallow foreground plane of their own. Salvi's attitude toward the placement and composition of the sculpture for the Trevi can best be termed classical. The architecture of his fountain, like a classical *scaenae frons*, determines the choreography of the sculptural figures. It is precisely in Salvi's subordination of sculpture to architecture that he departs from the prevailing Baroque tradition of fountain design, exemplified by Bernini, in which sculpture constitutes the predominant element.

As a sculptor and late follower of Bernini, Giovanni Battista Maini was naturally opposed to Salvi's more architectural view of sculpture. An unpublished drawing in Switzerland shows, I believe, one of Maini's early studies for the central sculpture (fig. 149).[9] This sketch belongs to a group of eight other sheets by the same hand, one of which is inscribed with Maini's name and several of which represent projects on which he is known to have been engaged. Maini's figures are linked by complex curving lines with a strong Baroque concentration of forms at the center. However, the composition is emphatically volumetric and sculptural; figures spill out into the foreground plane, while others lead the eye back in depth across a considerable distance. The same characteristics are evident in another sketch by Maini in the Berlin Kupferstichkabinett, which, significantly, was once attributed to Bernini (fig. 150).[10] Here, indeed, we see manifested all of the characteristic elements of Baroque sculptural compositions, only softened by the use of lighter and more gently curving forms, which are especially obvious in the warmer tonalities of the red chalk original. As represented in these two drawings, Maini's style is a milder version of Bernini's more dynamic high Baroque style. I am inclined to think that both sketches represent Maini's small clay and wax *bozzetti* set against Salvi's large wooden model, *bozzetti* for which he was paid in 1734. By the time Maini's large-scale stucco models were placed on the fountain itself in 1740 the sculptor had made a number of compromises, no doubt at Salvi's insistence, but even these, as we have seen, were not sufficient to satisfy his colleague.

I believe that a small print by Piranesi which appeared as an illustration in the 1741 edition of a Roman guidebook gives an accurate, if somewhat summary, impression of Maini's large-scale models, to which Salvi objected (figs. 151, 152).[11] The asymmetry of Maini's composition is immediately evident, one triton positioned on the inside of his steed, the other on the outside. Moreover, Maini has placed the group to the right of Oceanus much further forward than its counterpart on the left. While the left-hand group appears in profile and parallel to the facade, the right-hand group breaks forward perpendicular to the facade. Neither triton blows a conch shell to herald the arrival of Oceanus, as in Salvi's design. To sum up: while Maini obviously made concessions in response to Salvi's suggestions—the different groups have been untangled and are now clearly distinct from one another— his full-scale models still appear to function independently of the architecture. We are confronted by two opposing views of the relationship between sculpture and architecture which, no doubt due to the personal temperaments of Salvi and Maini, could be resolved only through outside mediation. Salvi presented his objections to Maini's design for the central group in a revealing letter addressed to Cardinal Neri Corsini.[12] In it Salvi states that he had repeatedly tried unsuccessfully to resolve his differences with Maini but that the sculptor would not cooperate with him. Salvi further remarks that although the central group of Oceanus was his own invention he was still willing to allow Maini the liberty to alter its composition, so long as the sculpture did not prejudice his architecture and the *scogli*, on which his reputation as an architect would rest.

How was the conflict resolved? Agostino Masucci's memorandum of 1741

Fig. 149. G. B. Maini, study for the Oceanus group

Fig. 150. G. B. Maini, study for the Oceanus group

describes the compromise solution that resulted from his intervention. Masucci wrote as follows:

> Having been named superintendent of the model of the Fontana di Trevi by the eminent Cardinal Neri Corsini, and having repeatedly studied the problem on the site . . . I have advised that changes should be made in the actions of the tritons, and in the position of the calm horse with his triton. . . . The sculptor has made small clay models showing these changes, which have satisfied both myself and the architect Signor Salvi.[13]

The "actions of the tritons" must refer to what they are doing—violently restraining the two sea horses—and the problem concerning the position of the calm sea horse with his triton (the right-hand group) very likely has to do with its placement so far in front of the other two groups. How, specifically, did Masucci suggest that these be changed?

I believe that two drawings by Salvi reflect his own efforts at realizing a compromise solution, no doubt following the suggestions of Masucci. The first of these is an unpublished working drawing now in London bearing instructions to Maini on the verso (fig. 153).[14] Note particularly the stocky

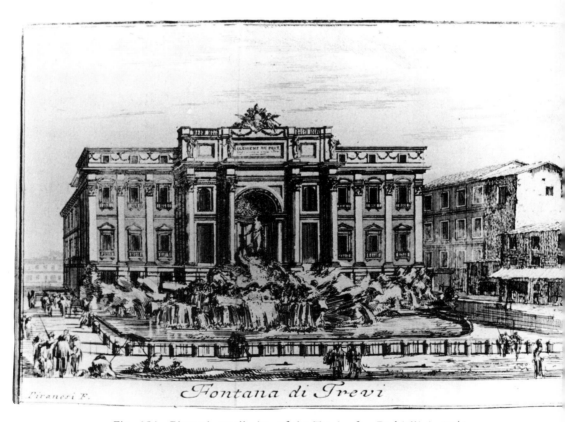

Fig. 151. Piranesi, small view of the Trevi, after Barbiellini, 1741

Fig. 152. Piranesi, small view of the Trevi, 1741, detail showing central
group of sculpture

proportions of Oceanus, whose head does not reach the level of the niche columns and whose right arm projects forward. The second drawing, which was in the Bracci Archives at the time of its publication by Constanza Gradara in 1920, is now lost (fig. 154).[15] This sheet was thought by Cooke to be Salvi's *prima idea* for the fountain, but in this he was certainly mistaken, for it shows the inscription of Benedict XIV, which was added only in 1744. Like Salvi's working drawing, the lost Bracci sheet depicts a stocky Oceanus with outstretched right arm, features that were thought to have been intro-

Fig. 153. Nicola Salvi, section through the central niche of the Trevi, circa 1741

Fig. 154. Nicola Salvi, elevation of the Trevi, 1744–51, after Gradara, *Pietro Bracci*

duced by Pietro Bracci in 1759, but which now must be attributed to Salvi and Maini around 1740.

The lost drawing shows that the right-hand triton group has been moved back somewhat to occupy the same plane as the group on the left, with the result that the entire composition has become more symmetrical and relieflike. This triton also blows a conch shell, as Salvi desired. Due to these alterations Maini's full-scale stucco models of the central group as depicted in the drawing conform much more closely to Salvi's wishes, especially regarding the relation of the sculpture to the architecture of the fountain. If Salvi's drawing dates from 1744 to 1751, it follows that it should show Masucci's compromise solution for the central group, namely the revised versions of Maini's stucco models, which were set in place on the fountain in 1743.

Of the numerous prints representing the Trevi while Maini's revised models were in place on the fountain between 1743 and 1759, Piranesi's *veduta* of 1751 is perhaps the most revealing (fig. 155). The large format of the *veduta* allowed Piranesi to include a wealth of detail; moreover, the oblique viewpoint helps to clarify the three-dimensional relationship of the different figures comprised in the central group of sculpture. It confirms the placement of the two triton groups in the same plane parallel to the facade, which though suggested in Salvi's lost frontal elevation, was more difficult to judge there. Maini's commanding figure of Oceanus appears very clearly at the center of Piranesi's oblique *veduta*, which, together with an oil sketch painted by Gian Paolo Panini around 1744, provides a detailed depiction of this lost statue (fig. 156).[16]

Veduta della vasta Fontana di Trevi anticamente detta l'Acqua Vergine.

Fig. 155. Piranesi, oblique *veduta* of the Trevi, first state, 1751

Fig. 156. G. P. Panini, oil sketch of the Trevi, ca. 1744

These two representations depict Maini's definitive stucco model of Oceanus with sufficient accuracy to allow his design first to be characterized and then to be compared with the marble statue by Bracci that replaced it. Maini's figure holds both of his arms relatively close to his body and maintains a well-balanced stance, his feet firmly planted on the edge of the seashell. A voluminous mass of drapery, the shaded folds of which serve to set off the powerful limbs of the deity, reinforces this impression of strength and solidity. From his elevated position on top of the *scogli* Oceanus gazes upward, ignoring the action below him and leading our eye outward and away from the composition.

A group of three unpublished drawings in the collection of Sir John Soane's Museum provides by far the most complete visual documentation of Maini's second set of full-scale models for the sculpture of the Trevi, as well as of Salvi's *scogli* as they appeared before 1758 (figs. 157–59).[17] Taken together, these drawings convey a remarkably vivid impression of what it was like to move around the fountain basin at this time, a sensation enhanced by the draughtsman's skillful use of colored chalks and white highlighting to represent the play of water. While I have been unable to identify the artist responsible for these sheets, he was most likely one of the group engaged by Robert Adam during his stay in Rome from 1755 to 1757 "to do the fountains, the buildings, the statues and the things that are of use for drawing after and for giving hints to the imaginations of we modern devils."[18]

The anonymous draughtsman focused his attention on the central group of sculpture and the *scogli* and provided only a summary impression of the architecture.[19] The naturalistic appearance of Salvi's cascade dramatically emphasized the central axis. In so doing it harmonized effectively with the jagged masses of the *scogli* and provided a sharp contrast to the architectural backdrop. The oblique perspective drawn from the left offers the best surviving view of Maini's giant snakes coiling around the great vase and spitting water into the trough below (fig. 157). The foreground figures give an accurate indication of scale and suggest the extent to which the naturalistic aspect of Salvi's fountain assumes a dominant role when viewed from the edge of the basin.

If we compare Maini's Oceanus as depicted by Piranesi with a later state of the same print representing Bracci's statue (figs. 155, 37), and Panini's *veduta* with a comparable photograph of the central group (fig. 156, 160), a number of small but nonetheless significant differences become apparent.[20] The most obvious change introduced by Bracci is the right arm of Oceanus, which now boldly projects from the central niche. Bracci's Oceanus looks down and to the right, his gaze directing our attention to the sculpture below him and effectively closing the composition. Bracci also makes a more limited use of drapery, which appears far less substantial, and his Oceanus stands further back on his heels in a more transitory pose. Furthermore, his legs are not spread so far apart and occupy different planes, with the result that the triangular stability of Maini's Oceanus gives way to a more elegant *figura serpentinata*. These are precisely the qualities that prompted Wittkower's in-

Fig. 157. The sculpture, *scogli*, and basin of the Trevi, viewed from the west, 1755–57

Fig. 158. The sculpture, *scogli*, and basin of the Trevi, frontal view, 1755–57

Fig. 159. The sculpture, *scogli*, and basin of the Trevi, viewed from the east, 1755–57

cisive characterization of Bracci's statue as a "slightly frivolous Neptune (*sic*), standing like a dancing master on an enormous rocaille shell."[21] Wittkower's remarks, however, while admirably characterizing the statues of Bracci and Della Valle, apply neither to Salvi's original design nor to Maini's full-scale models for the Trevi.

In addition to overseeing the placement of the marble statues by Bracci and Della Valle on the Trevi, Salvi's successor as architect of the fountain, Giuseppe Panini, was also responsible for a significant change made to the *scogli*. As we have seen, the main feature of Salvi's *scogli* was an axial cascade down which the main flow of water rushed before falling precipitously into the basin below. An unpublished plan by Salvi, which corresponds to his section depicting Oceanus, provides a detailed record of his conception of the cascade (fig. 161). The central niche and the shell chariot appear at the top of the sheet; even the positions of Oceanus's feet are carefully noted. Below appear the irregular shell forms that curve upward at the center to channel the flow of water. At the very bottom are the scalelike facets over which the cascade rushed before falling into the basin.

As conceived by Salvi, the cascade was a logical extension of the *scogli*. Its irregular forms produced the illusion of a natural waterfall rushing directly from its source to the basin below. In the process of placing Bracci's statues on the *scogli*, however, workmen damaged Salvi's cascade, which was replaced by three segmental basins designed by Giuseppe Panini (fig. 115). These

Fig. 160. Fontana di Trevi, detail of Oceanus

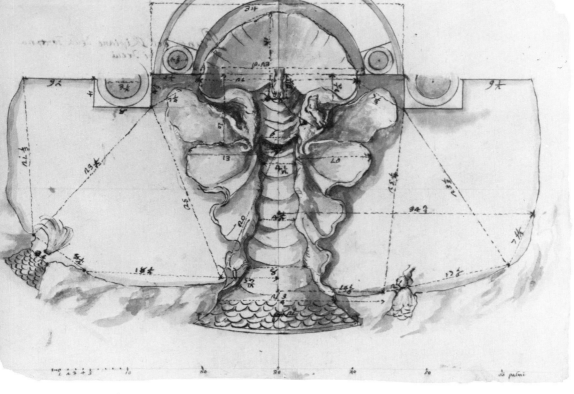

Fig. 161. Nicola Salvi, plan of the central niche and cascade of the Trevi,
circa 1741

basins were severely criticized by one of Salvi's partisans, who justly observed
that their smooth, regular lips of polished Carrara marble provoke an undesirable contrast with the naturalistic forms of the travertine *scogli*.[22] Once
again, when Wittkower comments on "the artificial union of formalized basins
with natural rock" it should be remembered that his remarks apply to Panini's
unfortunate alterations and not to Salvi's organic and unified conception of
the Fontana di Trevi.[23]

The departures from Salvi's original design, particularly those sought by
Maini for the sculpture, at once enlivened the composition and diminished
its coherence. The classical restraint of the architect's initial conception, while
unifying the fountain's component parts, also produced a somewhat static
effect at its heart. Maini's more dynamic vision of the central sculptural group
brought greater movement and life to the sculpture, complementing the
eddying water and rough-hewn *scogli*. But in fact, as executed, the sculpture
of the fountain is neither so symmetrical as Salvi planned nor so exuberant as
Maini wished. Still, as a result of the compromise imposed by outside arbitration, and in spite of later additions, Salvi's genius informs the Trevi in its
entirety. This harmony may be attributed to the inspired collaboration of
scores of artists and artisans who subordinated their personal styles to that of
the architect.

8

Salvi's Iconographical Program for the Trevi

In the course of describing the Fontana di Trevi, tracing its long construction history, and illustrating the evolution of Salvi's design, it has become obvious that the fountain's complex interplay of forms must have been largely determined by the architect's desire to convey an equally sophisticated expressive content. Salvi's literary inclination, reflected in the richly allusive poetry of his contemporary Arcadians as well as in the prevailing tradition of visual allegories in late Baroque art, supports this view. While early guidebooks systematically identify each of the allegorical figures on the fountain, they do not attempt to explain the embracing philosophy that unites the different themes and justifies many of the details. As a result, the essential meaning of the Trevi was generally either overlooked or misinterpreted by writers who concerned themselves with the fountain.

Fortunately, Salvi's own written program, in which he explains the iconography of the Trevi in great detail, survives intact as part of a manuscript in the Vatican Library.[1] This codex, perhaps by the architect's brother Abbate Dottor Francesco Salvi, was written in 1762, more than a decade after Salvi's death.[2] However, a portion of the manuscript was copied verbatim from Salvi's own papers in the possession of his heirs; this is transcribed in appendix 2.[3] Salvi's statements are written in the future tense and describe some features of his design that were never executed, suggesting that they may have been written as early as 1732, perhaps to accompany his drawings made for the competition. While the manuscript was consulted by Stanislao Fraschetti as early as 1900, the significance of Salvi's comments on the Trevi was recognized only in 1956 by Hereward Lester Cooke.[4] Cooke's exemplary translation of Salvi's passage on the iconography of the fountain allows the architect to speak directly and is quoted here in full.

> Oceanus, whose statue will be placed on the Fountain of Trevi, should certainly be considered as belonging to the same series as the other ancient deities who, under the cloak of mysterious imagery, have always symbolized useful lessons in moral philosophy or have contained hidden explanations of natural phenomena. This god, according to those authors who have had occasion to speak of him, has never been the subject of fanciful legends, but has always

220

been referred to in terms which denote a Power as superior to other Powers, as a universal Cause is superior to particular Causes. This clearly shows us that he was thought of by ancient philosophers as one of those prime, most powerful agents among natural phenomena, and was one of the original sources of an infinite number of products which depended on him.

In more specific terms he may be described thus. Oceanus has been represented at times as a figure traversing the seas on a chariot drawn by dolphins, preceded by Tritons, and followed by a numerous train of sea Nymphs. This image signifies that the visible and immense body of ocean waters are held together and constrained in the broad bosom of the Earth, and this water when it is in its assigned place we call the Sea. This Sea is, so to speak, the perpetual source which has the power to diffuse various parts of itself, symbolized by the Tritons and the sea Nymphs, who go forth to give necessary sustenance to living matter for the productivity and conservation of new forms of life, and this we can see. But after this function has been served, these parts return in a perpetual cycle to take on new spirit and a new strength from the whole, that is to say from the sea itself.

At other times Oceanus has been called the father of all things, and was believed to be the son of the Sky and of the Earth; in this role he is not the symbol of the powerful operative forces of water gathered together in the sea so much as the actual working manifestation of these powers, which appear as moisture; in this form water permeates all material things, and winding through the veins of Earth, even into the most minute recesses, reveals itself as the everlasting source of that infinite production which we see in Nature, which water also is capable of perpetuating in its productivity by its untiring ministrations.

Thus, in whatever way we choose to visualize Oceanus, it will always be true that the image must embody an impression of power which has no limit, and is not restricted in the material world by any bounds. It is completely free and always at work in even the smallest parts of the created Universe. Here it is brought and distributes itself to make useful those parts of Earth which give nutrition and birth to new forms. At the same time it quenches the excessive heat which would destroy this life. Thus water can be called the only everlasting source of continuous being.

Oceanus, therefore, given all these attributes, must be shown on his feet riding on a majestic chariot of great sea shells. This shows the essential mobility of water, which never ceases in its operation and is incapable of ever remaining still, even for the briefest moment; thus Oceanus is different from Earth which, if represented, should be shown as a seated figure, stationary and immobile, and should be shown thus because the Earth is passive, and receives the imprints which external forces, and particularly water, form upon her.

Oceanus, moreover, should be shown as having a rugged, muscular body inclined to fat, and permeated with liquid substances. He should have a long full beard on his chin to show the damp and luxuriant nature of his being. In this way he will also show the power which he has over other bodies, for when he acts calmly he is capable of giving them what they need for their being, and is able to preserve, multiply and clothe them in new and everchanging forms. On the other hand, when he acts without a just balance with all the other forces which combine to produce living bodies, no force is more powerful than his to destroy these same bodies, and take away all the beauty and good which are their natural attributes.

To give spectators the idea of a dominion which is both completely free and absolute, such as is appropriate for an absolute Monarch of the world, his head should be crowned, and he should have as imperious an air as possible. His expression, as in the images of Jupiter, should have a certain fierce, and at the same time lordly, majesty. In his right hand he should carry a scepter, which he raises in the act of giving a command. His left hand should be placed firmly on his hip and at the same time should grasp the hem of a cloak, part of which should cover as much as decency dictates, and the rest should float over his shoulder, billowing in the wind (which is never separated or independent of water). He should accompany these gestures of command with a lively action in all the other limbs of his body, and thus he will be seen to be a sovereign of unlimited power, who has appeared before his people to make known his command.

The entourage which must accompany him should in every way accord with the nature of water, and must be in allegorical form to signify his principal attributes. In this case dolphins, which are proper when Oceanus is shown being transported over the sea (which produces such monsters), are inappropriate. Instead here there should be two Tritons and two marine horses, which should be placed in such a way that they appear immediately below Oceanus, who will seem to be emerging from the hidden veins of the Earth before the people on the Fountain of Trevi. Therefore, they shall be placed on either side of the chariot, leaving Oceanus in the open and in the place of honor; this is an entirely proper relationship for servants before their master who, as soon as he shall have stopped, will wish to issue an edict from his throne, and declare a law for his subjects who watch him from below.

The marine horses should have their foreparts (which are the most noble part of the. body of living creatures) similar to the horses here on land. This signifies that the proper and primary sphere of the power of Oceanus is the land where men have their being. The hind parts of these marine horses shall end in long scaly tails like those of fishes, and this means that the power of Oceanus extends also over the vast and unfathomed leagues of the sea. These beasts shall also have wings on their backs to show that Oceanus has the power to raise himself into the air, where the waters he commands can produce the many wonderful and varied effects which we can see.

Of these two marine horses, one should be shown as being as ferocious as possible, rearing up his forepart, pawing the air with his curved legs and thrashing the rocks with his upraised tail, as though he wished to dash into a crevasse among the rocks and gallop freely away to follow his too spirited impulses. But at the same time one of the Tritons (who may be shown with his back turned to the people), having his left hand on the bridle will turn the horse's head with all his strength, and pull him in the opposite direction. He shall have his right hand raised on high to strike the beast with his conch shell, thus bridling and controlling him with all his might. This shall signify that water, when it is in stormy flood, can produce fearful effects and destruction, which would be even more dreadful if Eternal Providence did not restrain it within just limits, and an everlasting power represented by the Triton did not regulate its force.

The other horse, however, although full of lively spirit in its motions, is placid and quiet, and should be in the act of moving freely over the water, without the need of a rein, as though the beast were sufficiently well aware (by his very nature) of his duties; thus he will show the peaceful and calm state of water, which is so delightful and useful, benefiting the whole world. The second Triton, freed of the duty of holding the rein of his horse, shall be seen as though going ahead to announce the arrival of Oceanus to his subject waters. He should carry in his right hand the conch shell raised to his mouth. Thrusting out his left hand and throwing forward his chest he should appear as though he were impelled by a strong desire to proclaim to a distant crowd, with a strident blast of his conch shell, their dutiful obeisance to Oceanus. Thus he shall be shown with cheeks puffed out and straining muscles on his chest.

All of the figures which have been described, since it is reasonable that whatever subject is represented should be in an appropriate and natural setting, shall be placed in a welter of water, which comes out in foaming cascades from around the chariot and the horses with their Tritons. This will make it appear that wherever they go, they take with them the source itself of water. These waters shall have for a basin a crown of stones, the greater part of which will jut up with natural imitations of rocky crags, and others sloping downwards in various shapes and forms will receive and break the falls of water with their rough edges. These, with a roaring noise, will spill the water in foaming cascades into another great basin below, the smaller part of which will be carved in the form of a rough-cut cup. Thus the same art which has been manifest in the other parts of the monument will be displayed in the design of the rocks, in order to make a becoming setting for Oceanus and his waters. The effect of this will be that the people, who will not be able to see over these rocks, will imagine that Oceanus and his train are going over the water. It would be an improbability if they were to go over the bare rocks, where the horses and Tritons could not move and live, because they belong to the water as fishes do, and in the water have their natural environ. This setting is even more proper for Oceanus, who is none other than water itself.[5]

Salvi's remarkable statement makes it clear that the grand theme of the Fontana di Trevi is nothing less than the role of water as the primary animating principle of all Nature: "Thus water can be called the only everlasting source of continuous being." It also clarifies the significance of numerous features that appear in Salvi's preparatory studies for the Trevi as well as on the fountain itself. Salvi's remark that Oceanus should be crowned in order to express his absolute dominion explains the crown that appears in his early presentation drawing in the Museo di Roma (fig. 45). Further on Salvi suggests that the triton engaged in restraining the rearing sea horse should be shown about to strike his steed with a conch shell held in his right hand, a detail that appears in Grimm's copy of Salvi's elevation (fig. 148). Salvi also indicates that the wings of the sea horses, which often strike observers as incongruous, are intended to illustrate the presence of moisture in the air. The benign power of water, which provides "nutrition and birth to new forms," is given both metaphorical and literal expression on the Trevi in the allegorical statues in the attic and in the plants carved onto the *scogli*. In much the same way, the destructive effects of water are manifested both by the rearing sea horse[6] and crumbling pilaster base.

Salvi's metaphor of organic growth and decay is amplified by other details, notably the twin serpents of gigantic proportions set below the monumental vase (fig. 157). Like the salamander crawling out from beneath the crumbling pilaster, they call to mind the inevitable fall and decay of even the grandest works of man. Salvi's fountain deserves to be viewed in relation to other variations on this theme, both literary and visual. Pope Pius II's celebrated passage describing the ruins of Hadrian's Villa stands as an eloquent Renaissance formulation of this literary topos:

> Time has marred everything. The walls once covered with embroidered tapestries and hangings threaded with gold are now clothed with ivy. Briars and brambles have sprung up where purple-robed tribunes sat and queens' chambers are the lairs of serpents. So fleeting are mortal things![7]

A revealing visual expression of the same theme, contemporary with the Trevi, may be found in one of Giovanni Battista Piranesi's *Grotteschi*, in which serpents coil amid broken urns and the shattered fragments of antiquity (fig. 162).[8] Jonathan Scott convincingly relates Piranesi's *Grotteschi* to the poetry of the Arcadians.[9] Salvi and Piranesi both were Arcadians and shared a distinctly poetic view of the organic relationship between Nature and architecture.

Altogether, Salvi's iconographical program for the Trevi constitutes a highly original accomplishment which unites traditional allegorical and classical themes with a characteristically eighteenth-century concern for enlightened philosophical inquiry. Francesco Milizia, who regarded the Fontana di Trevi as the most magnificent work of the eighteenth century in Rome, observed, "This century has come to be called the age of philosophy. . . . Everything pertaining to our way of reasoning, even the way we feel, is the true domain of philosophy."[10] Salvi's interest in the precise and accurate depiction of naturalistic effects—witness the snake heads studied from nature and the attention lavished on the placement of plants on the *scogli* so as to recall their natural habitats—may also be related to the growing interest in science during the Age of Enlightenment. Cooke was the first to suggest that the Trevi "was intended as a symbolic demonstration of certain principles in natural science and physics which had been discovered in the early eighteenth century," notably the Marchese Giovanni Poleni's explication of the principle of the circulation of water, made in 1717.[11] This may well be true, but there is no evidence that Salvi was aware of Poleni's scientific paper, which was presented to the Royal Society in London. In any case, the cyclical transfer of moisture from air to earth and back again was a phenomenon well known to ancient philosophers

Fig. 162. G. B. Piranesi, *Grotteschi: The Tomb of Nero*

writing on meteorology, and their texts provide an equally likely source for Salvi's ideas.

According to the cosmological myths of the Greeks, the earth was bounded by the stream of Oceanus, which was not the sea but a great river flowing in a circle. Homer wrote that the gods and all living creatures originated in the waters of Oceanus, which is the source of the earth's rivers, lakes, and springs.[12] Other early accounts of Oceanus, like Hesiod's, are concerned either with the place he holds in the ancient cosmogony or with mythical geography. Plato, in a well-known passage of the *Phaedo*, provides a mythical description of a region somewhere near the middle of the earth to which our souls will journey when we die.[13] Coursing through this "unseen world" are four rivers, the largest of which is Oceanus. These constitute the ultimate source of all water on the earth's surface.

Aristotle, writing in the fourth century B.C., took issue with Plato's theory concerning the subterranean origin of water and proposed a continuous cycle of moisture moving from the earth to the heavens and then back again. He argued as follows:

> The earth is surrounded by water. . . . Now the sun, moving as it does, sets up processes of change and becoming and decay, and by its agency the finest

and sweetest water is every day carried up and is dissolved into vapour and rises to the upper region, where it is condensed again by the cold and so returns to earth. This, as we have said before, is the regular course of nature.[14]

In another passage Aristotle related this natural cycle to the mythological deity: "If Oceanus had some secret meaning in early writers, perhaps they may have meant this river that flows in a circle about the earth."[15] While Aristotle's theory of the circulation of water falls short of Poleni's conclusive scientific demonstration of this principle, his text nonetheless introduces the essential themes taken up by Salvi in his design for the Trevi.

Even if Salvi were not familiar with Aristotle's discussion of Oceanus—and his command of classical languages suggests that he was—he could have read a similar argument in the epic verse of Torquato Tasso, which he certainly must have known. A complex allegory in Tasso's *Gerusalemme Conquistata* (1594) presents Oceanus as "il gran Principio immenso, Il gran Principio delle cose eterno," who nourishes all living things with life-giving rain.[16] Both Aristotle and Tasso provide the crucial connection between Oceanus as the personification of water and as observed meteorological phenomena, which forms the philosophical basis of Salvi's iconographical program for the Trevi.

Salvi may well have consulted another source: iconographical handbooks, often written as guides for artists, which contained information about classical divinities. Natalis Comes's late Renaissance compendium of mythology, for example, has an extensive entry treating Oceanus which cites the relevant passages in ancient literature and examines the controversy about evaporation.[17] Gian Paolo Lomazzo, in his influential treatise on painting, sculpture, and architecture (published in 1584), provides instruction to artists wishing to represent Oceanus.[18] Among other details, Lomazzo particularly recommends that Oceanus should be depicted in a chariot attended by tritons blowing conch shells. Cesare Ripa's description of Oceanus in the 1603 edition of his *Iconologia* specifically mentions billowing drapery and suggests that he be depicted standing on a seashell.[19] The authors of such handbooks often took liberties in inventing new symbolic imagery and bestowing added attributes on classical deities in an effort to produce detailed and vivid images more suitable as subjects for painters. This was particularly true in the case of Oceanus, who had always remained a rather ill-defined abstraction in classical literature. By the eighteenth century encyclopedic compilations of classical iconography, accompanied by extensive illustrations of ancient simulacra, became available. Salvi may have consulted one of these, Bernard De Montfaucon's monumental *Antiquity Explained and Represented in Sculptures.*[20]

Homer's famous description of the shield of Achilles, on which Oceanus figures as the encircling border, is the earliest recorded depiction of the deity.[21] The oldest anthropomorphic representation of Oceanus appears on the François vase of about 570 B.C., which shows the god riding a sea horse.[22] Oceanus was not often represented in Classical Greek and Hellenistic art, however, and his image appears to have become confused with the more common type of the reclining river god.[23] In this guise he is represented on late Hellenistic and Roman gemstones.[24] More significant, a reclining figure of Oceanus is known to have been a prominent feature of many Roman fountains, both large public nymphaea, like that of the Aqua Julia, and small domestic fonts like the example in the Villa Albani (fig. 163).[25] This association undoubtedly had its origin in early shrines sacred to Oceanus, like the one described by Virgil in the fourth Georgic, which with its "hanging roof of stone" had the appearance of a rustic nymphaeum.[26]

By far the most popular way of representing Oceanus in Roman art, however, was as a bust or mask with large, staring eyes, broad nose and cheeks, heavy mustache, and long, wet hair and beard, from which fish and hornlike lobster claws often emerge. This type appears in virtually all artistic media, including colossal busts and reliefs,[27] sarcophagus reliefs,[28] mosaics,[29] and silver plate.[30] Many examples were visible in eighteenth-century Roman collections and were repeatedly drawn by Salvi's contemporaries. Among Pier Leone Ghezzi's drawings after Roman antiquities are no fewer than four representations of Oceanus,[31] one of which appears to have been copied by a close associate of Salvi (fig. 164).[32] Some of the other antiquities drawn by Ghezzi and known to Salvi may well have influenced Salvi's conception of the deities represented on the

Fig. 163. Oceanus fountain in the Villa Albani

Fig. 164. Copy after Pier Leone Ghezzi, head of Oceanus

Trevi. In 1732 a sarcophagus with marine figures was excavated and acquired by Cardinal Neri Corsini, in whose collection it remains.[33] Ghezzi copied the reliefs on the two ends, which are adorned with tritons, commenting on the fact that they have one tail only, not two, as do the late sixteenth-century tritons on Bernini's Fontana del Moro (fig. 165).[34] Given the date of its discovery and the collection to which this sarcophagus belonged, it seems certain that Salvi would have studied it closely in designing the tritons on the Trevi.

Another Roman marine sarcophagus may have influenced the sculpture of the Trevi in a more general way. This example, dating from the first half of the third century, is now in the Vatican, but in Salvi's day it was displayed in the Palazzo Lancellotti, where it was repeatedly sketched (fig. 166).[35] The frontal presentation of Neptune—not Oceanus—enveloped by billowing drapery and standing in his chariot pulled by sea horses accompanied by tritons, may have suggested the arrangement of the figures composing the central group on the Trevi. The planar, relieflike organization of statues that is especially apparent in Grimm's copy after Salvi's design may, in part, be explained by such a source. Salvi was likely acquainted with other works of ancient art either lost or unknown to us, perhaps another version of the Oceanus mosaic in the Sala Rotonda of the Vatican, which was discovered only after his death (fig. 167).[36]

Judging from this brief survey of classical sources, we may say that while Salvi almost certainly studied and adapted specific ancient prototypes in formulating his iconographical program for the Trevi no single one of these, literary or visual, could have provided him with the basis for his overall design. The same is true of postclassical art. Renaissance and Baroque fountains representing Neptune and Oceanus may be said to anticipate specific aspects

Fig. 165. Pier Leone Ghezzi, study of a triton
sarcophagus in the Corsini collection

Fig. 166. Neptune sarcophagus, Vatican

of Salvi's design, but none could be considered as his model. An examination of a few select examples will serve to underscore the originality of the Trevi.

Most Renaissance fountains personifying water consisted of a freestanding central figure, usually Neptune, set apart from smaller subordinate figures. The composition invariably was sculptural, with no architectural backdrop or setting. Giovanni Montorsoli's famous Fountain of Neptune in Messina (1557) and Bartolomeo Ammannati's Neptune in Florence (1561–75) are characteristic examples of this type.[37] Ammannati's colossal figure of Neptune stands on top of a shell chariot pulled by four diminutive sea horses (fig. 168). In his right hand Neptune holds a scepter, an attribute more appropriate to Oceanus. While elements of Salvi's fountain are present here, nothing could be further removed from the essentially pictorial composition of the Trevi. Conforming to the same general type is Giovanni Bologna's Oceanus Fountain

Fig. 167. Oceanus mosaic, Vatican

Fig. 168. Bartolomeo Ammannati, Neptune Fountain, 1561–75, Piazza della
Signoria, Florence

in the Boboli Gardens, which was executed between 1567 and 1576 (fig. 169). Professor Malcolm Campbell argues convincingly that the crowning figure should, in fact, be identified as Neptune and that Oceanus is portrayed symbolically by the water collected in the *tazza grande*.[38] Crouching at the feet of Neptune are personifications of three rivers, the Euphrates, Ganges, and Nile. Salvi must have been familiar with Giovanni Bologna's superb fountain, which brilliantly uses silhouetting to produce constantly changing rhythms of form, as well as with Giovanni's Bologna's iconographical interpretation of Oceanus, but neither its form nor its content appears to have influenced his design for the Trevi.

A Renaissance fountain that points toward a more pictorial composition than those of the Florentine sculptors is the Fountain of Neptune at the Villa D'Este in Tivoli, which was never completed but figures in Etienne Dupérac's engraved view of the villa made in 1573 (fig. 170).[39] Dupérac's print shows a colossal figure of Neptune holding a trident and standing in a chariot pulled across a semicircular basin by four sea horses. An exedra articulated by aedicules framing vistas out over the countryside provides an architectural backdrop to the sculptural group. A written description of 1571 emphasizes that all of the water from the fountains situated on the terraces cut into the hillside above the Neptune Fountain would flow into its basin, which was to represent the sea.[40] Aspects of the content as well as the form of the Neptune Fountain anticipate the design for the Trevi, but Salvi could have studied it only through the medium of prints like Dupérac's.

In the seventeenth century Gianlorenzo Bernini single-handedly transformed prevailing attitudes toward fountain design, replacing the additive compositions of the Renaissance with more dynamic and unified forms. Salvi's debt to Bernini is considerable, whether one thinks of details, like the treatment of the *scogli*, or in more general terms of style. Indeed, Salvi's design for the Trevi contains multiple allusions to Bernini's fountains. Among the most direct and revealing of these were the giant serpents set below the monumental vase, which were inspired by the snake set on top of the rustic base of Bernini's Four Rivers Fountain (figs. 157, 171).[41] Not only did Salvi dramatically increase the scale of Bernini's snake, however, but he also transformed its meaning. Rather than signifying cunning and renewal, as did Bernini's snake, Salvi's serpents amplify the metaphor of organic growth and decay. Moreover, with calculated ambiguity the twin serpents of the Trevi, through their association with Ascelepios and Hygea, also emphasize the salubrious effects of water.

While acknowledging Bernini's influence on Salvi, however, one must recognize that in the Trevi Salvi created a fountain utterly unlike any of Bernini's designs both in form and content. Bernini's fountains were primarily sculptural compositions, while the Trevi is essentially architectural in character. To be sure, Bernini had represented marine deities on some of his fountains—the Neptune of the Villa Montalto and the Triton of the Piazza Barberini—but

Fig. 169. Giovanni Bologna, Oceanus Fountain, 1567–76, Boboli Gardens, Florence

Fig. 170. Tivoli, Villa D'Este, detail of Dupérac print
showing the Fountain of Neptune, 1573

he never appears to have taken up the theme of Oceanus. Moreover, the iconography of his most complex fountain, the Four Rivers Fountain, is predominantly Christian. The personifications of the four great rivers of the world, represented in different stages of enlightenment, all relate to the central obelisk symbolizing Divine Inspiration.[42] Bernini's fountain stresses the universality of Faith, Salvi's the animating principle of water.

Once we distinguish Salvi's intentions for the Trevi from later alterations to his plan, the originality of his design becomes more evident. Drawing on classical sources, time-honored iconography, and contemporary scientific inquiry, Salvi expressed a new outlook in the metaphorical content of the Trevi. The circulation of water, a principle long known but infrequently used in fountain design, provided an added level of meaning to an already ambitious iconographical program. Both the mythological symbolism and the spirit of rational inquiry that inform the sculpture of Salvi's fountain are quintessential characteristics of his age and of the man himself. Indeed, only when the Trevi is appreciated for the distinctly eighteenth-century attitudes and values it embodies can Salvi's design be fairly evaluated. Such an evaluation must

Fig. 171. Bernini, Fountain of the Four Rivers, detail of snake

necessarily stress Salvi's profound awareness of Rome's classical heritage as well as his intellectual engagement in the theoretical and philosophical issues of his time.

9

The Trevi and Its Place in the History of Art

A survey of the *fortuna critica* of the Trevi Fountain reveals a remarkable range of opinion regarding its style and artistic quality. Giovanni Bottari, writing while the Trevi was still under construction, was especially critical of what he felt to be Salvi's lack of imagination in producing a mere variation on Bernini's Four Rivers Fountain.[1] Bottari went on to criticize the *scogli* ("una enorme congerie di sassi rovinatisi addosso l'uno all' altro") and to comment on the narrowness of the piazza. He also singled out the undesirable "dissonance" resulting from the juxtaposition of the rough *scogli* and the elegant Corinthian order. Perhaps most significant, Bottari was concerned with what he took to be Salvi's failure to allow the water to dominate his composition and thereby express the true function of his fountain, its *utilitas*. In spite of all these shortcomings, Bottari reluctantly admitted that the Trevi has been "exalted above the stars," as if it had been designed by Michelangelo. Bottari's censure did not go unanswered, but it is a sign of how much theoretical attitudes toward architectural design had changed that Salvi's apologist and biographer could not find a publisher for his impassioned defense of the Trevi, in which he refuted Bottari's criticism point by point.[2]

Just six years after the completion of the Fontana di Trevi another rationalist critic, Francesco Milizia, characterized it in the following terms: "This Fountain is superb, grand, rich, and altogether of surpassing beauty. One can truly say that in this century nothing more magnificent has been done in Rome."[3] This is enthusiastic praise, to be sure, but qualified by the very next sentence, which begins a litany of twelve defects. Milizia touches on all the points made by Bottari and adds others, such as the impropriety of allowing the second-floor windows to break into the entablature of the giant order. Milizia's *Memorie* is an important statement of rationalist attitudes toward Baroque architecture, most of which he condemns for excess of ornament and unwarranted license in the use of the orders. The content of Milizia's remarks makes clear that in spite of his criticism he considered the Trevi to be one of the exceptional buildings of his century. As a result of Milizia's general condemnation of Baroque architecture and the overwhelming triumph of Neoclassicism, however, the Trevi came to be discredited, and for the next century most connoisseurs tended to repeat not his praise but his criticism.

Writing in the early nineteenth century, Joseph Forsyth criticized every aspect of the Trevi except the *scogli*:

> The sculpture of the Trevi is another pompous confusion of fable and fact, gods and ediles, aqueducts and sea monsters; but the rock-work is grand, proportioned to the stream of water and a fit basement for such architecture as a *castel d'acqua* required, not for the frittered Corinthian which we find here.[4]

Whether Forsyth's remarks echo Milizia or rather reflect a personal bias is difficult to ascertain. Such is not the case, however, with writers like Michelangelo Prunetti, whose censure may be traced back to Bottari and Milizia.[5]

The antiquarian Antonio Nibby provides a rare example of a balanced and independent critical view of the Trevi in this period.[6] After quoting Bottari's criticisms of Salvi's design, Nibby shrewdly observes that in condemning the Trevi out of hand Bottari undermined his own credibility and caused his readers to suspect that, like Vasari and Baldinucci, he had an ax to grind against non-Florentine artists. Implicit in Nibby's assessment is an acknowledgment of the enduring popular enthusiasm for the Trevi, which was untroubled by the erudite censure of critics like Bottari. If the critical response to the Trevi during the nineteenth century was predominantly negative, one has only to look at more popular literary forms to see that the fountain continued to be valued as a compelling metaphor of renewal and as a symbol of Rome itself. Madame de Staël, Stendhal, and Hawthorne all affirm the almost universal accessibility of the Trevi.

Jacob Burckhardt, the first art historian to use the word *Baroque* to denote a specific style rather than a term of abuse, included a very perceptive analysis of the Trevi in his *Cicerone* of 1869.[7] Burckhardt compared the Trevi with the fountains of the Acqua Felice and the Acqua Paola and pointed out how Salvi's painterly treatment of the architecture contributes to its striking overall effect. The great German art historians of the late nineteenth and early twentieth centuries do not appear to have shared Burckhardt's enthusiasm for the Trevi. Even Heinrich Wölfflin and Paul Frankl, in spite of their sensitivity to Baroque monuments, omit any discussion of the Trevi in their published work. To a certain extent the neglect of the Trevi by these scholars may be attributed to their preoccupation with certain building types, notably churches and palaces, at the expense of others, like fountains. The Trevi's popularity, too, may have prevented it from being taken seriously.

The Trevi was included in several early surveys of Baroque architecture published around the First World War, each of which emphasized the Berninesque sources of Salvi's design.[8] The view that the Trevi is a monument to the unconscious survival of Bernini's attitudes toward fountain design, first suggested by Stanislao Fraschetti in 1900, was reinforced by Brauer and

Wittkower in their fundamental study of Bernini's drawings, which appeared in 1931.[9] Only in 1956, in an important article by Hereward Lester Cooke, was the idea that the Fontana di Trevi is a posthumous realization of a design by Bernini contested.[10] Cooke's analysis of the documents and visual records, while far from complete, conclusively proved this point.

A year later Cesare D'Onofrio published a book on the fountains of Rome with a lengthy and informative chapter devoted to the Trevi.[11] Working independently from Cooke, D'Onofrio arrived at conclusions that contradicted those of his American colleague. Basing his analysis on a drawing that he believed to be a copy of Bernini's lost design for the Trevi, D'Onofrio argued that Salvi's fountain was directly modeled on Bernini's project. The drawing in question is no longer thought to reflect an original design by Bernini, however, and was omitted by D'Onofrio in the second edition of his book.[12]

Rudolph Wittkower's magisterial survey of Italian Baroque art and architecture, which appeared in 1958, contains a remarkably sensitive analysis of the Fontana di Trevi.[13] Wittkower acknowledged the presence of Borrominesque motifs and marginal Rococo features but considered them subordinate to Salvi's particular brand of Late Baroque Classicism. Wittkower took care to distinguish the Trevi from Bernini's fountain designs but nonetheless saw it as the swan song of an epoch that had largely been formed by his genius. While it is possible to qualify certain of Wittkower's observations, the research of more than a quarter century has tended to confirm his broad vision of the period.

Wittkower used the term *Late Baroque Classicism* generically to characterize a coherent body of work executed in painting, sculpture, and architecture in the period 1675–1750.[14] He was careful to differentiate Late Baroque Classicism from previous classical trends, stressing the remarkable variety and flexibility of attitudes it embraces. By the early eighteenth century, the repertory from which an architect was able to choose had grown to include not only the acknowledged masterpieces of antiquity and the Renaissance, but the works of the great seventeenth-century masters as well. Wittkower singled out as an important sign of the new period the fact that architects were fully aware of this variety and regarded it as an asset. He also stressed the deliberate scenic quality of Late Baroque Classicism, which is manifest not only in Salvi's design for the Trevi, but in the unexecuted projects of Juvarra, Fuga, and Vanvitelli as well.

I believe that the rubric of Late Baroque Classicism most correctly describes the style of Salvi's overall design for the Trevi. However, certain of the Trevi statues, in particular those executed by Bracci and Della Valle long after Salvi's death, are more difficult to describe by this term. Once again, Wittkower's sharp eye was quick to detect different characteristics of style in the main statues of the Trevi, which he considered to be Rococo. While I acknowledge these differences, which reflect the passing of a generation between the design of Salvi's architecture and the completion of the sculptural component of the Trevi, I am not satisfied with the use of the term *Rococo* to describe them.[15]

In my view the incipient Rococo tendencies apparent in the main sculptural ornament of the Trevi, in particular a certain lightness and gentle grace, are not sufficient to justify the application of the term *Rococo*, with its French and south German associations, to the statues of Bracci and Della Valle. To my eye the dynamic Baroque exuberance of the statues composing Bracci's central group provides the primary impression, to which Rococo features are only secondary and quite marginal. It may be protested that Bracci's figures constitute a special case, since he was obliged to follow closely the models of his predecessor Giovanni Battista Maini. What of Della Valle's allegorical figures then? None can deny the corporeal abundance of *Fertility* or the classical pose and inspiration of *Health*, which seem to me to stand comfortably in the tradition of seventeenth-century sculpture in Rome and to fulfill the essential prerequisites of Late Baroque Classicism.

Salvi's relationship to the great monuments of the past as well as to the architectural theory and practice of his own day underscores his originality and the unique position of the Fontana di Trevi. Placing the Trevi against a broader background that embraces not merely Italy but northern Europe as well makes apparent the particular nature of Salvi's synthesis of Rome's architectural heritage.

The Fontana di Trevi could never be mistaken for any other monument and reflects Salvi's highly personal approach to architectural design. At the same time, however, it attests to the rich variety born of Salvi's architectural heritage. To examine Salvi's use of sources is in no way to diminish his originality but rather to explore the relationship of forms, the art of architectural allusion, which characterizes monuments in the grand classical tradition. My purpose is not directed at mere source-hunting, but rather at illuminating the dynamic process of assimilation, whereby an artist creatively transforms his sources into an original and personal statement.[16]

We have already seen how Salvi's design for the Fontana di Trevi recalls the great *nymphaea* of classical antiquity. The other ancient building type to which Salvi consciously alludes is that uniquely Roman structure, the triumphal arch. At first glance the centerpiece of the Trevi strongly resembles a two-dimensional projection of a triumphal arch with a single opening, like that of Titus in the Roman Forum (fig. 172). However, the rich surface texture of the Fontana di Trevi as well as its use of boldly projecting features recalls rather more the Arch of Constantine (fig. 173). The attic of the Trevi, too, with its four allegorical figures framing the central inscription, clearly reveals Salvi's debt to the same arch. Salvi's study of the Arch of Constantine extended to its overall design, particularly the way in which running bands of relief sculpture slide behind its projecting columns. These relief bands, like the string course of the Trevi, serve to knit together the component

Fig. 172. The Arch of Titus

elements of the arch and to enhance its three-dimensional effect. The particular
form and placement of the relief plaques on the Trevi may even have been
suggested by yet another ancient triumphal arch, the so-called Arco di Portogallo, which used to span the Via del Corso.[17]

The most important feature contributing to the remarkable range of chiaroscuro effects on the Trevi, as well as to the dynamic play of mass and void,
is the central niche, against which the commanding figure of Oceanus is
brilliantly silhouetted. This niche is crowned by an apsidal vault articulated

by a swirling pattern of diamond-shaped coffers (fig. 174). The twin apses of the Temple of Venus and Rome provide the most obvious classical source for this coffering (fig. 175). As we might suspect from the way in which Salvi creatively interpreted ideas and motifs drawn from several different triumphal arches, here too he was concerned to give this feature his personal stamp. On the geometric regularity of the coffering from his classical prototype Salvi has superimposed a second system of ribs that interrupts the primary pattern and provides an added measure of relief.[18]

Fig. 173. The Arch of Constantine

Fig. 174. Fontana di Trevi, detail showing swirling pattern of vault coffering

For Salvi the substantive remains of classical buildings shed valuable light on ancient architectural theory. Salvi's anonymous biographer relates that he memorized the entire text of Vitruvius. More important, Salvi seems to have approached the study of built architecture, both ancient and modern, from a Vitruvian perspective that stressed the three precepts of strength, utility, and grace.[19] The emphasis Vitruvius placed on the orders and their correct use, while not preventing Salvi from breaking the rules when the situation demanded it, emerges in the clarity and legibility of his design for the Trevi. Salvi subordinated ornament to the sustaining role of the orders, not allowing it to interfere with the clarity of the overall design. Salvi's "antico gusto," which distinguished him from most of his contemporaries, resulted not so much from his study of ancient monuments—all architects studied the antique—as from how he studied them.[20] His method, based on a flexible reading of Vitruvius, showed the way to a consistent and rational approach to architectural design.

As an architect practicing in Rome just before the middle of the eighteenth century Salvi was heir to an immense architectural tradition by no means limited to the period of classical antiquity. Specific Renaissance architects and buildings also exerted a powerful influence on his creative imagination. One of Salvi's biographers mentions that he devoted special attention to the work of Michelangelo. In connection with Salvi's project for the Lateran we have already seen how much he learned from Michelangelo's early design for the facade of San Lorenzo. Michelangelo's later Roman works, in particular the Campidoglio and Saint Peter's, appear to have been especially stimulating to Salvi in designing the Fontana di Trevi.

Michelangelo's Campidoglio shows a number of similarities to Salvi's design for the Trevi (fig. 176). Both the Senators' Palace and the Fontana di Trevi are raised above basements vigorously articulated by drafted masonry, from which spring colossal Corinthian pilasters. Moreover, in each case the architects applied facades as veneers to already existing palaces, a similarity that suggests Michelangelo's solution was of particular interest to Salvi.[21] On the facade of the neighboring Conservators' Palace Salvi could have observed the essentials of Michelangelo's gridlike structure based on post-and-beam construction. Michelangelo's dramatic juxtaposition of a smaller order supporting the portico with the colossal pilasters extending the full height of the building may have inspired the columns framing the central niche of the Trevi.

By the eighteenth century the work of Michelangelo and other masters of the High Renaissance constituted part of a heritage with which every architect was expected to be familiar. For example, Salvi's great contemporary Filippo Juvarra was instructed by his master Carlo Fontana to study the work of Michelangelo, in particular the Campidoglio.[22] Seen in this light Salvi's close study of Michelangelo is by no means unusual; the real significance lies in the particular lessons he learned and how he applied them in his own work. Here, again, the parallel with Juvarra is instructive. While Juvarra exploited the scenographic potential of the Campidoglio in his later designs, Salvi was struck by the powerful interplay of horizontal and vertical forces in Michelangelo's buildings on the Capitoline Hill.[23]

In my view Michelangelo's architecture influenced Salvi's design for the Trevi in other ways as well. Salvi's bold sculptural treatment of the central *mostra* of the Trevi as well as his exploitation of the rough texture of the travertine recalls the exterior elevations of Saint Peter's. There he could have studied Michelangelo's use of cast shadows as an animating feature of design and also become familiar with the great niches scooped out of the wall mass, some of which appear to be supported by consoles like Salvi's windows on the Trevi.

Salvi's biographer mentions only Michelangelo among the Renaissance architects he studied. No doubt Salvi was also familiar with the designs of Michelangelo's great contemporary Andrea Palladio. Palladio's treatise on architecture as well as his collaboration on the Barbaro edition of Vitruvius would have sufficed to ensure Salvi's acquaintance with this master's published buildings and principles of design. However, there is no evidence to suggest

Fig. 176. Michelangelo, Piazza del Campidoglio

that Salvi ever saw any of Palladio's executed buildings, all of which are situated in the Venetian *terra firma* and in Venice itself.

For this reason Palladio's influence on Salvi was altogether different from that exerted by Michelangelo. While Salvi's continuous and direct experience of Michelangelo's powerfully expressive architecture evoked a more emotional response, his study of Palladio's treatise understandably led to a more rational consideration of theoretical principles. Paolo Portoghesi has stressed the influence of specific Palladian buildings on Salvi's design for the Trevi.[24] Two of Palladio's palaces, the Palazzo Valmarana and the Palazzo Porto-Breganze, employ features—a high basement of drafted masonry, a colossal order, pedimented windows, and projecting balconies—that also appear in the Trevi. While acknowledging the similarity of these individual features as they are employed by Palladio and Salvi, I would consider them to be parallel, rather than consciously related examples. Given Salvi's creative adaptation of earlier monuments, for him underlying principles and overall structure clearly were concerns of primary importance, to which mere details were always subordinate.

◀ Fig. 175. Temple of Venus and Rome, apse with swirling pattern of coffering

In one respect, however, Palladio did influence Salvi's design for the Trevi, albeit indirectly. The Loggia del Capitaniato in Vicenza, like the Valmarana and Porto-Breganze palaces, bears a generic relationship to the Fontana di Trevi (fig. 177).[25] A colossal order of engaged columns frames bays, in the upper story of which are windows with projecting balconies. While these window frames do not include tympana, they break into the entablature of the colossal order much as the second-story windows on the Trevi do. By violating the physical integrity of the entablature in this way Palladio stimulated later architects to do likewise. In the next century Francesco Borromini made use of a similar solution in the facade of the Oratory of the Filippini as well as in the courtyards of the monastery, which were certainly known to Salvi.[26] Palladio's Loggia was not illustrated in his treatise, and I am of the opinion that Salvi arrived at his own formulation—certainly the most elegant of the three—indirectly through Borromini's inspired transformation of Palladian design.

As this last comparison suggests, in addition to consulting the acknowledged masterpieces of antiquity and the Renaissance, Salvi made extensive use of seventeenth-century sources as well. Salvi's biographer singled out Bernini from the ranks of "modern" architects whose work he studied. We have already seen how influential Bernini's treatment of the *scogli* in his Four Rivers Fountain was for Salvi. Bernini's sculptural treatment of architectural forms identified him as the heir of Michelangelo, and in some cases it is difficult to say whether Salvi was responding directly to Michelangelo or seeing him through the filter of Bernini.

Bernini's palace designs, in particular the Palazzo Ludovisi-Montecitorio, the Palazzo Chigi-Odescalchi, and his projects for the Louvre, all display a triadic organization, contrasting a central motif with flanking wings. Great rusticated basements composed of rough-hewn blocks figure prominently in Bernini's designs for the Ludovisi Palace and the Louvre. In the corner bays of Bernini's final project for the Louvre colossal pilasters frame two vertically stacked windows separated by a string course, which may have suggested Salvi's treatment of the Palazzo Poli facade. Salvi also took up the variety of texture and dramatic play of light and shade Bernini brought to all of his designs, both secular and ecclesiastical, though here it is indeed difficult to separate Bernini from the broad tradition going back to antiquity by way of Maderno and Michelangelo. Salvi's mastery of illusionism and his intuitive sense of theater undoubtedly reflect Bernini's influence too, but these may also be traced to Salvi's awareness of such great contemporaries as Pietro Metastasio. Some historians have seen specific elements of the Fontana di Trevi, notably the central niche, as deriving from Bernini,[27] but I am inclined to see the postclassical sources of Salvi's niche in the work of Michelangelo and Pietro da Cortona.[28]

Salvi undoubtedly learned much from the other great masters of Roman

Fig. 177. Palladio, Loggia del Capitaniato, Vicenza

Baroque architecture, Francesco Borromini and Pietro da Cortona. I have already suggested that Borromini's adaptation of Palladio's Loggia del Capitaniato provided the inspiration for Salvi's treatment of the entablature on the Trevi. We have also seen how Pietro da Cortona's remarkable project for a monumental display of the Trevi at Piazza Colonna anticipated the essential features of Salvi's design for the Fontana di Trevi (fig. 40). To this may be added the predilection of both Borromini and Cortona for triadic compositions with focal concavities. Pietro da Cortona's design for the Pignetto Sacchetti, with its grottoes and basin set in front of a highly scenographic facade, would have been especially relevant to Salvi in formulating his design for the Trevi (fig. 178). Subsuming as it does the Renaissance tradition of villa and garden design from the Belvedere Court through the *nymphaeum* of the Villa Giulia, Cortona's Pignetto Sacchetti reminds us that the dynamic assimilation of earlier monuments is an essential process in the formulation of new artistic conceptions. This was as true for Salvi practicing in the eighteenth century as it was for Cortona in the seventeenth.

In describing the art historical context of the Trevi it is as important to understand Salvi's attitude toward his contemporaries as it is to establish his relation to architects of the more remote past. Salvi belonged to a generation of architects, including Luigi Vanvitelli, Ferdinando Fuga, and Alessandro Galilei, who came to dominate the architectural profession in Rome from 1730 until after the middle of the century. Unlike most of the successful architects of the preceding generation, the members of this group had not been trained in the studio of Carlo Fontana, whose practice and teaching had formed a link between the seventeenth and eighteenth centuries. While these architects were in certain respects Fontana's artistic heirs, in subtle yet significant ways Salvi and his colleagues reacted to Fontana's reductive synthesis of Baroque design to develop more highly expressive and independent personal styles.

Salvi reacted even more negatively to the style that prevailed in Rome during the pontificate of Benedict XIII Orsini (1724–30). The Orsini pope favored south Italian architects, notably Filippo Raguzzini, whose architectural designs emphasized atectonic surface decoration. Salvi's attitude reflected the views of the Roman architectural establishment, which had been denied important papal commissions during the reign of Benedict XIII. Even more important, Salvi's personal style, stressing the sculptural play of large masses and striving for a Roman *grandezza*, embodies a conscious shift in taste on the part of his patrons, the Corsini pope and his family.

As Florentines, members of the Corsini entourage were naturally looked upon as outsiders by the Romans. The first architectural competition they initiated, which was won by a Florentine, Alessandro Galilei, sufficed to confirm the worst suspicions of the Roman architects (fig. 179). Galilei's design for the facade of the Lateran Basilica, particularly in its original con-

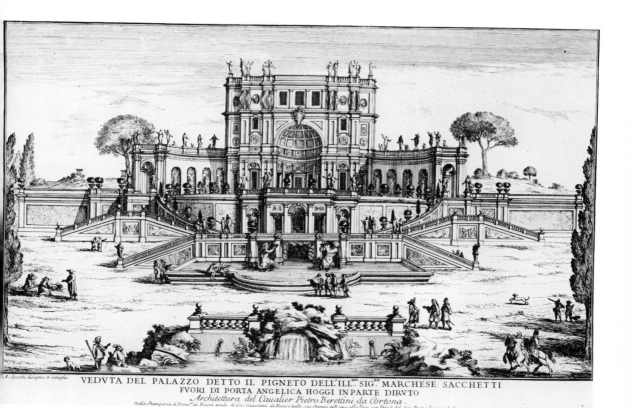

VEDVTA DEL PALAZZO DETTO IL PIGNETO DELL'ILL.^{MO} SIG.^{RE} MARCHESE SACCHETTI
FVORI DI PORTA ANGELICA HOGGI IN PARTE DIRVTO
Architettura del Caualier Pietro Berettini da Cortona.

Fig. 178. Pietro da Cortona, Villa Pignetto Sacchetti

ception, projected an austere monumentality that breaks with the more exuberant Roman Baroque. Its planarity, its emphasis on trabeated forms, and above all its insistence on a horizontal crown for the facade reflect Galilei's close study of Vitruvius and Michelangelo. In contrast, Salvi's designs for the Lateran facade, especially the one in the Accademia di San Luca, appear more sculptural and stand directly in the tradition of the Roman Baroque (fig. 82).

It is natural, therefore, that Salvi, and to a lesser degree Vanvitelli, should have been championed by the Roman camp in this debate over taste. I suspect Salvi won the competition for the Trevi not merely because of his superior design but because the award to a Roman was intended as a belated act of artistic diplomacy on the part of the Corsini. Salvi's architecture constituted an acceptable compromise between Galilei's reforming style favored by the Corsini and the tradition of Late Baroque Classicism espoused by the Roman architectural profession. Not that Salvi consciously set about formulating a personal style that would appeal equally to the divergent tastes of his patrons and the Roman public, but his training and theoretical principles naturally led him to design in a way that would be appreciated by both groups.

Two of the most important components of Salvi's training were his close study of Vitruvius and Michelangelo. As a member of the Arcadian Academy

Fig. 179. Alessandro Galilei, S. Giovanni in Laterano, facade, 1732

he was naturally predisposed to temper the excesses of Baroque imagery and metaphor and to value the example of Renaissance models. At the same time, however, Salvi's association with the *Arcadia* also led him to explore and master a range of irregular, picturesque forms analogous to pastoral imagery that are so expressively embodied in the *scogli* of the Trevi. Moreover, Salvi highly esteemed the great Roman architects of the seventeenth century, from whom he learned how to use the classical orders to achieve bold sculptural effects. As a result of Salvi's unusual training and background he was in a position to effect a synthesis of Roman tradition and Florentine reform that was acceptable to both sides.

That the patronage of the Corsini pope and his family represented a return to many of the values of classicism has long been noted. Giovanni Bottari, the secretary of the pope's influential cardinal-nephew, makes this very clear in his treatise on the fine arts, which was written during the early 1730s.[29] It would be a mistake to read too much into this critical attitude, however. The Corsini were unusual not so much in fostering the classical strain of Baroque art by their patronage, as in articulating, through Bottari, their own definition of classical art with such clarity. Classicism, after all, is an important component of Baroque art and particularly in Rome was always present, even in the most exuberant Baroque compositions.[30] It is a mistake, therefore, to argue, as does Sandro Benedetti, that architects like Salvi and Vanvitelli were "anti-Baroque."[31] To be sure, classical principles of clarity and utility (as defined by Bottari) are prominent in their work, but the increased prominence of the classical component in their art only tempers, and does not deny, their essentially Baroque character. In this sense I feel that Rudolf Wittkower's rubric *Late Baroque Classicism* remains the most valid way to describe the Fontana di Trevi and related monuments.

A pronounced classicism was by no means limited to artists practicing in Rome. Two examples will suffice to make this point. The first of these is the Donnerbrunnen in Vienna, by Georg Raphael Donner, and the second is the Fontaine de la Rue Grenelle in Paris by Edme Bouchardon (figs. 76, 180). The Donnerbrunnen was begun in 1737 and the Fontaine de la Rue Grenelle in 1739; both were completed while the Fontana di Trevi was still under construction.

The classicism of Donner's fountain is immediately evident.[32] He employs a stable triangle to enclose the figures composing the central group and clearly separates each of the component parts. This, together with the calm repose of the allegorical figures and the restrained use of water, is in marked contrast to the Fontana di Trevi. Only the leg of the river Traun, which extends over the edge of the basin to occupy the observer's space, calls to mind the Baroque models Donner must have known from his Italian master, Giovanni Giuliani.

Bouchardon's Parisian fountain resembles the Trevi rather more in its emphasis on an architectural backdrop, to which the sculpture is subordinated. Still, it is decidedly classical in its composition, which recalls features of the unsuccessful project Bouchardon entered in the competition for the Fontana di Trevi (fig. 75). The central group of sculpture framed by an architectural frontispiece appears to be a French translation of his earlier Italian project, and other details, especially the drafted masonry of the basement, suggest that Bouchardon had familiarized himself with Salvi's winning design for the Trevi. The restraint of the sculpture, which stands aloof from the observer, as well as the minimal role afforded water in the composition is in even greater contrast to the Trevi than is its Viennese counterpart.

These brief comparisons certainly are not intended to suggest that all fountains on the Continent dating from the decade of the 1730s were classical in appearance. Nothing could be further from the truth, as Adam's fountain of Neptune and Amphitrite in the Bassin de Neptune at Versailles, which was finished in 1740, illustrates. But clearly classicism was by no means limited to the Rome of Clement XII. Moreover, if one views the Trevi against a broader perspective its classicism appears less remarkable, while its Baroque features tend to predominate.

Salvi's synthesis of classical and Baroque forms was no doubt one of the factors contributing to the close study devoted to the Trevi by architects practicing throughout Europe. We have already seen that Salvi counted a Moravian architect, Franz Anton Grimm, among his students. The numerous

Fig. 180. Georg Raphael Donner, Donnerbrunnen, Vienna, 1737

drawings Grimm executed under Salvi's directions, including academic exercises in addition to measured drawings after Roman monuments like the Trevi, suggest that Salvi's studio may have become the successor of Carlo Fontana's atelier as a training ground for architects. In addition to Grimm we know that other foreign architects followed the construction of the Trevi with interest.

A few select examples of studies after the Fontana di Trevi will suffice to suggest the range of the fountain's influence. In the superb collection of architectural drawings in Stockholm is a sheet representing the Fontana di Trevi (fig. 181).[33] This handsome drawing is by Carl Hårleman (1700–52), the Swedish architect who, together with Nicodemus Tessin, was responsible for the formation of the great collection to which it belongs. Hårleman traveled extensively in Italy, spending most of 1726 in Rome. He cannot have drawn directly from the actual building, which was only begun six years after his departure.[34] More likely, Hårleman secured a drawing after Salvi's project, or perhaps after the building itself, from a young Swedish architect studying in Rome. In any event, close inspection reveals that Hårleman's own study is a free version, rather than an accurate copy, of Salvi's design for the Trevi. In particular, Hårleman's rendering of the sculpture departs from the designs of Salvi and Maini. Hårleman also inserts consoles into the frieze of the centerpiece of the Trevi. The consoles, while accentuating the sculptural relief of the central *nostra*, also weaken the horizontal unity of Salvi's design by interrupting the entablature. It is fascinating to visualize Hårleman, busily engaged in completing the Royal Palace on the shores of the Baltic, turning his hand to explore some of the implications of the Trevi for his northern clime.

Among the numerous architects who trained with Hårleman in Stockholm was Simon Louis Du Ry (1726–99), born of a French family that practiced throughout northern Europe over the course of several generations.[35] On his departure from Stockholm in 1748 Du Ry began an extended period of travel that brought him to Italy, where he stayed for more than three years between 1753 and 1756. By this time Salvi had died, but his design for the Fontana di Trevi attracted the attention of the young Du Ry, who made a measured drawing of the main prospect (fig. 182).[36] As is appropriate for a drawing made at this time, Du Ry's elevation shows the Trevi as it had been left by

Fig. 181. Carl Hårleman, elevation of the Trevi

Fig. 182. Simon Louis Du Ry, elevation of the Trevi, 1753–56

Salvi and Maini and does not record the alterations made later in the decade under Clement XIII. After his Italian study trip Simon Louis Du Ry returned to northern Europe, settling in Kassel, on which his architecture and planning left an indelible stamp.

English architects, too, expressed a lively interest in the Fontana di Trevi. Much as Hårleman, long after his Italian sojourn, followed the construction of the Trevi, so James Gibbs (1682–1754) was informed of the competition for the fountain.[37] Gibbs had been in Rome from 1703 to 1708–09, when the Trevi was very much under discussion, and the competition of 1730 must have recalled something of the challenge and excitement of his youthful study to the mature and successful London architect.

The most important English architects of the next generation, Robert Adam and Sir William Chambers, also took pains to document the progress of work on the Trevi. We have already seen the three drawings Adam commissioned to nourish him after his return to his native country (figs. 157–59). In like fashion Chambers had an elevation of the Trevi drawn for him by the French painter Laurent Pecheux (1729–1821), a pupil of Battoni and Mengs (fig. 183).[38] Pecheux's rendering is dated 1753, which coincides with Chambers's travels in Italy between 1751 and 1755. While the architectural backdrop of the Trevi is represented accurately by Pecheux, he took considerable liberties with the sculpture. There is no indication that Salvi, Maini, or any other artist associated with the Trevi ever considered placing allegorical figures of Prudence and Faith in the lateral niches.

Fig. 183. Laurent Pecheux, elevation of the Trevi, 1753

Chambers also drew the Trevi himself; a small sketch by his hand representing the large vase on the parapet of the Via della Stamperia is in the collection of the Victoria and Albert Museum (fig. 184).[39] Chambers has masterfully captured the effect of metamorphosis whereby living rock gives way to human artifice. Judging from remarks Chambers made twenty years after drawing this beautiful sketch, the impression produced by the Trevi on the youthful architect remained vivid. In a letter of 1774 he wrote

> Naples has never been famed for architects, they are now I apprehend worse than ever. You will see some execrable performances there, and there about, of Vanvitelli, Fuga, and some blockheads of less note, avoid them all, as you must Borromini with all the later Architects of Rome, excepting Salvi, who had indeed no general principles to guide him, yet sometimes fortunately hit upon the right, as appears by parts of his fountain of Trevi, and parts of his Dominican church at Viterbo.[40]

The attic of the Strand front of Somerset House, executed around 1776, bears testimony to the Trevi's influence on Chambers's own designs.[41]

Interest in the Fontana di Trevi was by no means limited to European architects; in the twentieth century the influence of the Trevi has extended to American architects as well. During the eighteenth and most of the nineteenth century, America was not receptive to Italian Baroque architecture, but with the triumph of Beaux-Arts Classicism at the Chicago Exhibition of 1893 the scenographic potential of monuments like the Trevi came to be recognized by American architects. One building that consciously imitates the Trevi is,

Fontana di Trevi

116

Fig. 184. Sir William Chambers, sketch of the colossal vase on the Trevi,
1751–55

most appropriately, the Chestnut Hill pumping station, designed in 1899 by the firm of Shepley, Rutan, and Coolidge. (fig. 185). While not actually a fountain like the Trevi, this pumping station, which looks out over the Brookline reservoir, nonetheless performs a function analogous to the great terminal displays of the Roman aqueducts. The architects have employed a stripped-down version of the Trevi facade, but in place of sculpture they have introduced windows to provide glimpses of the great machinery that, in Pope's words, "tells the waters or to rise or fall." As is fitting for the twentieth century, the presiding genius of the place is no longer a classical deity, but the pumps and dynamos of the industrial age.

In the course of the last decade many American architects have again turned to European models and consciously employed historical allusions and a classical vocabulary for expressive purposes. Among these Post-Modernist architects Charles Moore is remarkable for the range of his allusions and the subtlety with which they are made. Among the most controversial of his public designs is the monumental fountain in New Orleans known as the Piazza d'Italia, begun in 1975 (fig. 186).[42] Moore's fountain is emphatically scenographic

Fig. 185. Shepley, Rutan, and Coolidge, Chestnut Hill pumping station, Boston, 1899

Fig. 186. Charles Moore, Piazza d'Italia, 1975

and makes use of screening elements that function like stage flats to create vistas and effects of transparency. The centerpiece of the fountain's architectural backdrop evokes the central *mostra* of the Trevi in both formal and symbolic terms. Here, as at the Trevi, the water rushes forth to begin its downward course to the basin, or metaphorical ocean, below. The role of the *scogli* is played by a sequence of irregular steps representing the Alpine watershed over which the water washes on its way down the Italian peninsula to the surrounding basin. Also like the Trevi, the Piazza d'Italia is intended to provide the focal point for a neighborhood and invites the viewer to move about and to play an active part in experiencing the water as it transforms the familiar urban environment.

Charles Moore's fountain alludes not only to formal features of Salvi's design, but to its guiding philosophical premise as well. In his stimulating doctoral dissertation of 1957 on water and architecture, Moore quotes Salvi's memorandum on the symbolic meaning of the Trevi, giving particular emphasis to his allegorical treatment of the water cycle.[43] Like the architects of the Chestnut

Hill pumping station, Moore dispenses with the sculpture Salvi employed to express his mythological allegory. Instead he concentrates on the medium of water itself, and in keeping with the cultural background of his patrons and intended audience he introduces topographical references to Italy. The water cycle is expressed more specifically in geographical, rather than mythological, terms.

The Piazza d'Italia suggests the enduring value of the Trevi as an artistic metaphor. The Fontana di Trevi deserves recognition as one of a select group of monuments, the form and meaning of which produce a resonance transcending the culture and age that conceived them. Such rare monuments are interpreted and transformed by successive generations of artists, who, whether in music or prose, architecture or film, offer new and refreshing insights into their universal meaning.

Appendix 1.
Documents and Published Reports
Pertaining to the History
of the Trevi Fountain,
Arranged in Chronological Order

Abbreviations: ASR/AV: Archivio di Stato Roma, Presidenza degli Acquedotti Urbani, Acqua Vergine; BAV: Biblioteca Apostolica Vaticana: DO: *Diario Ordinario di Roma*; Valesio: Valesio Diary, followed by citation to Scano and Graglia edition.

1. 8/13/1704: È stato hoggi misurato il sito che è dietro la fontana di Trevi, meditando S. Beatudine di formare a quell' acqua una sontuosa facciata e porvi la gran colonna Antonina di Monte Citorio e formare avanti la detta fontana una spaziosa piazza con tirare quella addietro a filo della chiesa della Madonna de' Cruciferi. (Valesio, 3:144–45)

2. 8/28/1704: È stato ordinato a tutti gl'architetti di fare il disegno per ornamento della facciata della fontana di Trevi, essendo stato di già misurato il sito delle case e cortili che gli stanno dietro e a' fianchi, pensandosi portarla all'istesso filo della chiesa de'Cruciferi, et è in oltre intenzione di S. Beatitudine di porre la sudetta colonna Antonina per ornamento nella detta facciata. (Valesio, 3:158)

3. 6/18/1708: È stata inalzata più di quattro palmi la fabrica della mostra d'acqua di Trevi et in tal guisa si è inalzata anco l'acqua che viene a cadere sopra le tazze molto più grandi e spaziose delle antiche con bellissima vista. (Valesio, 4:97)

4. 7/5/1728: Mons.re Sardini lucchese e presidente delle Acque fu a persuadere il papa di volere adornare la mostra dell'acqua di Trevi e, avendogli detto il papa che non avea denari, egli si compromesse di trovargli e il Papa gli diede licenza di farla; pertanto sua signoria illustrissima, che si picca di poeta, communicò il suo pensiero ad un certo scultore napoletano Paolo Benaglia, che ha servito il papa ne'stucchi, uomo ardito ma di poco o niun sapere nella sua arte, ed egli ha di già fatto il modello, veduto da molti. Nel luogo più elevato è posta a sedere la Beata Vergine del Rosario e questa ve la ha voluta S. Beatitudine; sotto a questa, alla sinistra de' risguardanti, v'è la vergine Trivia, nata dalla testa del prelato come Pallade da quella di Giove: questa con una mano accenna la Vergine SS.ma e con la sinistra l'acqua che esce da alcuni scogli; alla destra v'è una Roma armata in piedi e accanto ad essa, senza alcun proposito, una scrofa con alcuni porchetti, e dalla banda della vergine Trivia un alicorno. Coronarà questa bell'opera una iscrizione della stessa eleganza già composta dal medesimo prelato che fece la breve che è alla fontana del cortile de'frati della Minerva: "Minervae aquas ministrat Trivia virgo." Mi era dimenticato che, acciò non manchi il vitto alla scrofa, vi sono due querce una per lato. (Valesio, 4:966)

5. 7/29/1729: Sono stati portati molti travertini per la fontana di Trevi, da farsi,

secondo il ridicolo pensiero di monsignor Sardini lucchese, eseguire da Paolo Benaglia napolitano, già intagliatore di legname, onde può da ciò arguirsi come sia per riuscire questa opera. (Valesio, 5:94)

6. 8/18/1729: Si portano travertini su la piazza [per] la fontana di Trevi. (Valesio, 5:102)

7. 4/8/1730: The mason Matteo Caramaschi submits a bill for work carried out between 2/8/1730 and 4/8/1730, including the unloading of "il sasso di marmo venuto dà Massa di Carrara p. la statua Principale della Fontana di Trevi." (ASR/AV, busta 69, no. 35)

8. 8/19/1730: Si è sospesa l'opera delle statue della fontana di Trevi abbozzate dal Benaglia e si fanno nuovi disegni. (Valesio, 5:264)

9. 11/24/1730: Aveva la casa Conti lasciato un vano nel mezzo della balaustrata fatta sopra la fabbrica che unisce gli due palazzi sopra la fontana di Trevi, ed avea disegnato porvi l'arme di papa Innocenzio XIII, il che gli è stato proibito per volere S. Beatitudine ornare la fontana, per la quale non sono piaciuti gli disegni e modelli fatti, onde adesso sono stati deputati quattro architetti per farli, ma si crede non vi sia molta intenzione di eseguirne alcuno. (Valesio, 5:304)

10. 8/6/1732: Ha S. Beatitudine fatti fare molti desegni per l'ornamento della fontana di Trevi oltre gli fatti altre volte ed ha scelto uno de' più belli, che è quello del Vanvitelli, che ne avea fatto altro per la facciata di S. Giovanni Laterano ed era stato reputato de' più belli. (Valesio, 5:504–05)

11. 9/16/1732: Ha S. Beatitudine passato il chirografo di scudi 17,000 per la fontana di Trevi e per il disegno è stato scelto quello del Salvi. (Valesio, 5:516)

12. 10/2/1732: *Chirografo* of Clement XII authorizing work to begin on the Trevi under the direction of Nicola Salvi.

Monsig. Felice Passerini Chierico della nostra Camera, e Presidente delle Acque.

Avendo le due Fontane dell'*Acqua Felice*, ed *Acqua Paola* il suo ornamento nel loro Prospetto, fattogli dai nostri Predecessori *Sisto V. e Paolo V.* respettivamente, abbiamo stimato ben giusto, e ragionevole, che simile ornamento si faccia ancora a quella denominata l'*Acqua Vergine*, detta anche di *Trevi*, come che più antica, e più accreditata dell'altre Acque suddette; al qual effetto abbiamo per detta opera assegnata la somma di scudi 17647.71, ritratta dal sopravanzo della terza estrazione del Lotto di Roma delli 12 maggio prossimo passato: e perche detto ornato non può effettuarsi senza servirsi di un sufficiente spazio intorno a detta fontana; siccome ancora di qualche porzione di quello occupato per la fabrica del muro, e palazzo del Duca di Guadagnola, e Poli nella parte della facciata di detta fontana sopra la piazza, a cui devono appoggiarsi le colonne, statue, e marmi necessarj giusta il modello fatto da Niccola Salvi architetto, che noi abbiamo prescelto per detta opera, ad esclusione di altri diversi modelli fatti da altri professori di maggiore spesa, e maggior latitudine; lo che sarebbe stato di pregiudizio al palazzo di detto Duca di Poli, ed all'alzata del medesimo: ed all'incontro dubitandosi, che ciò potesse dal medesimo impedirsi per qualche Indulto, Chirografo, o Privilegio concessoli da' nostri Predecessori, e specialmente dalla Sa: Me: di *Benedetto XIII.* in vigore di un rescritto di Monsig. Sardini, allora Presidente dell'*Acqua Vergine*, in data di 9 luglio 1728., fatto coll'oracolo di detto Pontefice; cosi abbiamo determinato, affine di stabilire, e perfezionare detta opera pubblica, e necessaria, di commetterne a Voi l'intiera, e totale esecuzione; NON OSTANTI gli asserti Indulti, e Privilegi, e nè tampoco il ricorso a Noi fatto dal predetto Duca per rimostrarci li suoi pregiudizj, che poteano sovrastargli coll' esecuzione di quest' opera nel suo palazzo, muri, e fenestre; e però col presente nostro Chirografo, in cui abbiamo per espresso, e di parola in parola inserto l'intiero tenore di detti asserti Indulti, Chirografi, o Privilegi, in qualunque modo, e tempo emanati, e concessi a detto Duca di Poli, e di Guadagnola, e Rescritto di detto Monsig. Sardini, e qualunque altra cosa quanto si voglia necessaria d'esprimersi, e benchè degna di speciale, ed individua menzione; commettiamo a Voi la fabbrica dell'ornato della detta fontana dell'*Acqua Vergine*, detta di *Trevi*; valendovi del suddetto denaro assegnato, e depositato nel Monte di Pietà a tenore degli ordini da darvisi dal Rm̄o Cardinale Corsini; con servirsi ancora a tal effetto del muro del palazzo del predetto Duca di Poli nella parte della facciata, con perforarlo, e penetrarlo anche nelle stanze interiori, e colla clausura ancora di finestre di detta facciata secondo porterà il bisogno, e l'effettuazione di detto disegno, e modello dell' architetto Salvi; *senza che possa darvisi veruno impedimento, o ritardo* per parte di detto Duca, e suoi ec.; in virtù non meno di detti Privilegi, Chirografi, e Indulti, che di qualunque altra ragione, e motivi de jure, e di fatto, che le potessero competere; quali tutti Noi di nostro Moto proprio, certa scienza, e pienezza della nostra suprema, ed assoluta potestà, atteso che trattasi di opera pubblica, e per altre cause giustamente moventi l'anima nostro, revochiamo, invalidiamo, ed affatto annulliamo, e vogliamo, *che quelli non possino in conto alcuno allegarsi* per impedire, e ritardare l'incominciamento, prosecuzione, e perfezione della fabbrica dell'ornato suddetto; quale vogliamo resti pontualmente adempito *senza verun ostacolo, o impedimento, che potesse darsi dal predetto Duca di Poli, e di Guadagnola:* intendendo però, che debba rimanere assicurata la fabbrica di Casa Conti, in guisa tale, che non possa patire detrimento alcuno, se non in quella parte, che sarà puramente necessaria per l'esecuzione del predetto modello; dandovi Noi per l'effettuazione delle cose premesse tutte, e singole facoltà, ed autorità in qualunque modo necessarie, ed opportune privativamente quanto a qualunque altro, *per esser così mente, e volontà nostra espressa.* Volendo, e decretando, che il presente nostro Chirografo benchè non ammesso, e registrato in Camera vaglia, e debba aver sempre il suo pieno effetto, esecuzione, e vigore colla nostra semplice sottoscrizione; e che non gli si possa mai opporre di subrezione, obrezione, nè di qualunque altro vizio, o difetto della nostra volontà, ed intenzione; e che così e non altrimenti debba sopra ciò giudicarsi, definirsi, ed interpretarsi da Voi, e da qualunque altro Giudice, e Tribunale ancorchè collegiato, e composto di Revm̄i Cardinali: togliendo loro, ed a ciascheduno di essi ogni facoltà, ed autorità di giudicare, definire ed interpretare diversamente; e dichiarando d'adesso preventivamente nullo, irrito, ed invalido tutto ciò, che scientemente, o ignorantemente si facesse in contrario; *ancorchè non ci sia stato chiamato, citato, nè sentito* il detto Duca di Poli, e qualunque altra persona, che vi avesse, o pretendesse d'avervi interesse; *non ostanti* le cose premesse, l'Indulti, Chirografi, Brevi, Moti proprj, o altri privilegi in qualsivogla modo, e tempo, e per qualsivogla causa, e motivo conceduti, ed emanati da Sommi Pontefici nostri Predecessori; e specialmente dalla Sa: Me: di *Benedetto XIII.* a favore del predetto Duca di Poli, e Guadagnola, mediante l'accennato Rescritto; sebbene contenessero, e fossero muniti di clausule insolite, e derogatorie di derogatorie; *e non ostante ancora* il ricorso estragiudiziale come sopra a Noi fatto dal detto Duca, la Costituzione di *Pio IV.* nostro Predecessore *de registrandis*, la regola della nostra Cancellaria *de jure quaesito non tollendo*, e qualsisiano altre Costituzioni, ed ordinazioni Apostoliche nostre, e de'nostri Predecessori, leggi, statuti, riforme, usi, stili, consuetudini, ed ogni altra cosa, che facesse, o potesse fare in contrario; alle quali tutte, e singole avendone il tenore quà per espresso, e di parola in parola inserto; e supplendo Noi colla pienezza della nostra Suprema, ed assoluta potestà a qualunque vizio, e difetto, quantunque sostanziale, e formale, che in ciò potesse intervenire, questa volta sola, e per l'effetto suddetto amplamente deroghiamo. Dato dal nostro Palazzo Apostolico Quirinale, questo di 2. ottobre 1732. CLEMENS PP.XII (Archivio Segreto Vaticano, Fondo Boncompagni, protocollo 682, folder 16. Transcribed by C. Fea, *Storia delle acque antiche*, 72–74)

13. 10/17/1732: Alla fontana di Trevi si demolisce la fabrica che vi era con tre bocche fatto dal cavaliere Bernini. (Valesio, 5:528)

14. 11/22/1732: Bill for 916:78 *scudi* submitted by the plumber Giovanni Battista Tognotti on 11/22/1732 for work done between 10/4/1732 and 11/4/1732 "in servizio della nuova Fabrica et Ornato della Facciata di Fontana di Trevi." Tognotti's bill is signed by Salvi. (ASR/AV, busta 69, no. 2)

15. 12/20/1732: Bill for 138:10 *scudi* submitted by the ironmonger Simone Moretti covering work done between 10/10/1730 and 8/11/1732, which was approved by Salvi on 12/22/1732. Above Salvi's signature appears the following note: "Tutti li sudd.i e Retriscritti lavori approvo essere stati fatti, et ordinati da me sottoscritto questo di 20 Xmbre 1732 Maffeo Angelo Contini." (ASR/AV, busta 69, no. 5)

16. 12/21/1732: Per rendere asciutta dall'acqua la cava del fondamento della fontana di Trevi, ancor oggi vi erano gli operai che con due trombe cavavano acqua. (Valesio, 5:548)

17. 5/12/1733: Ha S. Beatitudine distribuiti 50,000 scudi delli 120,000 guadagnati col lotto ed ha dati 12,000 per la fabrica della facciata di S. Giovanni della nazione fiorentina, 10,000 per quella da farsi di S. Celso, 6,000 al Bambino Gesù conservatorio per terminare la chiesa e il resto per la Consulta e la fontana di Trevi. (Valesio, 5:595)

18. 7/24/1733: 1733. A di 24 Lug.o al S. Nicola Salvi per il Modello della Facciata . . . 110 (ASR/AV, busta 64, fasc. 160, "Pagamenti fatti per l'Ornato di Fontana di Trevi," p. 4)

19. 9/5/1733: In occasione di qualche dilazione fatta nel pagamento di coloro che hanno vinto al lotto, sono stati attaccati alcuni cartelli allusivi alla perdita fatta dalla Camera: alle colonne non ancora terminate della fontana di Trevi "Non plus ultra," alla fabrica della Consulta di Monte Cavallo dalla parte dove il muro è sopraterra "elemosina per la fabbrica" e dall'altra parte "sito da dare a canone," del che il Papa si è inquietato. (Valesio, 5:628–29)

20. 4/28/1734: Nella fabrica della fontana di Trevi cadde sopra un povero scarpellino un gran pezzo di travertino, dal quale rimase schiacciato e morto. (Valesio, 5:689)

21. 8/17/1734: A di 17 Agosto a Gio: Batta. Maini p. il Modello di cera . . . 50 (ASR/AV, busta 64, fasc. 160, "Pagamenti fatti per l'Ornato di Fontana di Trevi," p. 4)

22. 10/2/1734: Paolo Benaglia scultore: 1734. A di 2 Ott.re per p.zo de marmo Statuario . . . 300 (ASR/AV, busta 64, fasc. 160, "Pagamenti fatti per l'Ornato di Fontana di Trevi," p. 4)

23. 10/13/1734: È stato dato ordine all'architetto Salvi di terminare la facciata della fontana di Trevi fin al cornicione e poi di dare i conti, vedendosi che è d'una altezza grandissima. (Valesio, 5:732)

24. 3/29/1735: Bartolomeo Pincellotti scultore / 1735 A di 29 Mzo. 100 / A di 17 Agosto 100 / A di 15 Xm.re 50. . . . 250

Agostino Corsini Scultore / 1735 A di 29 Mzo. 100 / A di 14 Xm.re 100 / 1736 A di 7 Sett.e 50. . . . 250

Bernardino Ludovisi Scultore / 1735 A di 29 Marzo 100 / A di 6 Xm.re 100 / [1736] A di 25 Sett.e 50. . . . 250

Francesco Queirolo Scultore / 1735 A di 29 Marzo 100 / A di 17 Agosto 100 / A di 15 Xm.re 50. . . . 250 (ASR/AV, busta 64, fasc. 160, "Pagamenti fatti per l'Ornato di Fontana di Trevi," p. 5)

25. 5/17/1735: S. Beatitudine ha dati 5000 scudi per l'arma e finimenti da porsi sulla fontana di Trevi, non volendo poi dare altro per la mostra dell'acqua. (Valesio, 5:785)

26. 6/1/1735: *Stima e misura* of work done by the stone carver Francesco Tedeschi between 4/15/1733 and 6/1/1735 "Pella piana fatta dalla parte di dentro alla detta cimasa, cioè rivolta che fa parapetto indetta Balaustrata longa stesa attorno 37½ largha inpelle stesa p. 1¼ segue l'altro dal altra parte sim.e misura . . . 95:08" (ASR/ AV, busta 69, no. 63)

27. 6/1/1735: *Stima e misura* submitted by Nicola Giobbe and Matteo Caramasca on 6/1/1735, containing references to alterations made to the facade of the Palazzo Poli: "Seguono i muri che riempiano il prospetto dietro l'ornato di travertino sino addosso al muro di Casa Conti. Seguono altri lavori in levar d'opera Li Sassi di trav.no delle fenestre di facciata di Casa Conti, che sono state murate in occasione del Prospetto della Fontana di Trevi. Per aver scalzato, e levato d'opera la ringhiera di ferro della d.a fenestra." (ASR/AV, busta 69, no. 88)

28. 6/8/1735: Bill for 4058:11½ *scudi* submitted by the stonecutters Giuseppe Poddi and Francesco Pincellotti, which was approved by Salvi on 6/8/1735: Segue La Scudella che forma Cuppolino di trav.o Intagliato a cassette tutte à mostaccioli degradati al punto con fiori in luogo delli rosoni Intagliati a fiori di quercia frappanti di varie sorti con ghiande e semi, et in altre cassette simili tramezzate con dentro diversi grotteschi intagliati a conchiglie dritte e roverse con l'intreccio di un fiore lumacato nel mezzo con suoi semi, e ricavatoci n.o 4 costole degradate parimente al punto e riquad.e con fascia e intaccat.ra, e nello sfondo di d.i ritrovatoci le cocciole intagliate degradate al punto con un laccio che finge d'esser infilate una con l'altra à ciasched.a di d.e quattro Costole il tutto ricavato dal masso in opera con molto scomodo e tempo rinettato pulito a sodisfatione. (ASR/AV, busta 69, no. 119)

29. 6/14/1735: 1735. A di 14 Giug.o à M.ro Carlo Camporese p.zo e fattura del Modello Grande di legno. . . . 120 (ASR/AV, busta 64, fasc. 160, "Pagamenti fatti per l'Ornato di Fontana di Trevi, p. 4)

30. 6/17/1735: Il Papa ha dati 15,000 scudi per proseguire la fabrica della fontana di Trevi e si è posta mano ad adornarne i lati guastando quello ornamento del loro palazzo che vi aveano fatto gli duchi Conti di Poli. (Valesio, 5:794)

31. 8/1/1735: The painter Antonio Bicchierari paid 70 *scudi:* Nota delle Pitture a guazzo per servizio della nuova Fabrica della Fontana di Trevi fatte per ordine del Sig. Nicola Salvi Architetto della med.ma. Per aver dipinto a chiaro scuro colore di Travertino l'Arma di S. Santità, che fà finimento nel mezzo alla Cima della Sud:a Fabrica, con le due Fame, che la sostengono, come ancora li due Festoni di frutti, e suo basamento di larghezza p.mi 40, e alta p.mi 26. Dovendosi considerare, che si sono disegnate prima in picolo a casa dello scultore, e poi in grande il cartone di

grandezza, come sopra; acciò il Falegname potesse fare il Fusto con suoi riporti. Per le quattro Figure che stanno più passo dipinte come sopra di grandezza alte p.mi 16, disegnate parimente in casa di ciascheduno de' scultori in piccolo, e poi in grande, come è l'Opera. Tutto fatto da me Antonio Bicchierari. (ASR/AV, busta 69, no. 69)

32. 8/20/1735: Conto di Lavori di falegname fatti da me Carlo Camporese di ordine del Sig. Nicola Salvi Architetto consistenti in modelli armature fusti et altro per servizio della fontana di Trevi da Luglio 1735 A tutto Maggio 1740 come appresso ... A 20 Agosto [1735] P. servizio delli Intagliatori ... Per haver fatto una tavola p. modellare li scogli sotto li casini longha pmi. 3 larga pmi 1 ... Per aver fatto un altra armatura p. modellare altri scogli delle parti di mezzo ... A 24 Settembre [1735] Per haver fatto un modello di una delle parte delli casini fatto di tutta l'altezza del zoccolo con pilastrelli membretti finestre con grossezza di muri squinco e battenti con cornice da capo che gira attorno scorniciata tale è nel opera. (ASR/AV, busta 70, no. 295)

33. 8/29/1735: Era stata posta, non incisa ma scritta, l'iscrizione alla fontana di Trevi, benché non ancora terminata, ed era "Clemens XII aquam Verginem copia et salubritate commendata augustius exornavit etc.": ora è stato mutato il quarto verso e invece di "augustius" è stato posto "magnifico cultu." (Valesio, 5:808)

34. 9/17/1735: Bill for 560:47 ½ scudi submitted by Nicola Giobbe and Matteo Caramaschi, which was approved by Salvi on 12/17/1736. In date of 9/17/1735: Per haver revoltato sotto sopra con leve diversi pezzi di med.mi nella piazza alli Crociferi à causa, che non vi era altro da impiegrare li Omini p.che non erano terminati li modelli messovi di tempo n. 2 giornate di due M.ri con N. 10 garzoni con aver med.mte revoltato in parte anche incontro al Palazzo di Scavolini. (ASR/AV, busta 69, no. 118)

35. 9/21/1735: De' denari guadagnati nel lotto S. Beatitudine ne ha dati scudi 10,000 per la fontana di Trevi, della quale si era quasi che sospeso il lavoro. (Valesio, 5:813)

36. 10/25/1735: Sono venuti nuovi travertini per terminare la fontana di Trevi, nella quale se ne consuma una prodigiosa quantità per formare i finti scogli su'quali si finge fondata la fabbrica. (Valesio, 5:819)

37. 11/16/1735: Si proseguisce la fabrica della fontana di Trevi, impiegandovisi un numero infinito di trevertini. (Valesio, 5:822)

38. 6/16/1736: Oggi cadde dalla più alta parte della fabrica della fontana di Trevi un muratore, che immediatamente morì. (Valesio, 5:888)

39. 7/31/1736: Misura, e stima delli Lavori di Scarpello, et altro fatti fare da Cecilia Tedeschi Ved. Rel. del. q.m. Fran.co Tedeschi in ornare di travertini li due Casini laterali al prospetto di mezzo della Nuova Fontana di Trevi che fà fare la Santità di Nro S.re Papa Clemente XII il tutto con ord.e dell' Emo e Rmo S. Card.l Corsini e di Mons. Illmo, e Rmo Passerini Presid.te dell'acque fatti d.ti lavori a tutta robba spese e fattura della med.a Cecilia misurati da me sottoscritto, e stimati in conformità della loro qualità, e fatture il tutto come segue principiati detti lavori dal p.mo Luglio dell'anno 1735, e terminati à tutto Luglio 1736. (ASR/AV, busta 69, no. 117)

40. 9/5/1736: Simone Moretti, chiavaro / Conto de Lavori fatti alla Rev. Camera Apostolica per Servizio della Fabrica del Novo Ornato della Facciata à Fontana di

Trevi come siegue, cioè . . . a 5 detto [9/5/1736] per havere fatto otto spranche di rigetta da botte lunghe un palmo e mezzo . . . che servono per tenere li sassi dell'Arma del Papa di peso N. 23 L . . . a 9 detto [11/9/1736] per haver fatto n.o 25 zeppe grosse di ferro larghe oncie 4 e longhe parte trè quarti, e parte mezzo palmo che servono per inzeppare li Travertini delle Fame . . . (ASR/AV, busta 70, no. 125)

41. 9/17/1736: *Misura e stima* of the stone carvers Giuseppe Poddi and Francesco Pincellotti . . . "Per il trasporto de' trav.ni dalla Piazza de Barberini, e dalla Pilotta, e Campo Vaccino à Fontana di Trevi in Carrettate n.o 40 . . . Per la fattura, et intaglio di d.a Arme con Triregno isolato e guarnito di gioie, e ricavato p. la parte di sotto, e ornato con chiavi dalle parti, che scappono da due cartocci, parimente isolate, con targa contornata con diversi contorni, e Impresa di Nro Sig.re nel mezzo." (ASR/AV, busta 69, no. 119)

42. 9/1736: Antonio Carelli, pittore / Conto di Lavori fatti di Pittura à Fresco e di Bianca di Venetia color di Travertino à Oglio per accompagnare alle statue che sono nella facciata della Fontana di Trevi fatti dal Mese di 7bre 1736 . . . Più per haver dato di Color di Bianca color di Travertino come, e sopra, a Tutti li fiori che regge in mano la Statua con li fiori che escono dal Seno che sono di metallo, ed agli trè mano, e alli quattro acciò accompagnino come e d.a con più pericolo maggiore che e di d.a ed accompagnato si li fiori come le foglie, ed altro, che sono di metallo . . . 5:40 (ASR/AV, busta 70, no. 122)

43. 12/17/1736: Bill submitted by Nicola Giobbe and Matteo Caramasca . . . Per la spesa de proprij p. fare la forma dell'Arme di gesso, e modello degli scogli, di cera, e formature di gesso p. detti scogli assieme." (ASR/AV, busta 69, no. 118)

44. 12/17/1736: Hora che è stata posta l'arma alla fontana di Trevi, si è dato ordine all'architetto Salvi di dar fuori i conti, contrassegno che non si abbia a procedere più avanti. (Valesio, 5:919)

45. 8/11/1737: Si vede in stampa un epigramma latino composto dal cardinale del Giudice con due elegie, una del Lorenzini ed altra dell'abate Lelli, per animare il Papa a dar compimento alla fontana di Trevi, ed è stata presentata al papa. (Valesio, 6:73)

46. 8/31/1737: Sono state stampate alcune composizioni latine senza nome di autori, ma questi sono: il cardinale Del Giudice, che ha fatto un epigramma assai buono, con due elegie del Lorenzini e Lelli, e queste supplicano il Papa acciò voglia terminare la fabbrica della fontana di Trevi per far comparire fuori l'acqua. (Valesio, 6:77)

47. 1/29/1738: È stato dal papa pagato alla casa Conti il danno cagionatole dalla nuova fabrica della fontana di Trevi con l'occupazione di alcune finestre d'una rimessa per farvi il bottino, ed è stata la somma di circa 4,000 scudi ed i scarpellini hanno ripreso il lavoro per formare il labbro della vasca. (Valesio, 6:112)

48. 5/21/1738: Ha S. Beatitudine dati scudi 10,000 per il proseguimento della tazza per la fontana di Trevi. (Valesio, 6:137)

49. 9/15/1738: Il Computista dell'Ornato dell'Acqua Vergine faccia il mandato di scudi cinquecento mon.ta al S.e Gio. Batt.a Maini Scultore di d.o Ornato, quali facciamo pagare a conto di scudi cinquemila concordati per la fattura della statua grande di mezzo, e gruppo de Tritoni, e due Cavalli marini per servitio di d.o ornato et in fede. / Casa 15 7bre 1738 / Felice Passerini Presid.te dell'Acque (ASR/AV, busta 70, no. 142)

50. 10/20/1738: È stata levata l'acqua di Trevi, essendo andati il medico del papa ed altri al Salone per esaminare la qualità d'un acqua, che si pretende con essa aumentare quella viene a Roma per lo stesso condotta per rendere più copioso d'acqua il nuovo fonte. (Valesio, 6:180)

51. 12/4/1738: Per terminare la fabrica di fontana di Trevi ha il papa fatto una nuova aggiunta di luoghi di Monte. (Valesio, 6:189)

52. 1/16/1739: Ha S. Beatitudine fatti dare 10,000 scudi al Salvi architetto per proseguire la fabbrica della fontana di Trevi, opera di molta spesa e poca riuscita. (Valesio, 6:197)

53. 2/26/1739: Sono giunti i marmi per le statue di fontana di Trevi, per terminare la quale si è fatta nuova giunta alli luoghi de'monti. (Valesio, 6:208)

54. 3/9/1739: Si continuano a portare marmi per statue e bassirilievi che devono porsi alla fontana di Trevi. (Valesio, 6:210)

55. 3/19/1739: Il Comp.ta dell'Ornato dell'Acqua Vergine faccia il Mandato di scudi mille al Sig. Fran.co Ceroti quali sono cioè scudi ottocento in conto del prezzo de Marmi, che deve dare per servizio di d.o Ornato, e venuti da Massa di Carrara, e che verranno in avvenire, e scudi dugento sono per il trasporto de Marmi sud.i ed un altro Marmo grosso, che era riposto nello studio del q.m. Benaglia allo studio del Sig. Giov. Batta. Maini cosi d'accordo, assumendosi esso Ceroti il peso di pagare d.i 200 all' Huomini, che vi hanno lavorato altrimente et in Fede 1000 / Casa 19 Marzo 1739 / Felice Passerini Presid.e dell' Acque (ASR/AV, busta 64, fasc. 160)

56. 3/20/1739: Conto de Lavori fatti ad uso di Faleg.me Cominciati li 9 Gennaro 1739 a tutto Luglio Sud.o Anno fatti per l'Ornato di Fontana di Trevi per Ordine del Sig.e Nicola Salvi archit.o e Monsig.re Ill.mo Passarini Presidente di d.ta Acqua il tutto come Seg. fatti dalli Eredi del q.m Fran.co Polveroni e per essi à Mro. Nicola Enrico Falg.mi / A di 20 d.o [3/20/1739] Per hav. fatto un fusto di Tavole d'Albucco lavorate, e pol: inccollato per il Modello della Tazza del Ornato Long.o p.mi 12 e larg. pmi 2 ½ è poi contornato conforme il segno fatto dallo Scarpellino. / A di 6 Aprile [1739] Per N.o 4 giornate con dui Omini, et il Mastro più e meno volte considerato esser andato a Mettere in Op.e il Modello di Legnio della Facciata del Ornato allo Studio del Sig. Maini rimesso assieme à pocho à pocho, e rincollato quantita di Tavole di pezzi di ritolti, e rinchiod.o cornice bollette chiodi colla, e Tempo e Centaroli . . . / [4/6/1739] Per hav. fatto un Tavolone per il modello dove deve cadere l' acqua dalla tazza di inanzi fatta di Tavola grossa d'Abb.co lavorata e polita long.a pmi 9 larg.a p. 3 ½ intaccata tutta accio che entri nelli piedestalli Tonda d'Avanti conforme il Modello di Carta fatto dal Sig. Maini, e Sig. Salvi. (ASR/AV, busta 70, no. 187)

57. 5/19/1739: Il Computista dell'Ornato dell'Acqua Vergine faccia il mandato al S.e Nicola Salvi Architetto di d.o Ornato di scudi trenta mon.ta, quali facciamo pagare per la mercede ad esso dovuta per la fattura e delineatura della pianta giuditiale fatta nella lite, che verte frà il V. Capitolo, e Canonici di S. Maria Maggiore, e d. fabrica dell' ornato in occasione della pretentione dalli medemi eccitata di voler il prezzo di quell'acqua, che d'ordine di N.S. si vuole introdurre nella forma Maestra che conduce tutto il corpo dell' Acqua Vergine nella Citta di Roma . . . / Casa 19 Maggio 1739 / Felice Passerini Presid.te dell' Acque (ASR/AV, busta 70, no. 146)

58. 6/23/1739: Si proseguisce la fabrica della fontana di Trevi, non si sa che cosa riuscirà, con poca speranza di buono, non essendosi fatto sin ora che fare e disfare i scogli con gran consumo di trevertini. (Valesio, 6:237)

59. 11/27/1739: A di 29 Mzo 1752 / Nota di tutto il Denaro a Gio: B.a Maini Scultore per Conto dell' Ornato di Fontana di Trevi mediante li Inf.ti Ordini tratti dalla Fel. M. Monsig. Passerini già Presid.e dell'Acque come distinta in app. . . . / 1739. A di 27 Nov. gli fù spedito altro ord. n. 211 di 150 à della fattura del modello della statua grande, e gruppo che stà facendo per d.o ornato come alla Giustificaz.e n. 203 . . . 150 . . . / 1740. A di 24 Ag. gli fù spedito altro ord.e n. 240 di 150 perche disse à tenore della Giustifica.ze 231 per resto, saldo, e final pagam.to di 500 concordati per l'intiera fattura del Modello della Statua grande gruppo de'Tritoni, e Cavalli Marini post'in opera nella Fontana con obligo di coreggere ed emendare quello si stimarà necessario per compime.to di d.o Modello senza spesa, ed Emolu. alcuna . . . 150 (ASR/AV, busta 64, fasc. 160)

60. 2/10/1740: Da' turchi fatti schiavi a Fiumicino si è ricavato che tra le prede fatte era stato un legno genovese che portava i marmi per la statua e bassi rilievi della fontana di Trevi e che l'avevano affondato. (Valesio, 6:303)

61. 3/10/1740: Alla fontana di Trevi si è portato il masso della gran statua dell'Oceano, da terminarsi con lo stucco per modello. (Valesio, 6:320)

62. 6/13/1740: Un giovane portoghese allievo del Maini scultore, nel lavoro della fontana di Trevi caduto e percossa gravamente la testa, se ne morì. (Valesio, 6:350)

63. 8/19/1740: Alle 22 hore andarono il cardinale Corsini e Valenti a vedere la fabbrica della fontana di Trevi. (Valesio, 6:378)

64. 8/24/1740: Il Computista dell'Ornato dell'Acqua Vergine faccia il mandato al S. Gio. Batt.a Maini Scultore di d.o Ornato di scudi centocinquanta, quali facciamo pagare per resto e final pagamento di scudi cinquecento concordati per l'intiera fattura del modello della Statua grande e gruppo de Tritoni, e Cavalli Marini posto in opera nella fontana da farsi, con l'obligo di emendare e coregere quello si stimara necessario per finale compimento di d.o modello senz'altra spesa, et emolumento perche cosi et in fede / Casa 24 Agosto 1740 / Felice Passerini Pres.te dell'Acque (ASR/AV, busta 70, no. 231)

65. 9/7/1740: Si è sospeso il lavoro della fontana di Trevi, sì perché si è consumato il denaro, sì anche per il ricorso dello scultore Maini per non storpiare secondo l'idea dell'architetto il suo lavoro. (Valesio, 6:391)

66. 3/15/1741: Essendo insorta lite fra l'architetto Salvi di fontana di Trevi e lo scultore Maini, si sono incominciati a guastare i modelli di stucco delle figure, cioè dell'Oceano, de' due Tritoni e de' due cavalli marini, uno de' quali con le ale. (Valesio, 6:451)

67. 3/30/1741: S. Beatitudine andò questa mattina privatamente alla basilica Vaticana a fare le sacre funzioni della Settimana Santa e darvi la solita benedizione. Nell'andare fu scoperto il recinto di tavole della fontana di Trevi per fargliela vedere ora che si mutano i modelli delle statue, e la sera ritornò al Quirinale. (Valesio, 6:455)

68. 5/22/1741: Volendo S. Beatitudine che si ponga fine alla fontana di Trevi, si è fatto fare dall'architetto lo scandaglio della spesa per terminarla, ed è stato dato di 14,000 scudi, senza fare le statue e bassi rilievi, ma lasciarle, come sono, di stucco. Questa opera di grandissima spesa fin da principio non piacque. (Valesio, 6:477)

69. 8/13/1741: Il Computista dell'Ornato dell'Acqua Vergine faccia il mandato al Sig. Gio. Batta. Maini scultore di d.o Ornato di scudi cento mon.ta, quali sono per recognitione delle nuove fatiche per il risarcimento del Modello di Stucco presentato nella Piazza della Fontana di Trevi secondo la nova idea del Sig. Agostino

Masucci Pittore eletto dal E.mo Sig. Cardinal Corsini, come si vede nel suo attestato dato in computisteria, qual somma si paga per resto, e final pagamento di d.o modello, e che si sia altro, che possa pretendere sino al p.nte giorno, per d.o titolo et in fede. / Casa 13 Agosto 1741 / Felice Passerini Presidente dell Acque.

Il sottoscritto, essendo stato Eletto dall' E.mo Sig. Card. Corsini per sopra intendere al modello della Fontana di Trevi, e perche era cosi contento il Sig. Gio: Batta. Maini scultore, che operava d.o Modello, ed' anco il Sig. Nicola Salvi Architetto di d.a Fontana, fù da mè accettata la d.a sopraintendenza per sodisfare alli comandi di d.a Sua Em.a onde più volte andiedi, viddi, e considerai, è secondo il mio debol talento Consigliai, che si dovesse mutare l'atione delli tritoni, ed il sito del Cavallo Placido col suo tritone, è qual cosa ancora nella prima figura; è questa mutazione prontam.te Lo scultore ne fece modeletto di Creta à sodisfazione mia, e del Sig. Salvi, e questa mutazione fù idea mia, è non già sbaglio dello scultore, è perciò moltiplicata la fatica, è di questo ne faccio piena ed indubitata fede. / Agostino Massucci Pittore Accad.co (ASR/AV, busta 70, no. 260)

70. 9/21/1741: Si proseguisce il lavoro della fontana di Trevi, ma lentamente e fin ora vi sono stati spesi scudi 114,000 e per darle il compimento con statue e bassi rilievi di marmo giungerà alla somma di 115,000. (Valesio, 6:518)

71. 12/24/1741: *Misura e stima* of work done by Nicola Giobbe and Matteo Caramaschi between 1/2/1737 and 12/24/1741, including scaffolding: "Per il Ponte reale fatto à posto à causa di mettere in Op.a li modelli tanto della Statua, che Cavalli Marini e Tritoni. (ASR/AV, busta 70, no. 289)

72. 2/7/1742: Si è posta di nuovo mano alla fontana di Trevi, avendo S. Beatitudine date alcune migliaia di scudi acciò si termini con far venire l'acqua. L'architetto Salvi, dopo aver consumate montagne di trevertini, ha di nuovo variato pensiero, ammontonatine altri fin al mezzo della gran nicchia, e si sta attendendo che cosa riuscirà. (Valesio, 6:558)

73. 4/12/1742: A di 12 Aprile 1741. Misura e stima delli lavori d'intaglio de scogli, piante, erbe diverse, alberi, et altro fatto da Giuseppe Poddi e Francesco Pincellotti Intagliatori compagni per l'Ornato della Nuova Fontana di Trevi incominciata sotto il Ponteficato di Clemente XII, il tutto con ordine dell' E.mo e R.mo Sig. Cardinal Corsini e di Monsig. Ill.mo, e R.mo Passerini Presidente dell'acque misurati, e stimati da me sottoscritto secondo le loro qualità, e fatt.ce, il tutto come segue.

References to plants carved on the *scogli:* una pianta di capperi, che nasce da sotto l'architrave . . . con suoi rami e frondi . . . diversi rami di ellera . . . una pianta di lingua di cane, che resta sotto il terzo pilastro . . . una pianta di cardo, che resta sopra li scogli nell' angolo . . . un'albero di ceraso marino che resta superiore al misurato, intagliato con n.o 3 tronchi, rami, foglie, e frutti che scherzano in diverse maniere . . . diverse piante di pampani, e canne che restono nel sito sotto il pezzo di mezzo . . . una pianta di tasso che resta nell'altra punta incontro . . . una pianta di courbita, che resta nel sasso maggiore . . . una pianta di ciambrusco . . . un albero di cerqua . . . diverse piante di giaro, carciofi, e cavoli, che restano nel terrazzo incontro la porticella delle botte . . . un' altra pianta di foglie ad acqua . . . targa, con ramo attaccato di lauro con cordoni, e cappello . . . una pianta di fava grassa, che resta addosso il secondo pilastro verso S. Martino . . . una pianta di Tasso . . . un ragano . . . una pianta di semprevivo, che resta nella rivolta verso S. Martino . . . una pianta d'edera terrestre . . . un albero di fico nella rivolta con rami, foglie, e frutti . . . frondi di cerqua con foglia ad acqua in mezzo che . . . restano sotto il corpo del vaso . . . ovolo con baccelli che resta dalla parte di sopra di d.o vaso . . .

Per la spesa di cera, e gesso, giornate del formatore per le molte e diverse forme si di tutti i scogli, erbe, e carro di conchiglie modellati in piccolo dal Sig. Salvi, come di tutte le med.me erbe e di molte parti di scogli ridotte dagl' Intagliatori per ordine del med.mo in maggiore grandezza, e di due serpi modellati in opera dal Sig. Maini, seg. per spese di tende, e corde per commodo degl'Intagliatori si d'estate à causa del gran sole, come d'inverno per l'acqua . . . Seg. per . . . il prezzo del modello de i due serpi sud. fatti in grande nel suo luogo pagato al Sig. Maini, e del carro di conchiglie fatto nella sua grandezza naturale sopra i scogli dal Sig. Francesco Ruggieri stuccatore, e suoi huomini e stabilito di stucco come doveva esser l'opera per potervi situar sopra il modello della statua principale, e per altro regalo dato al Sig. Bartolomeo Pincellotti che accommodò le due Fame accanto l'arma in più luoghi dopo morto il Sig. Benaglia. Seg. la fatt.ra di tutti i modelli sud.i dall'istessi Intagliatori trasportati in maggior grandezza dalli piccoli del Sig. Salvi, cioè erbe, scogli, carro et altro, e fatti formare, e gettare per il regolamento dell' intaglio, che comprese tutte le sud.e partite insieme importano . . . scudi 500 (ASR/AV, busta 70, no. 290)

74. 6/16/1742: Si vide poi quasi terminata la magnifica fabrica della fontana di Trevi, mentre in questi giorni vi è stato collocato il giro marmoreo, che forma la gran Vasca di essa Fontana; ed in oggi si vanno faccendo alcuni piccoli fondamenti da eriggervi una scala a cordonata, per la quale potrassi commodamente calare al sudetto Vascone. (D.O., no. 3882, p. 8)

75. 12/5/1742: The merchant Giuseppe Bartoli submits a bill for canvas and other supplies:

A di 5 Dec.re 1742 / Conto del appresso Canevaccio dato d'ord.e di Monsig. Ill.mo e Rev.mo Felice Passerini Presidente dell'Acqua Vergine, servito p. fare una tenda p. l'ornato di Fontana di Trevi di 20 teli longhi di Canne 7 l'uno di Canna Romana. (ASR/AV, busta 71, no. 311)

76. 2/1/1743: Il Computista dell'Ornato dell'Acqua Vergine faccia il mandato di scudi dugento mon.a a Gio. Batta. Maini scultore di d.o Ornato, quali gli si fanno pagare in conto del Lavoro del novo modello, che fà nel Vascone della fontana di d.a acqua Vergine in fede / Casa p.o febr.o 1743 / Felice Passerini Presid. dell'Acque (ASR/AV, busta 71, no. 307)

77. 4/7/1743: Il Computista dell'Ornato dell'Acqua Vergine faccia il mandato di scudi cento mon.ta al Gio. Battista Maini scultore di d.o Ornato quali facciamo pagare a conto del modello, che presentamente lavora nel Vascone di d.o ornato et in fede / Casa 7 Aprile 1743 / Felice Passerini Presid. dell'Acque (ASR/AV, busta 71, no. 312)

78. 8/24/1743: In questi giorni è stata smantellata in parte la Piazza di Trevi dal gran steccato di tavola ivi fatto da lungo tempo per dar comodo al lavoro di quella sontuosa Fontana, la quale si vede quasi terminata in tutte le sue parti, e magnificamente eretta con nobile simetria, e disegno; poiche oltre le grandiose Colonne, che la decorano, vi è nel mezzo la Statua rappresentante l'Oceano, con scettro in mano; e più abbasso due Tritoni, che reggono il freno di due Cavalli marini; vi sono ancora molti abbellimenti di Statue, scogli, erbe, conchiglie, serpi, & altri varj ben intesi

ornati; dovendo il tutto essere scolpito in marmo, benchè alcune delle dette cose, che non sono terminate di marmo siano per ora di stucco, state poste ad uso di modello per goderne la comparsa, in effetto al sommo maestosa, e nobilissima; e già fino da Martedì circa le ore 23., alla presenza di molti riguardevoli Personaggi, che vi stiedero però in privato, e di numeroso Popolo, assistendovi l'Architetto di sì cospicua Fabrica Sig. Nicola Salvi Romano, fu data l'Acqua universalmente, ma non in quella gran copia, che si darà in appresso, per tutta quella vasta Mole marmorea, cadendo rapidamente dalla bocca principale nell'ampio Vascone, ed a sufficienza ripartita l'altra in altre parti con varj scherzi; ma più specialmente in quello addattato al pubblico comodo, ove ogn'uno potrà prenderne con tutta facilità, formato in un scoglio separato dalla Fontana, sopra del quale, che sta in atto di cadere, scherzando due Serpi gettano dalla bocca copiosa Acqua. Questo sì utile, ed insieme magnifico ornamento della Città, quando si vedrà del tutto compito, benchè principato dal Sommo Pontefice suo Predecessore, sarà uno de più manifesti contrasegni, tanto della somma munificenza di Sua Bne, che del suo distintissimo amore per i suoi Sudditi, verso de' quali è sempre intento a promuovere tutto ciò che puo ridondare in loro beneficio, e vantaggio. . . . Il giorno la Santità Sua . . . facendo la strada della Piazza di Trevi si compiaque osservare con particolare sua sodisfazione la struttura di quella nuova quasi terminata nobilissima Fontana, di già arricchita della sua preziosa Acqua, e smantellata in buona parte dal ricinto di tavole, come si è detto. Fermovvisi la Santità Sua per qualche spazio di tempo in discorso con Monsig. Maggi . . . Presidente delle Acque . . . ; essendovi presente anche il disopranominato Architetto di quella Fabrica per ragugliare Sua Bne di ciò avesse desiderato sapere circa tale Edificio. (D.O., no. 4068, pp. 13–15; 17)

79. 10/31/1743: *Stima e misura* of work done by Nicola Giobbe covering work carried out between 6/25/1742 and 10/31/1743:

Per giornate numero tre di un Mastro con numero 8 garzoni il giorno serviti in scalzare, e levare di opera li modelli calati a basso e portati con curoli alla fabbrica dell'Elmi con avere anche per d.i piantato il tiro, e doppo levato di opera dato in nota come sopra con consumo de ferri . . . 7:80 / Per il tempo di numero 20 giornate di due huomini il giorno serviti in disfare li Tritoni, e Cavalli, e fatto portare via tutto il calcinaccio, ed altro in quantità di numero 60 carrettate cosi dato in nota dal Mastro . . . 14:50 (ASR/AV, busta 71, no. 333)

80. 5/11/1744: A fragmentary letter addressed to Ridolfo Venuti concerning the inscription of Benedict XIV on the Trevi, which he composed. Also see 5/13/1744 below: Di Casa li 11 Maggio 1744 / Dovendo in pochi giorni ritornare l'Aqua alla Fontana di Trevi, nel qual tempo dovrà essere interam.te compito il lavoro. Quindi è che il Presidente dell'Aque, nell'atto che riverisce con piena stima l'Ill.mo Sr. Can.co Venuti, lo prega ancora sollecitare l'iscrizione da affigersi ed incidersi nel Fontanone sud.o, acciò vi si possa vedere espressa . . . [gap] . . . l'Aqua . . . [gap] . . . (BAV, Cod. Ottob. Lat. 3128, f. 23)

81. 5/13/1744: Di Casa 13 Mag.io 1744 / Essendosi Ieri sera portato Giancostanzo Caracciolo dall' Emo Seg.rio di Stato, ed avendo discorso coll' E.S. tanto dell'Iscrizzione quanto del nome di Nro Sig.re da ponersi in mezzo del Cornicione della Fontana di Trevi, approvò il tutto, a riserva delle due parole *Aquam duxit*, credendo il Sig.r Cardinale, che ciò non sia propriamente vero; onde in luogo di quel *duxit* vi vorrebbe una sola parola la qual . . . [gap] . . . perfetta terminazione dell'opera. Di tutto ciò

esso Caracciolo ne porge la notizia all'Ill.mo Sig.r Can.co Venuti, al quale raccomanda ancora, che voglia scegliere la parola, che crederà col suo prudente intendimento, adattarla alla mente del d.o Emo Porporato . . . [gap] . . . (BAV, Cod. Ottob. Lat. 3128, f. 22)

82. 5/29/1744: Misura e stima della terminaz.e delli Lavori d'intagli di scogli, carro, serpi, et altro fatti p. la terminazione dell'ornato di Fontana di Trevi sotto il Pontificato di Papa Benedetto XIIII sino al presente giorno [5/29/1744] da Giuseppe Poddi e Francesco Pincellotti Intagliatori Compagni, et ordinati, misurati, e stimati da me sottoscritto Architetto con la considerazione delle loro qualità e fatture il tutto come segue.

Per la fattura, e intaglio del serpe, che finge passare dietro il sopradetto fico long.o in due partite p.mia 29 ½ larg. girato p.m i 2 ½, ed il med.o serpe contiene per la fatture della testa studiata dal vero con bocca aperta con suoi denti straccati, e bocca traforata per il condotto e voltata staccata con diligenza tutte le voltate, che in essi serpi contengano il tutto studiato dal vero, e lustrato consideratone la fattura, e durezza della Pietra . . . 88:50 . . . Per la fattura e intaglio dell'altro serpe della med.a fattura, mà con scherzo diverso fingendo la coda di abbracciare il vaso per la parte dello scoglio, e inciamellandosi viene a passare la terra sopra à un pezzo di scoglio vicino l'altra serpe sudetta long. girata pmi 29 ⅚ larg. girata nel maggiore p.mi 2 ½ rotata impomiciata, e lustra simile alla retroscritta . . . 89:50 (ASR/AV, busta 71, no. 340)

83. 7/4/1744: Vedendosi ormai quasi perfezzionata la magnifica Fabrica della Fontana di Trevi di cui è stato l'Architetto il Sig. Niccola Salvi Romano, si è intanto discoperta una breve Iscrizzione scolpita a gran caratteri di lastra d'ottone nella fascia di marmo sotto il cornicione della facciata, del seguente tenore: PERFECIT BENEDICTUS XIV.PONT.MAX.—e la medesima è stata apposta sotto quella, che già vi era nel riquadro di mezzo sotto l'Arme dalla san. mem. di Papa Clemente XII Corsini. (D.O., no. 4203, pp. 19–20)

84. 7/11/1744: . . . la Sant. Sua . . . nel partire dal Quirinale volle fare la strada di Fontana di Trevi, che essendo stata smantellata dal gran steccato di Tavole, che la circondava, ed arricchita di tutta la sua preziosa, e copiossima Acqua, vi si fermò Sua Santità, e smontato di Carozza osservò con piacere quella magnifica Fabrica del tutto terminata, alla riserva delle Statue, che situate nelle proprie nicchie, ed altri luoghi fatte per ora di stucco, e di semplice pittura a chiar'oscuro sul legno, e conforme lo sono ancora alcuni ornati di basso rilievo, doveranno poi col tempo esservi apposte di marmo; e vi si trovò a ricevere, ed inchinare Sua Bne Monsignore Caracciolo di Santobono uno dei Chierici di Camera, e Presidente delle Acque, con il Sign. Nicola Salvi Architetto, a quali il S. Padre dimostrò di tutto l'operato molto gradimento. (D.O., no. 4206, pp. 7–8)

85. 7/21/1744: 1744. A di 21 d.o [Luglio] à Pietro Marchesini per mercede delli disegni di n. 16 Lettere Majuscole per farne li modelli per gettarle di metallo per l'iscrizione . . . 24 (ASR/AV, busta 64, fasc. 160, "Pagamenti fatti per l'Ornato di Fontana di Trevi, p. 10)

86. 7/23/1744: *Stima e misura* submitted by Giuseppe Poddi:

Misura del Carro / Per la fattura, e Intaglio del Conchiglione, che forma carro alla figura dell' Oceano lavorato a guisa di Ostricha intarterita da ogni parte imitando il vero, e la medesima è consistente in una Ostricha doppia cioè nel da Capo scherza slabrando il suo fine di contorno Iregolare con sua grossezza intarterita, come si dovesse aprire, da piedi à dette restringe, e forma due gran Corni intarteriti sopra ad uno di essi posa il piede la figura, e snodando per il di sotto scherzosa forma due orecchioni intarteriti per di dentro, e sopra terminando spumose, e rivolgendo verso l'Ostricha di sotto con la medesima grossezza forma due grandi occhi, che in mezzo alli medesimi dalli Tarteri de Corni ne nasce una bocca dove scatorirà l'acqua poi siegue la grossezza delle parti laterali di detti occhi, e con grandi scanelli parimente intarteriti formano un'altra Ostrica, dove dovrà correre la gran bocca d'acqua, et in mezzo ad essa dai Tarteri molto rilievati formano due tazze per fare cadute, e bullori dell' acqua, e tutta la sudetta Machina è lavorata con cavi, fondi, e vote da ogni parte . . . 2070:60 (ASR/AV, busta 71, no. 340)

87. 8/6/1744: Conto Di Pitture servite Per la Fontana di Trevi fatte d'Ordine dell' Ecc.mo Monsig.r Santobono da me Antonio Bicchierari.

Per due bassi rilievi di chiaro oscuro bianco dipinti à oglio alti palmi 14:, e Larghi palmi 10., che rappresentano in un Marco Agrippa, che ordina la Fabrica dell'Acquedotto, nell'altro la Vergine Trivia, che insegna à Soldati la sorgente dell'Acqua.

Per due Statue dipinte come sopra alte palmi 22: larg. pmi 12:, che rappresentano Li sud.i Marco Agrippa, e la Vergine Trivia.

Avendo concordato con il S. Nicola Salvi Architetto le sudette Pitture per prezzo di scudi 75 dovendosi fare a Guazzo, ma poi consideratosi esser più durevole si sono dipinte à oglio con l'approvazione di Sua Ecc.za, e però avendo cresciuto la fatica, e spesa de i colori, e oglio, Perciò si domanda il prezzo di . . . scudi 100.

Al Computista dell' Ornato di Fontana di Trevi spedira l'ordine per scudi novanta questo di 6 Agosto 1744. S.G. Caraciolo Presidente dell'Acque. (ASR/AV, busta 71, no. 345)

88. 9/5/1744: Nella nobilissima nuova Fabrica della Fontana di Trevi fu discoperta nelli scorsi giorni l'Arma di Monsig. Caracciolo de Principi di Santobono Presidente delle Acque, e come tale ha indefessamente invigilato all'adempimento della magnanima idea di Sua Bne in sì prospicua Opera; e la medesima Arma si vede scolpita con suo Cappello, e fiocchi in un scoglio laterale, che fa ornamento alla stessa Fontana, esistente dalla parte della strada, che conduce alla Chiesa di SS. Angeli Custodi. (D.O., no. 4230, p. 2)

89. 10/3/1744: Nell'Arma, che già si disse, di Monsig. Caracciolo de Principi di Santobono collocata nel nuovo Edificio della Fontana di Trevi vi è stato aggiunto l'ornamento di una fascia in cui si vedono scolpite le seguenti parole: JOANNE COSTANTIO CARACCIOLO AQUARUM PRAESIDE (D.O. no. 4242, p. 3)

90. 9/18/1745: Sopra la Porticella, che da l'ingresso alla conserva delle Acque della magnifica Mole di Fontana di Trevi, situata propriamente dalla parte laterale di essa Fontana, per la strada che conduce alla Chiesa della Madonna di Costantinopoli, e quasi dirimpetto al Palazzo de Sign. Scavolini, è stata collocata in questi giorni la seguente Iscrizzione: BENEDICTUS XIV, POM. / Rivos Aquae Virginis, / compluribus locis manantes, / quique in usu esse desierant / in Urbem reduxit, / Aquaeductus vetustate collapsos / restauravit / Fistulas, Tubulos, Castella, Lacus, / purgato Fonte, restituta forma / ingenti Liberalitate / in ampliorem formam redegit / Ann. Sal. MDCCXLIV, Pont. IV. (D.O., no. 4392, p.12)

91. 12/23/1745: Nota di spese fatte da Nicola Salvi p. servizio della Fontana di

Trevi. / Per la pigione di due stanze prese, e ritenute più anni in affitto p. comodo di fare i modelli e particolarmente de i scogli, e piazza, come p. ricevuta . . . 70 / Per tanti pagati in più volte allo scultore p. far eseguire in modelli i diversi pensieri delle figure p. l'ornato della fontana, come p. ricivute . . . 110 / Per spesa di cera, creta, modelletti di legno, ferri, assistenza d'un uomo, et altro . . . 32:25 / Per il calesse preso a vetture molte volte nel tempo, che si lavorava il cassone di legno temporaneo a Bocca di Leone p. rimandar l'acqua a Roma, come p. ricevuta . . . 17:75 / somma ass.e 230 / Il Comp. dell' Ornato di Fontana di Trevi spedirà l'ordine di scudi duecentotrenta pagabile al S. Nicola Salvi Arch.to di esso Ornato per rimborso di pag.ti comesr. A di 23 Xmbre 1745 / G. Caracciolo Presidente dell' Acque (ASR/ AV, busta 71, no. 363)

92. 12/2/1746: Matteo Caramaschi Murat.re per il Fondam.to e positura del Pilo per beverare, selciata di quadruccii, e Muro della Cortina. 1746 A di 2 Xm. per intiero . . . 300 (ASR/AV, busta 64, fasc. 160, Pagamenti fatti per l'Ornato di Fontana di Trevi, p. 3)

93. 9/1747 circa: Denari dati da S. me. di Clem. PP. XII: Dal Lotto di Roma . . . 58135:25 (ASR/AV, busta 64, fasc. 160, Pagamenti fatti per l'Ornato di Fontana di Trevi, p. 11)

94. 8/28/1748: Felice Botti Capom.ro Murat.re Conto de lavori di Muro, Cave di Terra, ed altro fatto al Lavatore publico nella Piazzetta a piè la strada, che va al Portone della Panateria di Mte. Cavallo. (ASR/AV, busta 87, no. 348)

95. 10/3/1748: Conto, e misura di lavori ad'uso di Scarpellino, e intagliatore di Pietra fatti da Fran.co Pincellotti, e dal q.m Giuseppe Poddi p. la nuova porta della Botte dell'acqua di Fontana di Treve, con Scrizzione, e Arma Sopra à d.a e Compreso l'arma di Mon. Illmo Presidente dell' Acqua fatta sopra lo scoglio della Fontana, et altro ornam.to d'intaglio, come in appro segue . . . / A di 3 Ott.re 1745 / Per la fatt.ra dell'intaglio fatto in opera l'arme di Mons. sopra lo scoglio della fontana, cioè aver scoperto la targa, che gia vi era dalli tartari, che in parte la ricoprivano, et aver tornato à lavorare la d.a arma, e ingrandita, con aver incavato, e rilevato lo scoglio di sotto accrescendovi parte delle soglie di lavoro, che la reggevano, et aver aggiunto li fiocchi, e il Cappello sopra con pezzo riportato, et intagliato l'impresa del Leone in mezzo il tutto ricercato alto d.o Lavoro p.i 8 lg. p.i 6 considerato l'incommodo d'averlo lavorato in opera . . . 57:60 (ASR/AV, busta 71, no. 364)

96. 11/25/1748: Acqua Vergine / Nota di diversi accessi et operazioni fatti da mè Luigi Vanvitelli Pro. Archi.to di detta acqua, con ordine di Mon.re Ill.mo e Reve.mo Pietro Petroni Presidente del tribunale delle acque a di 25 9mbre 1748. (ASR/AV, busta 64, fasc. 158, no. 3)

97. 2/13/1751: In detto giovedi mattina stiede esposto con pompa funebre nella chiesa di S. Maria in Aquiro, detta l'Orfanelli, sua Parrocchia, il defonto celebre architetto Nicola Salvi Romano, di cui tra le altre insigni opere, si ammira quella della famosa fabbrica della fontana di Trevi. (D.O., no. 5238, p. 13)

98. 3/14/1759: Monsig. Niccolò Perrelli Nostro Tesoriere Generale: Avendo noi determinato che il prospetto della Fontana dell'Acqua Vergine detta di Trevi, una delle più conspicue moderne fabbriche di questa nostra città di Roma venga intieramente compito, e perfezzionato mediante la costruzzione delli mancanti bassi rilievi, e statue di pietra, in luogo di quelle composte di stucco—che al presente vi esistono; Perciò col presente nostro chirografo, in cui abbiamo per espresso lo stato della

fabbrica della sudetta Fontana e qualunque altra cosa quanto si voglia necessaria di esprimersi vi ordiniamo, ed ingiongiamo, che dei denari della nostra Camera ne facciate passare per ora nella depositeria generale della Reverenda Camera a credito della medesima in conto a parte ed a libera disposizione del Rev.mo Cardinal Colonna Camerlengo la somma di scudi tremila moneta, per doverli, senza cura di veruna persona erogare nelle spese necessarie per la formazione delle dette statue e bassi rilievi, ed ornamenti della sudetta Fontana, ed in questa forma ne diriggerete alla Depositeria della detta nostra Camera, ed a chiunque spetta li vostri ordini pel detto pagamento, e farete ogni altra cosa necessaria, per esser tale la mente, e volontà nostra precisa, non ostante qualunque cosa, che facesse, o potesse fare in contrario. Dato dal nostro Palazzo Apostolico Quirinale questo di 14 Marzo 1759. / Clemens PP XIII (ASR, Computisteria Generale dopo la riforma di Benedetto XIV, Seria Verde, Giustificazioni del Libro Mastro Generale, busta 39, no. 41)

99. 6/2/1759: Per ordine della Santità di N. Sign., sono già molti giorni, che si è dato principio al lavoro delle statue, e bassi rilievi, che dalla magnanimità della Sant. Sua vogliono farsi collocare nei siti già opportunamente disposti fin da quando si fece la fabrica della nobilissima, e veramente magnifica Fontana di Trevi, per maggiore ornamento della medesima; e li virtuosi Scultori di tali opere sono li Signori Pietro Bracci, Filippo Valle, Giovanni Grossi, ed Andrea Bergondi. (D.O., no. 6537, p. 20)

100. 5/29/1762: In questi giorni passati è stato terminato il lavoro di perfezionare ne suoi abellimenti, restati fin'ora interrotti dopo essere stata costrutta di nuovo, e rimossa dalla sua antichità con la magnificenza, che si vede la famosa fontana di Trevi, Opera del celebre Architetto Salvi, poichè essendo mancante di alcune statue, e bassi rilievi postivi per allora in modelli di stucco, vi sono stati adesso messi di marmo, e questi in particolare vengono ad essere la statua, o sia colosso nel prospetto principale di mezzo rappresentante l'*Oceano*, e li due *Cavalli marini*, con li Tritoni reggenti il freno de suddetti, e questi sono opera del Sig. Pietro Bracci Romano.

Le due statue nelle nicchie laterali rappresentanti quella a mano destra *la Fertilità*, e l'altra alla sinistra *la Salubrità*, sono opera del Sig. Filippo Valle Fiorentino.

Il basso rilievo situato a mano destra rappresentante *Marco Agrippa, che ordina la fabrica degl'Acquedotti* è del Sig. Andrea Bergondi Romano, e l'altro a mano sinistra rappresentante *Trivia in atto d'insignare alli soldati di detto Marco Agrippa la sorgente dell'Acqua Vergine*, è del Sig. Gio: Battista Grossi Romano, tutti virtuosi scultori.

Nel frontispizio poi, o sia cornicione della stessa Fontana vi si legge scolpita a gran caratteri in metallo dorato la seguente Iscrizione: *Positis Signis, &, Anaglyphis / Tabulis / Iussu Clementis XIII / Pontificis Maximi / Opus, cum omni cultu absolutum / Anno Domini MDCCLXII*.

Essendo cosi del tutto compita in detti suoi mancanti abbellimenti, Sabbato della passata 22. del corrente il dopo pranzo, la Sant. di Nostro Signore in occasione di portarsi alla visita delle 40.ore nella Chiesa di S. Ivo de Brittoni, facendo ivi fermar la carozza, si compiacque trattenersi qualche poco tempo ad osservarla, ed allora fu scoperta per la prima volta al publico. Vi si trovarono ad umiliarsi al Santo Padre, e a dargli pieno ragguaglio del tutto il Sig. Giuseppe Pannini Romano, che ha cosi bene eseguito tutta l'opera come Architetto del Tribunale dell'Acqua Vergini, & il sudetto Sig. Bracci scultore, ed il primo di essi gli presentò il disegno di essa Fontana, clementissimamente gradito dalla Santità Sua. (D.O., no. 7005, pp. 4–6)

101. 7/14/1762: Monsig.r Saverio Canale Nostro Tesoriere Generale. Essendo intieramente compito, e perfezzionato l'ornato, e Prospetto della moderna ragguardevole fabbrica della Fontana dell'Acqua Vergine denominata di Trevi, mediante la costruzione delle statue, e Bassi rilievi mancanti, eseguita in vigore dei nostri ordini, e per il totale pagamento delli scultori ed artefici, che ci anno operato, mancando la somma di scudi due mila ottocento quarantasette, e Bajocchi settanta due moneta, a tenore della distinta nota presentataci dal Rev.mo Cardinal Girolamo Colonna Camerlengo, al quale ne abbiamo incaricato la sopraintendenza, e volendo inoltre che a credito, e libera disposizione dello stesso Rev.mo Cardinal Camerlengo si faccia passare la somma di scudi seicento per eseguirne la nostra mente ed intenzione comunicatagli; Perciò col presente nostro chirografo, in cui abbiamo per espresso lo stato di detta Fabbrica, e suoi ornati, la quantità de' denari somministrati a tal'effetto, li conti dei lavori fatti, e qualunque altra cosa quantosivoglio necessaria ad esprimessi ordiniamo, ed ingioniamo a voi, che oltre la somma di scudi ventun mila fatti somministrare con altri nostri chirografi segnati li 14 marzo, e 12 dicembre 1759, 23 febbraio 1760, 5 febbraio, 5 agosto, e 12 dicembre 1761, facciate dei denari della nostra camera passare nella di lei depositaria Camerale in conto a parte, a credito della medesima ed a libera disposizione del detto Rev.mo Cardinale Girolamo Colonna Camerlengo scudi tremila quattrocento quarantasette, e Bajocchi settantadue moneta; che sormonteranno in tutto alla somma di scudi ventiquattro mila quatrocento quarantasette, e Bajocchi settantadue moneta, per doverli senza cura di veruna Persona impiegare per la rata di scudi duemila ottocento quarantasette, e Bajocchi settantadue nel finale pagamento delle spese occurre per formare le dette statue, bassi rilievi, ed ornati della detta Fontana, e per la restante rata di scudi Seicento erogarli in tutto, e per tutto secondo la nostra mente, e volontà allo stesso Rev.mo Card. Camerlengo comunicata, ed in questa guisa ne dirigerete alla detta depositaria della nostra Camera, ed a chiunque altro spetta li vostri ordini, affinchè siegua detto pagamento, a farette ogni, e qualunque altra cosa necessaria, per esser tale la mente, e volontà nostra espressa, nonostante tutto ciò, che facesse o potesse fare in contrario date dal Nostro Palazzo Apostolico Quirinale questo di 14 luglio 1762 / Clement PP XIII.

Ristretto delle Spese occorse per la costruzione delle statue in marmo, Bassi Rilievi, et altri ornamenti per la Fontana dell'Acqua Vergine detta di Trevi / Al Sig. Pro' Bracci Scultore per la fattura del Oceano, Tritoni e Cavalli marini . . . 5000 / Al Sig. Filippo della Valle Scultore per fattura delle due statue laterali . . . 2300 / A Giuse Grossi Scultore per la fattura d'un bassorilievo . . . 750 / Ad And.a Beregondi Scultore per fattura d'altro Bassorilievo . . . 750 / A Bartolomeo Baroni Argentiere per p'zo delle sbranche, e Perni di metallo, e per le lettere di metallo dorate come da conti . . . 543:64 / A Fran.co Ceroti per p'zo de marmi come da conti . . . 2452.20 / A Paolo Campi per p'zo de marmi come da conti . . . 5616:77½ / A Giulio Cigni per il disegno delle lettere per la nuova iscrizione . . . 25 / A Pro' Pozzo Pittore per il disegno delle statue per incidente in rame . . . 30 / A Gio. Sassi Capo Mro' Muratore per i trasporti de marmi, e delle statue armatura de legnami per mettere in opera, ed altro . . . 4221:46½ / Ad Agostino Ancidoni Ferraro per lavori fatta per ferramenti, et altro per l'Armatura . . . 376:90 / A Gio. B.a Grossi per lavori fatti in riattare la scogliera, e vascone . . . 341:65 / A Gio. Dom.co Tognotti Stagnaro per lavori fatti come da conti . . . 320:59 / A Gius.e Alberigi Falegname per lavori fatti per d.a Fontana d. da d.a . . . 127:90 / Ad And.a Blasi e Lorenzo Perini Scarpellini per lavori fatti come da d.a . . . 912:95 / Per Piggione di due Rimessoni, ove sono state lavorate le statue dell'Oceani . . . 78:75 / E 30 = al Compa per ricog.e di fatiche fatte per spedire gl'ordini, e tenere il conto delle Sud.e spese . . . 30 / Somma in tt.o la Spesa occorsa . . . 23877.72. (ASR, Computisteria Generale dopo la Riforma di Benedetto XIV, Seria Verde, Giustificazioni del Libro Mastro Generale, busta 46, no. 127)

Appendix 2.
Documents Describing
the Trevi by Nicola Salvi

1. Copy of a letter and a memorandum on the sculpture of the Trevi, probably addressed to Cardinal Neri Corsini and dating 1740–41:

Queste mie poche qualunque si sieno riflessioni sulla maniera d'esprimere il gruppo dell'Oceano, soggetto principale da me introdotto nella fontana di Trevi, le quali prendo ardire di porre sotto gli occhi dell'Em.a v.ra, ed alla censura del di lei intendimento, posso giustamente temere, che, condannando in parte a ciò che ha stabilito di fare il Sig.r Fran.co Maini, professore meritevol.te prescelto per l'esecuzione di detto gruppo, sieno per farmi incontrare la taccia, o di presumere troppo di me med.o o delle mie operazioni, o di trascendere in un ardire eccedente, quasi che voglia stendermi oltre i confini che possano convenirmi come Architetto, e porre il piede nell'altrui provincia senza farmi scrupolo d'oppormi ad un Professore di tanto grido per la moltiplicità e perfezione delle di lui opere, io che per così dire appena incomincio adesso ad uscire dalle mie private applicazioni, e dalle mura del mio studio per rendermi cognito al Pubblico. Ma che poteva io fare se il Sig.r Maini per accomodare il gruppo in una maniera, siami lecito il dirlo, in tutto opposta alla verità di una giusta e conveniente espressione si è trovato in necessità di sconvolgermi la situazione de i scogli, e la caduta dell'acqua da i med. che mi era prefissa, e se proposte ad esso da me più volte particolarmente, et in privato tutte quelle ragioni, che potevano giustificare la mia elezione anno sempre incontrata la disgrazia, non solo di non essere per nulla considerate, per quanto strettamente elle dedotte si fossero da noi, a fondamentali principj, ma neppure rigettate, come tra ragionevoli professori suol farsi con altre riflessioni, a solo fine almeno, se non per altro, di render me istrutto di quegli errori, che averò facilmente in esse potuti commettere, e della preeminenza della scelta del di lui partito, che per certezza forse dal mio ingegno non ho saputa da per me stesso conoscere. Io so che dovendo il Sig.r Maini restare al mondo il debitore perpetuo di tutto ciò che di bene e di male sarà considerato nell'esecuzione del gruppo, deve avere tutta intiera la libertà di operare a seconda della propria intelligenza, e del proprio sapere senza che io possa pretendere in verun conto di limitarlo, ma so ancora altresì, che se mia doverà esser la lode, o il biasimo che sarà per nascere dal buono, o infelice esito dell'acqua per i scogli, deggio anch'io sodisfar me med.o, e non acquetarmi ciecamente alla sola di lui autorità, o di altrui, che egli asserisce aver'approvato il di lui modello, se non allora, che in quella guisa, che ho corroborate io le mie massime con quelle raggioni, che sarò per dire in appresso accompagneranno anch'essi la loro convenevole approvazione o disapprovazione con altre contrarie e convincenti, a fine di persuadermi a mutar parere, e concorrer di buona voglia col loro sentimento, come quello che mi si farà conoscere atto a condurmi alla maggior perfezione della mia opera. Oltre di che mi lusingo di restar facilmente assoluto di qualsivoglia taccia, e libero da qualunque rimprovero, che possa farmisi, se con equità, e con animo disappassionato si farà riflessione, che essendo mio parto, qualunque essa si sia l'idea di tutta l'opera, poteva, e doveva prendermi la libertà di suggerire al Sig.r Maini, quello che io aveva disegnato d'esprimere in essa senza che questo potesse imputarmisi ad una vana pretensione di volerlo circoscrivere nelle proprie operazioni, e che non persuaso da contrarie ragioni non v'ha cosa che potesse assolvermi dal fare ciò che io faccio, trattandosi di un'opera nella quale ha interesse la gloria del mio principe, che con paterna pietà si è degnato di comandarmela, quella dell'Em.a v.ra, alla di cui benignità assistendomi, e proteggendomi, deggio io corrispondere con tutto il trasporto dell'anima. Il decoro della mia Patria che indispensabilmente impegna ogni buon cittadino a procurarlo, per quanto si stendono almeno le proprie forze, ma sopra tutto la mia estimazione, per l'acquisto della quale non deggio trascurar cosa alcuna, e se pur troppa per la tenuità del mio ingegno, che non sa stendersi più oltre sarà quest'opera per uscire difettosa dalle mie mani, non voglio almeno, che mi resti il rammarico d'aver, tacendo, o adulando all'altrui autorità dissimulata alcuna di quelle cose, che possono renderla più degna di compatimento dinanzi agli occhi del pubblico, e meno esposta all'altrui maledicenza. Ma lasciando a parte queste digressioni, che non altro scopo anno avuto che la premura di giustificare le mie operazioni appresso l'E.ma V.ra, incomincerò a discendere metodicamente al particolare di questa materia e premettendo prima a guisa di puri e veri assiomi, che per tali credo che mi saranno ammessi da chi che sia, tutti quei principi sul fondamento dei quali ho appoggiato il mio raziocinio, passerò in appresso ad esporre il significato, e le passioni che ho avuto in mente doversi riconoscere nelle figure che compongono il gruppo, riserbandomi all'ultimo di esaminare se sia ragionevole tutto ciò, che il Sig.r Maini ha rappresentato nel suo modello.

Condusse ancora in Roma (cioè Marco Agrippa) l'acqua Vergine raccolta nel Campo di Lucullo. È chiamata Vergine, perché, cercando acqua i soldati, una verginella ne insegnò loro alcune vene, le quali, seguitando i cavatori, ritrovarono una gran quantità d'acqua.

Da questo passo di Giulio Frontino nel suo comentario degli acquedotti si cavano i quattro soggetti di scoltura da introdursi nella fontana di Trevi, cioè la statua della Vergine inventrice dell'acqua: Quella di Marco Agrippa condutore della med.a in Roma: il bassorilievo esprimente la sud.a invenzione, e l'altro, che doverà contenerne la condottura.

In quanto alle due statue, parlando in genere, la grandezza di esse, doverà essere quella stessa, che si vede dipinta nella fontana; Et il zoccola che anno sotto i piedi, non si farà maggiore di quello, che ivi comparisce, e se per il sostentamento della statua ve ne bisognasse di più, si farà in maniera, che possa incassarsi nel travertino, che forma pavimento nella nicchia senza che si veda esteriormente.

La statua d'Agrippa averà il ritratto cavato dalle medaglie, che di lui ci remangono. Il suo abito sarà di armatura romana con quegli ornamenti, che possono convenire ad un gran capitano, et ad un genero d'Augusto, pigliandone l'imitazione dalle buone statue, e da bassi rilievi antichi. La sua azzione principale esprimerà l'ordine, o il comando, che da agli artefici, quasi che fossero presenti, di fabbricare gli acquedotti, e di condurre l'acqua in Roma.

L'altra statua della Vergine sarà in sembianza di giovinetta vestita con abito semplice, puro, e confacente ad una verginella rustica ritrovata accidentalmente in campagna, come doveva esser questa di cui si tratta, avvertendo particolarmente di lasciare ogni pensiero della supposta, o sognata Vergine Trivia, che nulla a che fare nel caso nostro. La di lei azione necessaria sara di additar l' acqua o al Popolo, come dicesse, ecco l'acqua da me insegnata ai soldati, che or voi qui godete, ovvero ai med.mi soldati, mostrando loro ciò che cercavano.

Il bassorilievo sopra la statua d'Agrippa esprimerà la condottura dell'acqua. Doverà vedervisi l'istesso Agrippa col seguito di qualche soldato, che gli fa corte, il quale ordina ad alcuni artefici la costruzione degli acquedotti. Il campo dell'azione sarà di paese aperto in cui si osserverà porzione de med.i acquedotti già incominciato a fabricarvisi.

L'altro bassorilievo sopra la vergine conterrà l'invenzione dell'acqua. Vi sarà la med.a vergine, che ne addita alcune vene a i soldati, che la cercavano, alcuni dei quali potranno stare in atto d'essersi rivolti a guardarla al cenno di lei; et altri, piegandosi, la raccoglieranno desiderosi di beverla, e tutta l'azione sarà similmente espressa in campagna aperta.

È necessario riflettersi, che tanto i due scultori che faranno le statue, quanto quelli destinati per i bassirilievi dovrebbero convenire insieme, e mostrarsi vicendevolmente i modelli; i primi per non cadere nella med.a o in simile azione e far cosa, che conferisca all'armonia di tutta l'opera, et i secondi per stabilire una uniforme et uguale grandezza nelle loro figure, afine, che non sieno talmente diverse che facciano mostruosità in due bassirilievi compagni. (Biblioteca Nazionale Centrale Roma, Fondo Vittorio Emanuele, 580, ff. 43–45v)

2. Copy of Salvi's description of his design for the Trevi and his explanation of its iconography.

Descrizione del Prospetto della Fontana di Trevi, stesa, e scritta di proprio carattere da Niccola Salvi.

Si vede la nuova Fabrica della Fontana, di cui prendiamo a parlare, situata sopra una delle fronti del Palazzo dell'Eccellentissima Casa Conti, che risguarda la Piazza di Trevi, stendendosi da un angolo all'altro del medesimo in lunghezza di duegento venti palmi, la qual lunghezza divisa in tre porzioni, serve quella di mezzo di estensione di circa cento, e un palmo all'ornamento, che diremo in appresso, per l'esito, e sgorgo dell'acqua, restando le altre due laterali arricchite di fenestre, et altri ornamenti proprj per l'uso di Palazzo, a cui servono, e per un conveniente, e proporzionato accordo alla Parte Principale a cui formano fianco.

Nella parte di mezzo suddetta, s'inalza p. quanto essa si stende, uno scoglio in altezza dal piano della Piazza di ventiquattro palmi circa, e di trenta dal fondo del Vascone, o ricettacolo delle acque, dove ha il suo nascimento, il quale fra le sue rotture, e caverne lascia in alcune parti scoperto un gran zoccolo bugnato, che colla sua cimasa ne supera l'altezza, quasi che dall'Arte fosse stato così, come si vede, incominciato a lavorare, e cavare dallo scoglio, e sopra i suoi risalti sostiene un Ordine Corintio di quattro Colonne di cinque palmi, e mezzo di diametro, risaltate sino alla cima di tutto l'ordine medesimo, e di altretanti mezzi pilastri ad esse uniti, il quale uscendo in fuori verso la Piazza, fà, che li due fianchi detti di sopra, li quali formano

Palazzo, rimanghino più indietro di esso per uno spazio di circa dodici palmi. Il sudetto Ordine Corintio unito ad un Attico, che ha di sopra, terminante col balaustro, forma un'altezza di cento diecidotto palmi, la quale supera i due fianchi, quanto è necessario, che essa faccia, affinché la parte, che serve, et adorna il Soggetto principale dell'opera, rimanga, per quanto risguarda l'Architettura, più eminente, e maestosa delle altre. Per la sua larghezza poi, rimane diviso dalle quattro Colonne, e mezzi pilastri sudd. in tre parti, delle quali quella di mezzo il doppio maggiore delle altre due laterali, contiene un Nicchione, la di cui volta riquadrata, arricchita d'intagli, e fiori di varie sorti, viene sostenuta da altre quattro Colonne isolate di grossezza di tre palmi, et un quarto d'ordine Ionico-composito, co'i contropilastri a ciascheduna di esse, e cornice architravata al di sopra, la quale và a terminare sopra una fascia, che forma riquadro d'intorno all'arco esteriore della Nicchia medesima, e facendosi poscia rivedere col suo ricorso nelle parti laterali, le divide in maniera, che in esse lascia sotto di sé due altre nicchie quadrate, e fà sostegno al di sopra a due riquadri corrispondenti, ornati intorno di cornice intagliata.

Li due fianchi, li quali, siccome abbiam detto di sopra, formano parte del Palazzo dell'Eccellentissima Casa Conti, sono composti di quattro appartamenti, ciascheduno dei quali contiene tre fenestre, con pilastri d'ordine Corintio fra esse interposti, simili, e ricorrenti in tutti i membri con l'altro della parte di mezzo, non solo per quanto appartiene all'Architettura, mà ancora ad un Bassamento, parte bugnato, e parte rustico di scogli, simile al già detto di mezzo, scherzato in più luoghi con varie erbe, e con alcuni pezzi di masso, altri de'quali stanno quasi minacciando rovina, et altri già distaccati, si vedono caduti sopra un terrazzo, che stendosi per più palmi sopra la Piazza, forma piede al medesimo basamento. Il sudetto Scoglio terminando negli angoli dei due Palazzi, contiene dentro le sue cavità le fenestre del piano terreno, sopra le quali s'inalza in alcuni luoghi con varie punte, e prominenze, vedendosi alcune di dette fenestre già lavorate, e cavate in esso dall'arte, con un semplice rustico ornato di bugne all'intorno, rimanendo le altre in sembianza più di naturali, che di artificiose aperture di caverne. Degli altri tre ordini di fenestre superiori, due rimanendo compresi in tutta l'altezza de'pilastri, il primo è adornato di colonne d'ordine dorico in tutte le sue parti, alla riserva delle metope, e triglifi, terminante nella cima con frontespizio acuto; et il secondo (come che piu leggiero doveva comparire all'occhio per la vicinanza de'capitelli, et altri lavori d'intaglio ne'membri delle cornici appartenenti all'ordine de pilastri) resta arricchito per stipiti di fasce riquadrate, con mensole in cima, sopra le quali posa il resto dell'ornamento, consistente in Architrave, fregio con festone di lauro, e cornice con frontespizio circolare per ultimo termine; avendo ambedue questi ordini di fenestre sotto di se le ringhiere di balaustri, le quali formando ad esse parapetti, servono di ornamento, e di comodo a i medesimi Palazzi. Il terz'ordine componente un piano mezzanino, inalzandosi sopra il cornicione principale dell'opera, vi forma quasi un Attico con sua base, e cimasa, e frà le fenestre di esso ornate all'intorno di una semplice cornice, si rachiude un riquadro, dentro cui pende un sottil panno di basso rilievo, il quale appeso a tre chiodi, formando festone, arricchisce, e rende nel medesimo tempo leggero il detto ordine, facendo ricorso, et accordo agli altri ornamenti di tutta l'opera.

Ragioni Filosofiche, che rende Niccola Salvi dell'Invenione.

L'Oceano, la di cui statua dovrà situarsi nella Fontana di Trevi, non và certamente separato dalla serie delle altre antiche dietà, le quali, sotto la corteccia di misteriose imagini, racchiudevano sempre o utili insegnamenti di morale Filosofia, o recondite spiegazioni di naturali cose. Anzi il non ritrovarsi, che poco, o nulla adombrato da favolose invenzioni appresso quei Scrittori, a i quali è caduto in acconcio parlarne, mà chiamato bensì con nomi significanti una Potenza tanto maggiore dell'altre, quanto una causa universale può dirsi maggiore di altre particulari, ovvero de' suoi effetti medesimi, ci fà chiaramente conoscere rappresentar esso uno di quei Primi potentissimi Agenti stabiliti frà le materali cose dagli Antichi Filosofi, come fonti, e principj d'infinite produzioni, che da essi dipendono, e per discendere al particolare di ciò, che abbiam detto: l'Oceano considerato alcune volte passeggiar per il mare sopra carro tirato dalle Balene, preceduto da i Tritoni, e seguitato da numerosa schiera di Ninfe, non altro significa, che la visibile immensa mole dell'acqua marina, radunata, e ristretta ne i vasti seni della Terra, che col nome di Mare chiamiamo, da i quali, come da propria particolar sede, e quasi a dire da una miniera perpetua ha la potenza di diffondere varie parti di se medesima, rappresentante per i Tritoni, e per le Ninfe, le quali vadino a dar alimento necessario alla materia per la produzione, e conservazione delle nuove forme, che noi veggiamo, per indi ritornar poi con un perpetuo giro a prendere un nuovo spirito, et un vigor nuovo nel suo tutto, cioè a dire nel Mare medesimo: et altre volte chiamato Padre delle cose, e fatto Figliuolo del Cielo, e della Terra, si riconosce per simbolo, non tanto della potenza operative dell'acqua, allorche si considera radunata nel Mare, quanto dell'istesse di lei attuali operazioni, quando sotto sembianza d'Umido, pervadendo da pertutto la materia, e serpendo per le sue vene, e spazj anco più angusti, si fà riconoscere per una fonte perenne dell'infinite produzioni, che veggiamo in Natura, e per una causa instancabilmente conservatrice di esse. In qualunque maniera però si concepisce l'Oceano, sarà sempre vero, che ci darà l'idea di una Potenza non limitata, e circoscritta frà le materiali cose da alcuni termini; mà in tutto libera, e sempre operante in ciascheduna, benché minima, parte della materia creata, dove porta seco, distribuisce, e rende vivide le nutritive parti necessarie alla produzione delle nuove forme, e rattemperando il soverchio calore, che le distrugge, può chiamarsi l'unica perenne causa del di loro mantenimento.

L'Oceano, addunque, atteso tutto ciò, si doverà esprimere in piedi, sopra un Augusto Carro di grandi Conche marine, per significare la mobile, e sempre operativa sostanza dell'acqua, incapace di una, benchè minima, quiete, a differenza della Terra, la di cui imagine si rappresenterebbe sedendo, siccome quella, che stabile, e ferma in se stessa, non altro fà, che ricevere le impressioni, che dagli Agenti esteriori, e particolarmente dall'acqua, vengono in essa formate.

Doverà in oltre avere la robusta temperatura d'un corpo ben musculoso, ma inclinante alla pinguedine, e pieno di un vivido succo, con lunga, et abondante barba nel mento, per spiegare la di lui umida, e vegetante natura, e quel potere, che ha sopra i corpi nei quali operando pacatamente, e secondo la naturale esigenza di essi, si fà capace di conservarli, accrescerli, e vestirli di nuove, e sempre utili forme; laddove per il contrario, se agisce senza un guisto equilibrio con le altre parti, che concorrono alla produzione de i corpi medesimi non si da cosa più potente di lui per distruggerli, e togler loro tutto ciò, che di bello, e di buono sogliono in se contenere.

Per destar poi ne' Spettatori l'idea d'un dominio affato libero, et assoluto, qual potrebbe convenire all'Universale Monarca del Mondo; la di lui testa sia coronata, e di un aria la più imperiosa, che possa darsi, traspirando dal volto a guisa dell'imagini di Giove, una certa Maestà feroce, e nel medesimo tempo Signorile, la quale venga accompagnata dalla destra tenente lo Scettro, et inalzata in atto di comandare; e dalla Sinistra, che risolutamente appoggiata sul fianco, regga nel medesimo tempo per il lembo un panno, parte del quale lo ricopra quanto all'onesta si conviene, restandone parte sopra la spalla svolazzante, e mossa dall'aria, non mai separata, e disgiunta dall'acqua, e sostenendo tutto il peso del corpo sopra il piede destro, porti il sinistro con un azione libera, e risoluta a posarsi sopra il vicino nodo delle conchiglie, che formano il Carro, accompagnando questa azione d'impero con la vivezza di tutte le altre membra, in quella guisa, che farebbe un Sovrano d'illimitato potere alla presenza de suoi Popoli, a i quali publicamente parlamentar volesse.

L'accompagnamento poi che doverà avere, siccome non può essere affatto diverso dalla natura dell'acqua, e deve necessariamente comprendere sotto di se un allegorico sentimento, che insegni le sue principali proprietà, non potendo convenirgli nel caso nostro le Balene, le quali sono proprie dell'Oceano allora solo, che si considera condotto per quei vasti mari, dove sogliono prodursi simili mostri; così doverà esser formato da due Tritoni, e due Cavalli marini, li quali siano in tal maniera situati, che paia, che appena sorto l'Oceano dalle nascoste vene della terra, e fattosi visibile al Popolo sulla Fontana di Trevi, abbiano convenientemente fatto corte dall'una, e dall'altra parte del carro, lasciandolo intieramente scoperto nella sua principal veduta, come appunto ogni ragion vuole, che facessero i servi dinanzi a un lor Signore, il quale appena giunto, e fermato, dal Trono volesse promulgare una legge, e imporre un comando a i suoi sudditi spettatori.

Li Cavalli Marini, oltre la parte anteriore simile a i nostri terrestri, la quale siccome la più nobile d'un corpo, significa la propria sede, et il principale impero dell'Oceano sulla terra, abitazione destinata per gli uomini; e la posteriore, la quale terminando in lunga, e squammosa coda a guisa di pesce, fà vedere, che la sua potenza si stende egualmente ne i vasti, e profondi mari; doveranno ancora avere le ali sul tergo, per far conoscere l'Oceano niente meno atto a sollevarsi per l'aria, dove le di lui acque sono le produttrici di tante ammirabili cose, e così diverse, quante in essa ne veggiamo.

Di questi due Cavalli, uno doverà dar tutti i segni della maggior ferocia possibile, inalberandosi col petto, et attorcigliando ferocemente l'elevata coda, et inalzando le curvate gambe, co i crini svolazzanti per l'aria, stia gran parte fuori dello scoglio, come volesse furiosamente precipitarsi in una rottura del medesimo, e correr liberamente ad esseguire i sregolati impulsi d'un troppo fervido spirito. Ma nel medesimo tempo, uno de' Tritoni, che si potrà situare voltato di schiena al Popolo, con a sinistra sul freno, voltadogli a viva forza la testa dalla parte opposta al suo pricipizio, e con la destra alzata in atto di percuoterlo con la buccina, reggendolo, e governandolo a viva forza, faccia conoscere, che l'acqua soverchiamente agitata, e tempestosa produce funesti effetti, e maggiori sarebbe ancora capace di cagionarne, se l'Eterna Providenza non la facesse tener ristretta dentro giusti, e convenienti limiti da una regolatrice Potenza di cause naturali, rappresentata per il Tritone.

L'altro Cavallo poi, pieno bensi di vivezza ne i moti, mà però placido, e quieto, stia in atto di passeggiar libero per l'acqua senza bisogno di chi lo governi, quasi che per se stesso sia sufficientemente instrutto dall'istinto della propria natura di tutto ciò, ch'è suo obligo di fare; spiegando così lo stato pacifico, et in calma, nel quale stando l'acqua, si rende tanto deliziosa, utile, e profittevole al mondo; et il secondo Tritone libero dall'impiego di reggere il freno del suo Cavallo, si veda quasi precorso ad annunziare la venuta dell'Oceano alle acque soggette, e tenendo con la destra la buccina in atto di suonare alla bocca, spingendo avanti la sinistra spiegata, e secondandola colla piegatura del busto, come mosso da un forte desiderio di cosa lontana, colle gote turgide, e gonfi i muscoli del petto, faccia veder lo sforzo, che esso fà per convocarle con lo strepitoso suono della medesima buccina e rendere il doveroso tributo all'Oceano.

Tutto il discritto gruppo, essendo ragionevol cosa, che qualunque sogetto si prenda ad esprimere, sia posto in un luogo ad esso connaturale, e conveniente; cosi doverà esser situato dentro una mole d'acqua, la quale sorgendo a grossi bollori, tanto dal Carro dell'Oceano, quanto d'intorno a i Cavalli et a i Tritoni, quasi che dovunque essi vadino, portino seco la sorgente dell'acqua medesima, la quale averà per conca una corona di scogli, che la circonda, la maggior parte de'quali, con naturale imitazione inalzandosi, altri sporgendo in fuori le sue prominenze, et altri declinando in varie guise, la ricevino allor, che sversa, e frangendola con urto, e con strepito la gettino spumosa nell'altra gran conca sottoposta, restando la minor parte lavorata a guisa di rustica tazza, quasi che l'Arte, siccome è concorsa nel rimanente dell'opera, cosi abbia cooperato né i scogli ancora, per formare una propria, e decorosa sede all'Oceano, et alle sue acque, e dia luogo, che il Popolo spettatore, il quale per l'altezza de'medesimi scogli, non può commodamente mirarvi al di dentro, concepisca posarsi l'Oceano, e la di lui Corte nell'acqua, e non con irragionevole inverisimilitudine, sopra i nudi Scogli, dove non solo non potrebbero muoversi, e vivere i Cavalli, ed i Tritoni, che come pesci all'acqua appartengono, e nell'acqua devono avere il loro natural sito, mà lo stesso Oceano, il quale altro non rappresenta che l'acqua medesima. E questa è la ragione suddetta.

Siegue la descrizione dell'Edificio stesa, come sopra, da Nicola Salvi

Da tutti poi i scogli, non solo per quanto fanno basamento alla parte di mezzo, siccome abbiam detto; mà ancora sino alla metà de i due Palazzi, che formano fianco all'opera, esce da varj luoghi abondevolmente l'acqua, ora piombando libera in larga stricia ad unirsi con l'altra nella gran tazza inferiore, ora urtando, e riurtando nel cader, che essa fà, per le prominenze de'Sassi, balza ripercossa in aria disciolta in bianca spuma, et ora sorgendo a bollori per le aperte fibre dello Scoglio, scorre lambendo sempre i sassi divisa in rivoli, unendosi poi tutte nella tazza soggetta, dove mosse dal continuo impulso dell'altre cadenti, vanno placidamente ondeggianti a percuoterne il labro, il quale incominciando in ambedue le parti della suddetta metà de i Palazzi, rustico, e nascente da i medesimi scogli, come da essi cavato, esce in fuori per due linee perpendicolari alli medesimi, sopra le quali piegandosi ad angoli retti verso il mezzo, e proseguendo per non molta spazio, si rivolta poi in linea curva, formando la metà di un ellissi, d'intorno a cui, siccome anco agli altri lati suddetti, sono a coppia disposte alcune piccole colonne, che lasciando fra esse da una parte libero il passo al Popolo per accostarsi alla tazza, reggono coll'altra doppi ferri posti orizontalmente per difesa dell'opera, e commodo de Spettatori. Ne mancheremo di dire, ora, che ci cade in acconcio, che, siccome la strada, che conduce alla Chiesa dell'Angelo Custode, incominciando dolcemente a salire nel principio della Piazza di Trevi, giunta che essa è all' angolo de Palazzo, che forma fianco alla Fontana, suddetta parte, s'inalza per più palmi sopra il rimanente piano della piazza medesima; così affine, che la sunnominata irregolarità servisse in alcuna maniera per adornamento di tutta l'Opera, e commodo del Popolo, si vedono i scogli continuar sempre descrescendo in altezza per quanto essa si stende, reggendo sopra di se un rustico balaustro, che forma parapetto alla Strada, interrotto in alcuni luoghi da punte di scogli, una delle quali maggiore dell'altre, si vede parte restarsi nella sua naturale rozzezza, e parte scherzosamente intagliata a guisa di Vaso, che piantando con parte del suo piede sopra il balaustro suddetto, s'inalza con tutto il rimanente sopra di esso, e sotto questo vaso a perpendicolo sporgendosi più, che altrove le prominenze dello scoglio, vi si vedono attorno avviticchiati due grandi Serpi, che gettando acqua dalla bocca provvedono sufficientemente al bisogno delle Case vicine.

Parlando ora dell'altre Statue sparse per l'Architettura, le quali adornano la parte principale di mezzo, alcune delle quali seguono l'Allegoria già intrapresa, esprimendo altre quanto esponemmo rispetto alla Storia, et introduzione di quest'acqua in Roma. Nella nicchia quadrata, che si vede a destra dell'Oceano è posta la Statua di Marco Agrippa, che a proprie spese arricchì la Città di quest'acqua, sopra tutte le altre eccellente, il quale guardando il Popolo spettatore, pare, che colla destra mano elevata, comandi la erezione de' nuovi acquedotti, la quale poi si vede istoricamente scolpita in basso rilievo con figure di naturale grandezza nel riquadro già detto sopra la di lui nicchia, con diversi Artefici d'intorno all'opera impiegati, e lo stesso Agrippa, che loro impone ciò, che debbino farci; osservandosi nella aperta campagna l'acquedotto già in buona parte perfezionato. Nell'altra nicchia a sinistra dell'Oceano, è rappresentata la Vergine, la quale è fama, che per ristorare la sete di alcuni soldati di Agrippa, incontrata casualmente da essi, insegnasse loro la sorgente di quest'acqua. Stà essa vestita in abito semplice, come a rustica pastorella, (che tale forse doveva essere) si conviene, additando con una mano al Popolo l'acqua, e con l'altra al petto, pare, che voglia esprimere esserne essa stata l'Inventrice. Questo medesimo fatto rimane particolarizzato col basso rilievo nell'altro riquardo simile al già detto sopra la di lei nicchia, dove sono espressi diversi Soldati, uno dei quali si vede prender l'acqua colla celata, un altro più stimolato dalla sete, la sugge impazientemente colle labra dalla propria sorgente, et altri attentamente ascoltano la Vergine, che loro l'insegna. Sopra l'ordine delle quattro colonne, che, come dicemmo, formano il Prospetto principale dell'opera, sono poste in piedi le Statue di quattro Vergini rappresentanti ne'i simboli, che hanno nelle mani, quattro delle primarie, e più utili produzioni, che si fanno nella terra col mezzo dell'acqua, tenendo la prima delle due di mezzo alcuni fasci di spiche di grano, e la seconda grossi grappoli di uve, accompagnata da una tazza, che rassembra piena di generoso vino; e delle altre, l'una si vede col Cornucopia pieno di varie frutta; essendo la quarta coronata di fiori, e col grembo di essi ripieno. Fra le due di mezzo delle sudette quattro Statue, dentro un gran riquadro di marmo, è incisa la Memoria di Nostro Signore Clemente XII. felicemente regnante del seguente tenore: Clemens XII. P.M. / Aquam Virginem / Copia et Salubritate commendatam / cultu magnifico ornavit / Anno Domini MCCCXXXVI / Pont. VI.

Per ultimo termine, e finimento dell'opera, sopra la detta lapide si erge la grand'Arma di Sua Santità nascento da due cartelle ornate di festoni di fiori, e volute, le quali inalzandosi dal lato della medesima, nelle estremità esteriori fanno sostegno a due Fame, l'una delle quali insegnando l'arma, e l'altra suonando la tromba, propagano al Popolo la gloria del nostro Principe, in tante, e cosi grandi opere da lui magnificamente intraprese.

Notes

1. The Early History of the Trevi

1. Frontinus, *De Aquis* 1.10; Dio Cassius, *Roman History* 56.11.7. Pliny, *Natural History* 36.121, erroneously gives the date of completion as 33 B.C.
2. According to Dio Cassius, *Roman History* 54.2.7, the aqueduct was constructed at Agrippa's own expense.
3. For a comprehensive discussion of Agrippa's building projects, see F. W. Shipley, *Agrippa's Building Activities in Rome* (St. Louis, 1933). For the major classical sources bearing on the fabric of Augustan Rome, see D. Dudley, *Urbs Roma* (London, 1967), 14–17.
4. S. B. Platner and T. Ashby, s.v. "Campus Martius," *A Topographical Dictionary of Ancient Rome* (Oxford, 1929), 91–94.
5. Agrippa built the Aqua Julia either in 40 or 33 B.C. Between 34 and 33 B.C. he was responsible for repairs on the Aquae Marcia, Appia, and Anio Vetus. See Shipley, *Agrippa's Building Activities*, 28–34.
6. The Campus Martius was served by the Aqua Virgo alone for more than two centuries, until the Aqua Alexandrina was built to supply the Baths of Alexander Severus near the Pantheon.
7. *Natural History* 31.25.
8. *Variae Epistolae* 7.6. Thomas Hodgkin, ed., *The Letters of Cassiodorus* (London, 1886), 324.
9. *De Aquis* 1.10.
10. J. G. Graevius, *Thesaurus antiquitatum romanarum* (Venice, 1732), vol. 4, p. 1784. The print is signed "Pietro Monico." The accompanying essay by Joannis Chiflettii was first published in Antwerp in 1657.
11. For a general discussion of the ancient aqueducts, see T. Ashby, *The Aqueducts of Ancient Rome* (Oxford, 1935); R. Lanciani, *I commentarii di Frontino intorno le acque e gli acquedotti* (Rome, 1880); and E.B. Van Deman, *The Building of the Roman Aqueducts* (Washington, D.C., 1934).
12. L. Quilici, "Sull'acquedotto Vergine dal Monte Pincio alla sorgente," *Studi di topografia romana* (Rome, 1968), 125–60.
13. Aeneas Sylvius Piccolomini, *Memoirs of a Renaissance Pope: The Commentaries of Pius II*, trans. F. A. Gragg (New York, 1959), 328–29. For a nineteenth-century appreciation of the same site, see C. Fea, *Storia I. Delle acque antiche sorgenti in Roma, perdute, e modo di ristabilirle. II. Dei condotti antico-moderni delle Acque Vergine, Felice, e Paola, e loro autori* (Rome, 1832), 10.
14. D. R. Coffin, *The Villa in the Life of Renaissance Rome*, (Princeton, 1979), 265–67.
15. F. Ubaldini, *Vita di Mons. Angelo Colocci*, ed. V. Fanelli (Vatican, 1969), 54–55.
16. L. Quilici, *Collatia, Forma Italiae, Regio I*, X (Rome, 1974), 134 and fig. 222.
17. Van Deman, *Building of the Roman Aqueducts*, 169.
18. See A. Cassio, *Corso dell'acque antiche portate da lontane contrade fuori e dentro Roma sopra*

XIV acquidotti; e delle moderne e in essa nascenti coll'illustrazione di molte antichità che la stessa città decoravano, 2 vols. (Rome, 1756–57), 1:336, and G. Andres, *The Villa Medici in Rome* (New York/London, 1976), 1:288–90.

19. R. Lanciani, *Forma Urbis Romae* (Milan, 1893), tav. 9.

20. Lanciani, *Forma Urbis*, tavs. 15, 16; and *Carta Archeologica di Roma*, Ministero della Pubblica Istruzione (Florence, 1964), vol. 2, tav. 2, sector H.

21. The arcades show up prominently in the Dupérac–Lafréry plan of 1577. See A. P. Frutaz, *Le piante di Roma* (Rome, 1962), vol. 2, fig. 250. Several churches in the neighborhood— S. Lorenzo, S. Niccolo, and S. Stefano—were followed by the denomination *degli Arcioni*. Armellini traces this denomination to a family in the region whose members took their name from the neighboring arcade of the Aqua Virgo. See M. Armellini, *Le chiese di Roma dal secolo IV al XIX* (Rome, 1942), 1:326–28.

22. E. Nash, *A Pictorial Dictionary of Ancient Rome*, 2d ed. (New York/Washington, 1968), 1:56.

23. A portion of the arcade was uncovered in the courtyard of the Palazzo Sciarra in 1887. See Nash, *Pictorial Dictionary*, 1:55.

24. See Nash, *Pictorial Dictionary*, 1:102–03.

25. Frontinus, *De Aquis* 1.22. For the correct location of the Saepta, see Nash, *Pictorial Dictionary*, 2:291–93.

26. The remains beneath the facade of S. Ignazio were recorded by Padre Orazio Grassi, the architect of the church, and are now at Windsor Castle, Royal Library, vol. 186 A/12, nos. 10397–400. Grassi's drawings provided the basis for a print representing the arcade: A. Donati, *Roma vetus ac recens* (Rome, 1639), 294.

27. For a discussion of the course taken by the Aqua Virgo west of the Pantheon, see R. B. Lloyd, "The Aqua Virgo, Euripus and Pons Agrippae," *The American Journal of Archaeology* 83 (1979): 193–204; and H. B. Evans, "Agrippa's Water Plan," *The American Journal of Archaeology* 86 (1982): 401–11.

28. See C. Huelsen, *Die Thermen des Agrippa* (Rome, 1910).

29. Lloyd, "Aqua Virgo," 195.

30. Tacitus, *Annals* 15.37, trans. M. Grant, (Harmondsworth, 1956), 351.

31. Lloyd, "Aqua Virgo," 196. Also see F. Coarelli, "La topographie du Champ de Mars occidental dans l'antiquité," in *Le Palais Farnèse*, ed. A. Chastel, 3 vols. (Rome, 1980–81), 1:23–31.

32. Frontinus, *De Aquis* 2.84.

33. See, for example, Ovid, *Tristia* 3.12.22; and Martial, *Epigrams* 11.47.5–6.

34. Seneca, *Epistolae Morales* 83.5.

35. See Nash, *Pictorial Dictionary*, 1:393–94; and Lloyd, "Aqua Virgo," 196.

36. Recent restoration carried on the colossal bronze *Pigna*, or pine cone, in the Vatican, which was originally situated to the southeast of the Pantheon, confirms that it functioned as a fountain in antiquity. The *Pigna* was probably fed by the Aqua Virgo. S. Angelucci, "The Restoration of the Pigna di Belvedere in the Vatican," presented as a lecture to the American Academy in Rome on November 14, 1983.

37. The best general treatment of Roman nymphaea remains N. Neuerburg, *L'architettura delle fontane e dei ninfei nell'Italia antica. Memorie dell'Accademia di Archeologia, Lettere e Belle Arti di Napoli*, vol. 5 (1965), esp. 73–80.

38. See Nash, *Pictorial Dictionary*, 1.125–26, and G. Tedeschi Grisanti, *I "Trofei di Mario," Il ninfeo dell'Acqua Giulia sull'Esquilino* (Rome, 1977). For an extensive eighteenth-century survey and interpretation of this monument, see G. B. Piranesi, *Le rovine del castello dell'Acqua Giulia* (Rome, 1761).

39. See H. Mattingly, *Coins of the Roman Empire in the British Museum*, vol. 6, ed. R. A. G. Carson, 1962, nos. 323–25 and fig. 11; and Tedeschi Grisanti, *Trofei di Mario*, figs. 4–9.

40. Tedeschi Grisanti, *Trofei di Mario*, 17–26.

41. Tedeschi Grisanti reproduces many of these drawings, including those by Garnaud (1821), Burgess (1821), Canina (1836), and Gatteschi (1916).

42. Procopius, *Gothic Wars* 2.3; and R. Lanciani, *The Destruction of Ancient Rome* (New York, 1899), 83.

43. Procopius, *Gothic Wars* 1.19.

44. Procopius, *Gothic Wars* 2.9.

45. R. Krautheimer, *Rome, Profile of a City, 312–1308* (Princeton, 1980), 64.

46. Krautheimer, *Rome*, 64.

47. R. Lanciani, "L'itinerario di Einsiedeln e l'ordine di Benedetto Canonico," *Accademia dei Lincei, Monumenti Antichi* 1 (1890): 442, 467.

48. For the restorations of the Trevi carried out under Hadrian I, see L. Duchesne, ed. *Le Liber Pontificalis* (Paris, 1886), 505.

49. See R. Marchetti, *Sulle acque di Roma, antiche e moderne*, (Rome, 1886), 179–209, for the history of the governance of the Acqua Vergine.

50. K. J. Beloch, *Bevölkerungsgeschichte Italiens* (Berlin/Leipzig, 1937–39), 2:2.

51. Krautheimer, *Rome*, 252; and Duchesne, *Liber Pontificalis*, 505.

52. Lanciani, *Forma Urbis*, tav. 16; and G. Gatti, "Caratteristiche edilizie di un quartiere di Roma nel II secolo d. Cr.," *Quaderni dello istituto di storia dell'architettura* 6–8 (1961):31–48, 49–66, fig. 13.

53. For a discussion of the trivium in general, and that of the Trevi in particular, see A. Ceen, "The *Quartiere de'Banchi:* Urban Planning in Rome in the First Half of the Cinquecento" (Ph.D. diss., University of Pennsylvania, 1977), 70.

54. The earliest topographical references mentioning Trevi refer to a place, not a fountain. Significantly, an early seventeenth-century guidebook derived the name of S. Maria in Trivio, a church next to the Fontana di Trevi, from the intersection of three streets. P. M. Felini, *Tratado nuevo de las cosas maravillosas de la alma cividad de Roma* (Rome, 1610), 86.

55. For a survey of opinions regarding the etymology of *Trevi,* see A. Schiavo, *La Fontana di Trevi e le altre opere di Nicola Salvi* (Rome, 1956), 66; and C. D'Onofrio, *Le Fontane di Roma* (Rome, 1957), 228–29.

56. J. Chiflettii in Graevius, *Thesaurus*, vol. 4, cols. 1785–94. Frontinus makes no mention of the maiden's name.

57. D'Onofrio, *Fontane*, 228-29.

58. Krautheimer, *Rome,* 277.

59. R. Brentano, *Rome Before Avignon*, (London, 1974), 29; L. Hartmann, *Ecclesiae Scae. Mariae in Via Lata Tabularium,* 3 vols. (Vienna 1895–1913), esp. XLI–XLIV, LXXXI, LXXIV, LXXXX.

60. P. Fedele, "Tabularium S. Mariae Novae," *Archivio della Società Romana di Storia Patria* 23 (1900): 206–09.

61. V. Federici, "Registro del Monastero di S. Silvestro in Capite," *Archivio della Società Romana di Storia Patria* 22 (1899): 531–32.

62. Krautheimer, *Rome*, 277–78.

63. Lieven Cruyl's *veduta* of 1665 shows the portico enclosed. Sixtus IV was particularly concerned with the suppression of porticoes. For his bull of 1480, see E. Muntz, *Les arts à la cour des papes pendant le XVe et le XVIe siè cle: Recueil de documents inedits* (Paris, 1898), 3:1, 182; and T. Magnuson, *Studies in Roman Quattrocento Architecture* (Stockholm, 1958), 38–39.

64. For a list of similar porticoes, see Krautheimer, *Rome*, 294–95.

65. Frutaz, *Le piante*, 1:125–26; 2, fig. 149.

66. For a discussion of late medieval and Renaissance city images, see J. Pinto, "Origins and Development of the Ichnographic City Plan," *Journal of the Society of Architectural*

Historians 35 (1976): 35–50.

67. See A. Colasanti, *Le fontane d'Italia* (Milan/Rome, 1926), esp. figs. 30 and 44. The Trevi appears quite modest in comparison with the imposing fountains of medieval Siena.

2. The Trevi from 1453 to 1730

1. For the building program of Nicholas V, see Magnuson, *Studies*, 55–221, and C. W. Westfall, *In This Most Perfect Paradise: Alberti, Nicholas V, and the Invention of Conscious Urban Planning in Rome, 1447–1455* (University Park, 1974).

2. G. Vasari, *Le Vite de' più eccellenti pittori scultori ed architetti*, ed. G. Milanesi (Florence, 1878), 2:539.

3. See A. Coffin Hansen, *Jacopo della Quercia's Fonte Gaia* (Oxford, 1965).

4. G. D. Franzini, ed., *Descrittione di Roma antica e moderna* (Rome, 1643), 744. The source of this print is erroneously cited by D'Onofrio and Schiavo as Felini's *Tratado nuevo*. In fact, the print reproduced by D'Onofrio (*Fontane*, fig. 201) and Schiavo (*Fontana di Trevi*, fig. 13) dates from the nineteenth century: P. Letarouilly, *Edifices de Rome moderne* (Brussels, 1886), 709. G. Vasi's etching of 1777, reproduced in C. D'Onofrio, *Acque e Fontane di Roma* (Rome, 1977), fig. 640, was clearly made after Franzini's woodcut.

5. R. Lanciani, "Il codice Barberiniano XXX, 89 contenente frammenti di una descrizione di Roma del sec. XVI," *Archivio della Società Romana di Storia Patria* 6 (1883): 466.

6. Lanciani, "Il codice Barberiniano," 466: "Hà in facciata l'arme papale, che sono 2. chiavi incrocicchiate, et è in mezzo quella del popolo, con la solita inscrizione S.P.Q.R. nello scudo, che altro non v'è."

7. Vienna, Albertina, Topographie: Mappe, Rom II, folder 6, no. 4.

8. Colasanti, *Le fontane*, 53.

9. D. S. Chambers, "Studium urbis and gabella studii: The University of Rome in the Fifteenth Century," in *Cultural Aspects of the Italian Renaissance, Essays in Honour of Paul Oskar Kristeller*, ed. C. H. Clough (Manchester/New York, 1976), 77.

10. Fea, *Storia*, 9–28, 63–96; and L. Peto, *De restitutione ductus Aquae Virginis* (Rome, 1570). Richard Tuttle has called my attention to the relationship between the Trevi of Nicholas V and the Fontana Vecchia, which Pius IV built in Bologna. See M. A. Chiarini, *Piante con suoi alzati, profili, e notizie dalle origini dell'acque che servono al pubblico fonte in piazza maggiore della città di Bologna* (Bologna, 1763).

11. See Schiavo, *Fontana di Trevi*, 73–84; and D'Onofrio, *Acque*, 528–29.

12. Schiavo, *Fontana di Trevi*, 87.

13. See L. Patetta, *I Longhi, una famiglia di architetti tra Manierismo e Barocco* (Milan, 1980), 36–37; Schiavo, *Fontana di Trevi*, 84–96, 157–65; and J. Wasserman, *Ottaviano Mascarino and his Drawings in the Accademia di San Luca* (Rome, 1966), 104–05.

14. See Patetta, *I Longhi*, 37.

15. See Schiavo, *Fontana di Trevi*, 84–97; and S. Benedetti, *Giacomo del Duca e l'architettura del cinquecento* (Rome, 1973), 226–38.

16. See Benedetti, *Giacomo del Duca*, 155–71.

17. Archivio di Stato di Roma, Disegni e Piante, Coll. I, cartella 80, num. ord. 233. The designation of the Baldovino del Monte Palace on the plan as the site "dove si tiene la stampa" provides an approximate date for this plan, since the press of Paolo Manuzio was located there between 1561 and 1566.

18. Schiavo (*Fontana di Trevi*, 79–84) attributed this drawing to Guglielmo Della Porta and dated it 1571 on the basis of its presumed affinity with other sketches believed to be by Della Porta. D'Onofrio (*Acque*, 529) more convincingly related the plan to the office of the Maestri delle Strade.

19. Vienna, Albertina, Topographie: Rom, Mappe II, folder I, 6, Arch. Zeich., 4. See H.

Egger, *Architektonische Handzeichnungen alter Meister* (Vienna/Leipzig, 1910), 10, fig. 19; and D'Onofrio, *Acque*, 529.

20. Pietro Aldobrandini was created cardinal in 1593.

21. A. Schiavo, "Notizie biografiche su Giacomo Della Porta," *Palladio* 7 (1957): 41.

22. The relationship of sculpture to architecture is remarkably similar to that in Della Porta's memorial plaque of Gian Francesco Aldobrandini in S. Maria in Aracoeli, which was being assembled in 1602. See F. Fasolo, *L'opera di Hieronimo e Carlo Rainaldi* (Rome, n.d.), pl. 6.

23. See C. H. Heilman, "Acqua Paola and the Urban Planning of Paul V Borghese," *Burlington Magazine* 112 (1970): 656–62; and M. Fagiolo, ed. *La Roma dei Longhi. Papi e architetti tra manierismo e barocco* (Rome, 1982), 30–31.

24. Maggi's plan is known only in its second edition, by Carlo Losi, of 1774. See F. Ehrle, *Roma al tempo di Urbano VIII. La pianta di Roma Maggi-Maupin-Losi del 1625* (Vatican, 1915).

25. The Palazzo Barberini is the most prominent example; see Ehrle, *Roma al tempo di Urbano VIII*, 18–25.

26. See J. A. F. Orbaan, *Documenti sul Barocco in Roma, Miscellanea della R. Società Romana di Storia Patria* (Rome, 1920), 172; and R. Krautheimer, "*Il porton di questo giardino*: An Urbanistic Project for Rome by Alexander VII (1655–1667)," *Journal of the Society of Architectural Historians* 42 (1983): 35–37.

27. The document is transcribed by D'Onofrio (*Fontane*, 236), who relates the design recorded by Maggi to Vansanzio. On the basis of style the Trevi project might equally well be attributed to Flaminio Ponzio. For a discussion of Vansanzio's fountain designs, see G. J. Hoogewerff, "Giovanni Vansanzio fra gli architetti romani del tempo di Paolo V," *Palladio* 6 (1942): 49–56.

28. Vienna, Albertina, Topographie: Rom, Mappe II, folder I, 7, Arch. Zeichnung 12. See Egger, *Architektonische Handzeichnungen*, 10, fig. 20.

29. Pliny, *Natural History* 31. 25.

30. D'Onofrio, *Fontane*, 239–40.

31. H. Brauer and R. Wittkower, *Die Zeichnungen des Gianlorenzo Bernini* (Berlin, 1931), 1:147.

32. S. Fraschetti, *Il Bernini* (Milan, 1900), 127, cites an entry from the diary of Marcantonio Valena: "Anno 1635—si tramutò la fontana di Trevi dal luogo antico, e fu posta in faccia." Bernini's ideas for the Trevi may date as early as 1629.

33. This document is transcribed by D'Onofrio, *Fontane*, 237.

34. See O. Pollak, *Die Kunsttätigkeit unter Urban VIII*, (Vienna, 1927–31), vol. 1, Register, nos. 47, 48.

35. See Pollak, *Die Kunsttätigkeit*, reg. 50; Fraschetti, *Bernini*, 130; G. Baglione, *Le vite de'pittori, scultori ed architetti* (Rome, 1642), 182; and G. Gigli, *Diario Romano*, ed. G. Ricciotti (Rome, 1958), 232.

36. C. Montani, "Augusto Castellani orafo romano," *Capitolium* 4 (1928): 211. Cruyl's print is based on a well-known drawing of 1665 in the Albertina, reproduced in J. Pinto, "The Trevi Fountain: Unexecuted Projects from the Pontificate of Clement XI," in *Projects and Monuments in the Period of the Roman Baroque*, ed. H. Hager and S. Munshower (University Park, 1984), fig. 6b.

37. Pollak, *Die Kunsttätigkeit*, reg. 50–54; and C. D'Onofrio, ed., *Gian Lorenzo Bernini, Fontana di Trevi* (Rome, 1963), 26–28.

38. Pollak, *Die Kunsttätigkeit*, reg. 57.

39. Schiavo, *Fontana di Trevi*, 107; P. Romano, *Quod non fecerunt Barbari* (Rome, 1937), 61.

40. Pollak, *Die Kunsttätigkeit*, reg. 57. See L. Von Pastor, *The History of the Popes*, vol. 29 (1938), 382–401, for a discussion of the War of Castro.

41. Appendix 1.13.
42. The Wool Guild had been installed behind the Trevi in 1586 by Pope Sixtus V. See D. Fontana, *Della trasportazione dell'obelisco vaticano e delle fabbriche di Nostro signore Sisto V fatte dal Cavaliere Domenico Fontana* (Rome, 1590), 103.
43. Pollak, *Die Kunsttätigkeit*, reg. 51.
44. Biblioteca Corsiniana, Cod. Corsiniano 167, c. 14.
45. "Colla statua della Vergine et altri bellissimi fregi," Ubaldini, *Vita*, 56.
46. D'Onofrio, *Acque*, 334–36.
47. This passage from the inventory is cited by D'Onofrio, *Acque*, 535.
48. F. Zeri, *La Galleria Pallavicini in Roma* (Florence, 1959), 306.
49. See Fagiolo, *La Roma dei Longhi*, 42–46, for a discussion of the urban context of the facade of SS. Vincenzo e Anastasio.
50. Archivio di Stato di Roma, Disegni e Piante, Coll. I, cartella 86, no. ord. 537.
51. Joseph Connors argues convincingly that Borromini's projects of 1639–41 for the neighboring Palazzo Carpegna were stimulated by Bernini's design for the Trevi. See his forthcoming article in volume 2 of the *Papers in Art History from the Pennsylvania State University*.
52. See Patetta, *I Longhi*, 113–18; and J. Varriano, "The Roman Ecclesiastical Architecture of Martino Longhi the Younger" (Ph.D. diss., Univ. of Michigan, 1970), 37–47.
53. V. Rizzi, *La Facciata della Chiesa dei SS. Vincenzo e Anastasio di Martino Longhi il Giovane à Roma* (Rome, 1982).
54. Archivio di Stato di Roma, Disegni e Piante, Coll. I, cartella 86, no. 537 bis.
55. R. Lefevre, *Palazzo Chigi* (Rome, 1972), 128–54.
56. K. Noehles, "Die Louvre-Projekte von Pietro da Cortona e Carlo Rainaldi," *Zeitschrift für Kunstgeschichte* 24 (1961): 50; and R. Krautheimer, "Alexander VII and Piazza Colonna," *Römisches Jahrbuch für Kunstgeschichte* 20 (1983): 195–208.
57. Vatican Library, Cod. Chigi P VII, 10, fols. 10–12. Cortona's project exists in three versions, two of which depict variants in elevation.
58. R. Wittkower, "Pietro da Cortona's Project for Reconstructing the Temple of Palestrina," *Studies in the Italian Baroque* (London, 1975), 115–24.
59. Concerning Alexander VII's model, see A. Neri, "Saggio della Corrispondenza di Ferdinando Raggi, agente della Repubblica genovese a Roma," *Rivista Europea* 5 (1878): part 1, 676. Raggi, who was posted in Rome between 1663 and 1669, remarked that "Il Papa ha tutta Roma di legneame in Camera distintissima e curiosissima, come quello,che non ha maggior sfera che di abbellire la Città."
60. R. Krautheimer and R. B. S. Jones, "The Diary of Alexander VII: Notes on Art, Artists and Buildings," *Römisches Jahrbuch für Kunstgeschichte* 15 (1975):217, no. 584; Krautheimer, "Alexander VII and Piazza Colonna," 205.
61. Krautheimer and Jones, "Diary," 225, no. 939.
62. Brauer and Wittkower, *Die Zeichnungen*, 148.
63. M. De Chantelou, *Journal du voyage du Cav. Bernin en France*, ed. Lalanne (Paris, 1885), 40, in date of 6/25/1665: "Il a parlé ensuit de la proposition qu'il avait faite au Pape de transporter la Colonne Trajane dans la place où est la colonne Antoniane, et d'y faire deux fontaines qui eussent baigné toute la place; qu'elle eût été la plus belle de Rome."
64. B. R. Kommer, "Nicodemus Tessin und das Stockholmer Schloss" (Ph.D. diss., University of Heidelberg, 1974), 160. Cardinal Nini was a favorite of Alexander VII; see G. Moroni, *Dizionario Storico-Ecclesiastico* (Venice), vol. 48 (1848), 40–41. The Fondo Nini in the Archivio di Stato di Siena contains no references to Bernini's drawing.
65. Richard Krautheimer has suggested that a sketch in the Chigi Archives depicting a boat-shaped outline drawn around the Column of Marcus Aurelius may relate to a scaled-down variation of Bernini's project. Krautheimer, "Alexander VII and Piazza Colonna," 206.

66. See L. Pascoli, *Testamento politico d'un Accademico Fiorentino* (Cologne, 1733), 197.
67. Appendix 1.3.
68. Schiavo, *Fontana di Trevi*, 95.
69. A. De Montaiglon, ed., *Correspondance des directeurs de l'Académie de France a Rome* (Paris), vol. 6 (1896), no. 2359.
70. Archivio Segreto Vaticano, Fondo Boncompagni, protocolli 681–82. For the history of the Palazzo Poli, see Schiavo, *Fontana di Trevi*, 157–65; and A. Grelle, *Palazzo Poli* (Rome, 1979).
71. Pascoli, *Testamento politico*, 196–97; and A. Schiavo, "Un ignoto progetto di Innocenzo XIII per la piazza di Trevi," *Strenna dei Romanisti* 20 (1959): 197–201.
72. Schiavo, *Fontana di Trevi*, 114; Archivio Segreto Vaticano, Fondo Boncompagni, protocollo 882.
73. Appendix 1.9.
74. Letter of 9/3/1731 cited by A. Roserot, "La vie et l'oeuvre d'Edme Bouchardon en Italie," *Gazette des Beaux-Arts* 40 (1908): 32.
75. Appendix 1.26.
76. These spaces have been revealed by Architetto Maria Grazia Feretti of the Sopraintendenza per i beni ambientali e architettonici del Lazio, who graciously allowed me to explore them.
77. Appendix 1.4.
78. For the papal *chirografo*, see Appendix 1.12.

3. Unexecuted Projects for the Trevi Fountain

1. For a survey of artistic patronage under Clement XI, see Von Pastor, *History of the Popes*, vol. 33 (1941), 513–28.
2. Berlin, Kunstbibliothek, Hdz. 1018. See S. Jacob, *Italienische Zeichnungen der Kunstbibliothek Berlin* (Berlin, 1975), 158–60, and E. Berckenhagen, *Architektenzeichnungen 1479–1979* (Berlin, 1979), 86.
3. The inscription reads "PER ALZA / L'ACQUA VENTI PALMI E PIU VOLENDO / ANNO MDCC."
4. H. Hager, "Puntualizzazioni su disegni scenici teatrali e l'architettura scenografica del periodo barocco a Roma," *Bollettino del Centro Internazionale di Studi di Architettura Andrea Palladio* 17 (1975):119–25.
5. F. Valesio, *Diario di Roma*, ed. G. Scano and G. Graglia (Milan, 1977), 3:564, in date of 2/28/1706.
6. Appendix 1.3.
7. K. von Domarius, *Pietro Bracci, Beiträge zur römischen Kunstgeschichte des XVIII Jahrhunderts* (Strasbourg, 1915), 43.
8. H. L. Cooke, "The Documents Relating to the Fountain of Trevi," *Art Bulletin* 33 (1956):160. Cooke's attribution is convincingly dismissed by Jacob (*Italienische Zeichnungen*, 159).
9. D'Onofrio, *Fontane*, 242.
10. Hager, "Puntualizzazioni," 123.
11. See N. A. Mallory, *Roman Rococo Architecture from Clement XI to Benedict XIV, 1700–1758* (New York/London, 1977), 31–52.
12. Illustrated by D'Onofrio, *Fontane*, 523.
13. Four sheets relating to the Trevi—one signed, and three of which may be securely attributed to Bernardo Borromini on the basis of style—are in the collection of the Albertina in Vienna: Architektur Zeichnung, nos. 9, 11, 13, and Borromini Appendix X, 14.
14. See L. Pascoli, *Vite de'pittori, scultori ed architetti moderni* (Rome 1730), 1:304–06; and

P. Tournon, "Per la biografia di Francesco e Bernardo Borromini," *Commentari* 18 (1967): 86–89.

15. "Centina e schizzo del alzato della fontana de Trevi."

16. The inscription projecting above the attic center also calls to mind Michelangelo's Porta Pia.

17. See Nash, *Pictorial Dictionary*, 1:270–75; and L. Vogel, *The Column of Antoninus Pius* (Cambridge, Mass., 1973).

18. F. Posterla, *Istorico e perfetto ragguaglio osia esatta relazione di quanto si è operato per l'inalzamento & abassamento dell'antica Colonna Antonina trovata nel Campo Martio* (Rome, 1705), 6.

19. Biblioteca Nazionale Centrale Roma, Fondo Vittorio Emanuele, ms. 790, *Avvisi Marescotti*, vol. 4, 357v and 359r. Vatican Library, Cod. Ottoboniano latino 2732, 142v and 158. Also see Valesio, *Diario*, 3:144–45, 158.

20. Pinto, "Unexecuted Projects," 104.

21. Appendix 1.2.

22. Appendix 1.1.

23. London, Royal Institute of British Architects, Romano Carapecchia album on deposit from the Witt Collection, inv. no. 4649, fol. 92; Stockholm, Nationalmuseum, THC 5157.

24. Pinto, "Unexecuted Projects," 106.

25. See J. Tonna and D. de Lucca, *Romano Carapecchia, Studies in Maltese Architecture* (Valetta, 1975).

26. Pascoli, *Vite*, vol. 2 (1736), 549.

27. The fountain may be depicted from behind, which could be another reason why the palace in the background is not shown.

28. Two drawings in Stockholm, THC 2776 and 8414, may be studies for the capital of this project.

29. See J. Pinto, s.v. "Michetti," *The Macmillan Encyclopedia of Architects* (New York, 1982), 3:181–83.

30. Windsor 10329, 10765, and 10769. The drawings have been published by A. Braham and H. Hager, *Carlo Fontana: The Drawings at Windsor Castle* (London, 1977), 182, and J. Pinto, "An Early Project by Nicola Michetti for the Trevi Fountain," *The Burlington Magazine* 119 (1977): 853–57.

31. Michetti's section shows that some of the water from the upper of the two large basins was to be channeled back into a space behind this facade to power a mill.

32. While Michetti's project recalls aspects of Bramante's Belvedere Court and Pietro da Cortona's Villa del Pignetto Sacchetti, neither exerted a substantial influence on his design.

33. Turin, Biblioteca Nazionale, Riserva 59–4, 67v.

34. Inventory no. 8314; see H. A. Millon, *Filippo Juvarra: Drawings from the Roman Period 1704–1714*, part 1 (Rome, 1984), 331–32; pl. 153.

35. J. Pinto, "Filippo Juvarra's Drawings Depicting the Capitoline Hill," *Art Bulletin* 62 (1980): 598–616, fig. 20.

36. See L. Rovere, V. Viale, and A. E. Brinckmann, *Filippo Juvarra* (Milan, 1937), fig. 179.

37. FN 6717/32056

38. C. Gradara, *Pietro Bracci scultore romano, 1700–1773* (Milan, 1920), pl. 26; and L. Bianchi, "Disegni del Vanvitelli e del Fuga al Gabinetto Nazionale delle Stampe," *Atti dell'VIII Congresso Nazionale di Storia dell'Architettura* (Rome, 1956), 125.

39. Windsor Castle, Royal Library, vol. 169.

40. Braham and Hager, *Carlo Fontana*, 162–67.

41. Fontana drew two other plans of his projects, one of them preparatory to a model, but these differ only slightly from those we have just considered.

42. A copy after a presumed variant of this design is in Stockholm: Nationalmuseum THC 5158.

43. Fontana's interest in such naturalistic effects, which obviously derives from Bernini, is also evident in his other fountain designs, notably the Fontana degli Scogli in Lanuvio, which is reproduced in Colasanti, *Fontane*, tav. 214.

44. T. Marder, "Piazza della Rotonda e la Fontana del Pantheon: un rinnovamento urbanistico di Clemente XI," *Arte Illustrata* 7 (1974): 310–20.

45. Brauer and Wittkower, *Die Zeichnungen*, 2:25b.

46. Ibid., 2:110a, 176–77.

47. Vatican Library, Cod. Chigi, P. VII, 9, f. 117.

48. W. Eisler, "Concorso Clementino of 1706," in *Architectural Fantasy and Reality. Drawings from the Accademia Nazionale di San Luca in Rome, Concorsi Clementini 1700–1750*, ed. H. Hager and S. Munshower (University Park, 1981), 53–63.

49. Eisler, "Concorso Clementino," 57.

50. A preparatory drawing in the Victoria and Albert Museum shows that the embracing exedra in the attic is an afterthought and also illustrates the arbitrary breaks at the two ends of the screening wall: Print Room, Accession no. 3436.380. See Pinto, "Unexecuted Projects," 108.

51. Hdz. 1981/33 AOZ. See J. Pinto and E. Kieven, "An Early Project by Ferdinando Fuga for the Trevi Fountain in Rome," *The Burlington Magazine* 125 (1983): 746–49.

52. FN 1196/18519. Both the ground plan and the elevation are drawn to the same scale. See L. Bianchi, *Disegni di Ferdinando Fuga e di altri architetti del settecento* (Rome, 1955), 19–21.

53. See R. Pane, *Ferdinando Fuga* (Naples, 1956), figs. 47–50.

54. Pane, *Fuga*, figs. 52–53.

55. See M. S. Weil, "The Devotion of the Forty Hours and Roman Baroque Illusions," *Journal of the Warburg and Courtauld Institutes* 37 (1974): 218–48.

56. See W. Lotz, "Die Spanische Treppe. Architektur als Mittle der Diplomatie," *Römisches Jahrbuch für Kunstgeschichte* 12 (1969): 39–94.

57. "INNOCENTIUS.XIII.P.O.M. / FELICISSIMI.PONTIFICATUS / SVB.ANNO TERTIO. / HVNC. FONTEM.ORNAVIT. / SALVTIS.ANNO. / MDCCXXIII."

58. De Montaiglon, *Correspondance*, vol. 6, no. 2359.

59. Nationalmuseum, THC 264; reproduced by Werner Oechslin in *Kunstchronik*, vol. 31 (1978), 187–207, fig. 8b.

60. See P. Marconi, A. Cipriani, and E. Valeriani, *I disegni di architettura dell'Archivio storico dell'Accademia di San Luca* (Rome, 1974), 1: figs. 15, 32–34, 63–67, and Berckenhagen, *Architektenzeichnungen*, 74.

61. Nash, *Pictorial Dictionary*, 2:130–33, 144–47.

62. Ibid., 2:150–51, 153–54.

63. W. Oechslin, *Bildungsgut und Antikenrezeption im frühen Settecento in Rom* (Zurich, 1972), 34–35.

64. Appendix 1.4.

65. Ibid.

66. Ibid.

67. Archivio di Stato di Roma, Notaio Tribunale acque e strade F. N. Orsini, vol. 141, 262.

68. Archivio di Stato di Roma, Presidenza degli acquedotti urbani, Acqua Vergine, busta 69, nos. 3–33.

69. Archivio di Stato di Roma, Notaio Tribunale acque e strade F. N. Orsini, vol. 141, 255–256; 277 for the contract Benaglia signed with a quarry master at Carrara.

70. Appendix 1.15. M. A. Contini, son of the architect Giovanni Battista Contini, was born in 1686. Upon the elder Contini's death Maffeo succeeded him as architect of the

Acqua Vergine, a position he held until it was assumed by N. Salvi in 1732. See A. Del Bufalo, *G. B. Contini e la tradizioine del tardomanierismo nell'architettura tra '600 e '700* (Rome, 1982), 35, 48.

71. D'Onofrio, *Acque*, 548.

4. *Nicola Salvi and the Competition of 1730*

1. Appendix 1.9.
2. Appendix 1.8.
3. Appendix 1.9.
4. Roserot, "La vie et l'oeuvre d'Edme Bouchardon," 30–32. Some of these models were later exhibited in the Vatican; see G. P. Chattard, *Nuova descrizione del Vaticano osia del Palazzo Apostolico di San Pietro* (Rome, 1767), 3:135.
5. D. Calmet, *Bibliothèque lorraine, ou l'histoire des hommes illustres* (Nancy, 1751), 9–10. Adam's letter is transcribed by D'Onofrio, *Acque*, 551.
6. Appendix 1.10.
7. Appendix 1.11.
8. Appendix 1.12.
9. See Jacob, *Italienische Zeichnungen*, 158–62.
10. Hdz. 1017.
11. Hdz. 1016. Reproduced in H. Schmitz, *Baumeisterzeichnungen des 17. und 18. Jahrhunderts in der Staatlichen Kunstbibliothek zu Berlin* (Berlin/Leipzig, 1937), fig. 13.
12. Hdz. 1013.
13. Hdz. 1015.
14. See R. Wittkower, *Gian Lorenzo Bernini, The Sculptor of the Roman Baroque* (London, 1966), 223.
15. Hdz. 1014.
16. See Valerius Maximus, *Factorum ac dictorum memorabilium libri IX* 8.1.5; and Pliny, *Natural History* 28.3.
17. Rome, Biblioteca d'Archeologia e Storia dell'Arte, Coll. Lanciani, Roma XI, 12, I, p. 33, 1/21.
18. See, for example, Nicola Michetti's sets for *Carlo Magno* of 1727: J. Pinto, "Nicola Michetti and Ephemeral Design in Eighteenth-Century Rome," in *Studies in Italian Art History*, ed. H. Millon (Rome, 1980), figs. 2–8.
19. Rome, Biblioteca d'Archeologia e Storia dell'Arte, Coll. Lanciani, Roma XI, 12, I, p. 35, I/22.
20. Private collection, Rome, 465 × 430 mm, pencil and pen.
21. An architectural ornament composed of a reed intertwined with leaves and flowers set into the fluting of a column. See A. C. Daviler, *Cours d'Architecture* (Paris, 1710), 2:84.
22. An architectural ornament in the form of dripping water or icicles, frequently associated with fountains. See Daviler, *Cours*, 2:626.
23. Calmet, *Bibliothèque lorraine*, 9–10.
24. Transcribed by Roserot, "La vie et l'oeuvre d'Edme Bouchardon," 30–32.
25. Musée Vivènel, Compiègne. See P. Prouté, *Catalogue "Centenaire," 2e partie, dessins* (1978), 24, no. 41; and G. Weber, "Edme Bouchardon, Studien zu einer Stellung in der französischen Plastik des 18. Jhs." (Ph.D. diss., University of Vienna, 1965), 54, 195.
26. C. De Brosses, *Lettres familières sur l'Italie* (Paris, 1931), 2:58.
27. W. G. Kalnein and M. Levey, *Art and Architecture of the Eighteenth Century in France* (Harmondsworth, 1972), 59–60; A. Roserot, "La Fontaine de la Rue de Grenelle à Paris par Edme Bouchardon (1739–1745)," *Gazette des Beaux-Arts* 28 (1902): 353–72.
28. B. M. Santese, *Palazzo Testa Piccolomini alla Dataria; Filippo Barigioni architetto romano* (Rome, 1983), 160–61.

29. Vatican Library, Cod. Capponiano 177, par. 2a, fol. 238. This reference was noted by J. Garms, "Beiträge zu Vanvitellis Leben, Werk und Milieu," *Römische Historische Mitteilungen* 16 (1974): 139.

30. Appendix 1.10.

31. L. Vanvitelli, Jr., *Vita di Luigi Vanvitelli*, ed. M. Rotili (Naples, 1975), 19.

32. See G. L. Hersey, *Architecture, Poetry and Number in the Royal Palace at Caserta* (Cambridge, Mass., 1983).

33. FN 6718 (elevation) and FN 6716 (plan). A later copy—possibly a forgery—of one half of the elevation is in the Museo di Roma, Gabinetto Comunale delle Stampe, coll. Mūnoz, no. 16.750. This drawing, attributed to Vanvitelli, is reproduced in A. Mūnoz, *Roma Barocca* (Milan/Rome, 1919), 405. Also see M. Rotili, "Il progetto vanvitelliano per la Fontana di Trevi," *Samnium* 27, nos. 1–2 (1954): 54–64; "I progetti di Luigi Vanvitelli per la Fontana di Trevi," *Studi Romani* 21 (1973): 314–31; and *Vita di L. Vanvitelli*, 75–78.

34. See R. Pane's analysis of this detail in R. Di Stefano, ed., *Luigi Vanvitelli* (Naples, 1973), 48–49.

35. There are four inscription plaques on the facade, but the middle two repeat the first, recording the dedication to the Virgin and the date of 1730. The inscription at the far right commemorates the excavation of the column. A fifth plaque at the base of the column proclaims that it was reerected by Clement XII.

36. Salvi is known to have drafted four other projects in addition to his winning entry. See F. Milizia, *Memorie degli architetti antichi e moderni* (Bassano, 1785), 253. For descriptions of Salvi's other projects, see Vatican Library, Cod. Lat. 8235, 24–27; and Cassio, *Corso dell'acque*, 306–07.

37. See Bianchi, "Disegni del Vanvitelli e del Fuga," 115–16; and Gradara, *Pietro Bracci*, pl. 29.

38. FN 6715. A copy of this plan, in a private Roman collection, was called to my attention by Jörg Garms.

39. DR:66:001:102. 461 × 71 mm, pencil, gray ink, gray and blue washes. Phyllis Lambert and the staff of the Canadian Centre for Architecture kindly allowed me to study this drawing.

40. See Elisabeth Kieven's article "Rome in 1732: Alessandro Galilei, Nicola Salvi, Ferdinando Fuga," which will appear in the *Papers in Art History from the Pennsylvania State University*, volume 2.

41. See Gradara, *Pietro Bracci*, 120; and Marconi, Cipriani, and Valeriani, *I disegni di architettura*, 1, 557–62.

42. An echo of Salvi's design may perhaps be found in a drawing by the Danish architect Marcus Tuscher (1705–51), called to my attention by Elisabeth Kieven. Tuscher's drawing appears as plate XI in his unpublished manuscript entitled ABCEDARIO *dell'architettura civile*, (1743) in the Kunstakademiets Bibliothek, Copenhagen. Tuscher was in Rome from 1728 to 1741 and no doubt followed the competition for the Trevi closely.

43. There are two principal unpublished sources for Salvi's biography. The first was written in 1737 by the Florentine Niccolò Gaburri: Florence, Biblioteca Nazionale Centrale, Ms. Palat, E.B.9.5, vol. 4, p. 1975. The second, written anonymously around ten years after Salvi's death, is a biographical note included in a collection of critical essays concerning the Fontana di Trevi: Vatican Library, Cod. Lat., 8235, 10–14v.

44. The manuscript sources differ as to Salvi's birth date, Gaburri's *Vita* recording 1695 and the Vatican ms. 1699. The parish records of San Biagio della Pagnotta firmly establish that Salvi, baptized Gaetano Michele, was born on August 6, 1697. Archivio del Vicariato, Parrocchia di S. Lorenzo in Damaso, Liber XIV Baptzatorum, p. 291.

45. For a discussion of the Accademia degli Arcadi, see W. Binni, "La letteratura nell'epoca

arcadica-razionalista," *Storia della letteratura italiana, il settecento*, vol. 6 (Milan, 1968), 326–460; and C. Calcaterra, *Il barocco in Arcadia e altri scritti sul settecento* (Bologna, 1950), 1–35.

46. Vatican Library, Cod. Lat. 8235, 11r.

47. See Schiavo, *Fontana di Trevi*, 25–31. An unpublished drawing by Salvi for the baptistry is in the Museo di Roma, Gab. dei Disegni, no. 16.897.

48. See V. Moschini, "La prima opera di Nicola Salvi," *Roma* 7 (1929): 345–47; and Schiavo, *Fontana di Trevi*, 33–36.

49. Pinto, "Nicola Michetti and Ephemeral Design," 304–13.

50. See Wittkower, "Pietro da Cortona's Project," 115–24.

51. See W. Oechslin, "Un Tempio di Mosé. I disegni offerti da B. A. Vittone all'Accademia di San Luca nel 1733," *Bollettino d'Arte* 52 (1967): 167–73.

52. F. von Erlach, *Entwurff Einer Historischen Architektur* (Leipzig, 1725), fig. 18.

53. A. Pozzo, *De Perspectiva pictorum et architectorum*, 2 vols. (Rome, 1693–1700).

54. The identification of the sculpture in Salvi's fireworks *macchina* is given in the captions of the two prints illustrating his design, which are transcribed by Schiavo, *Fontana di Trevi*, 34.

55. For a summary of the history of the competition for the Lateran facade, see S. Jacob, "Die Projekte Bibienas und Doris für die Fassade von S. Giovanni in Laterano," *Zeitschrift für Kunstgeschichte* 35 (1972): 100–17. For a more detailed discussion, see E. Kieven's forthcoming monograph on Alessandro Galilei.

56. The copies of Salvi's projects for the Lateran facade made by his pupil, Franz Anton Grimm, were published by H. Lorenz, "Unbekannte Projekte für die Fassade von San Giovanni in Laterano," *Wiener Jahrbuch für Kunstgeschichte* 34 (1981): 183–87. Salvi's autograph drawing in the Accademia di San Luca was published by G. Matthiae, "Nicola Salvi minore," *Palladio* 4 (1954): 161–70.

57. L. Vanvitelli, Jr., *Vita*, 18.

58. Salvi died on February 9. Archivio del Vicariato, Parrocchia di S. Maria in Aquirio, Libro dei Morti, 1720–68, 128.

59. Vatican Library, Cod. Lat. 8235, 12v. F. Milizia, *Memorie degli architetti antichi e moderni, opere complete* (Bologna, 1826–27), 5:380.

60. Vatican Library, Cod. Lat. 8235, 13r; Milizia, *Memorie*, 380.

61. Archivio storico dell'Accademia di San Luca, Libro dei Decreti, vol. 49, 112; and Biblioteca Hertziana, Schede Noak, 7/3/1745.

5. *The Trevi Fountain, 1732–1762*

1. CLEMENS XII. PONT. MAX. / AQUAM VIRGINEM / COPIA ET SALVBRITATE COMMENDATUM / CULTV MAGNIFICO ORNAVIT / ANNO DOMINI MDCCXXV. PONTIF. VI.

2. PERFECIT BENEDICTVS XIV. PON. MAX.

3. POSITIS SIGNIS ET ANAGLYPHIS TABVLIS IVSSV CLEMENTIS XIII. PONT. MAX. OPVS CVM OMNI CVLTV ABSOLVTVM A. DOM. MDCCLXII.

4. Milizia, Memorie, 5:379.

5. F. Blondel, *Cours d'architecture enseigné dans l'Académie Royale* (Paris, 1698), 1:75.

6. See L. Du Jardin, "Del simulacro tiberino di Marforio e delle statue affini," *Atti della Pontificia Accademia Romana di Archeologia, Memorie* 3 (1932–33): 59–80; and H. Sichtermann, s.v. "Oceanus," *Enciclopedia dell'arte antica* (Rome, 1963), 5:619–21.

7. The statue of Oceanus is 26 *palmi*, or 5.8 meters high, as compared with the Dioscuri of the Quirinal, which are 5.3 meters tall. The height of the David is 5.1 meters.

8. Appendix 1.36, 37, 41, 79.

9. Appendix 1.58, 72, 73.

10. Vatican Library, Cod. Lat. 8235, 107r–v.

11. A. Del Lungo, "La flora nelle sculture della Fontana di Trevi," *Capitolium* 22 (1957): 18–21.

12. Del Lungo, "La flora," 18.

13. Appendix 1.82.

14. Madame De Stael-Holstein, *Corinne, ou l'Italie* [1807] (Paris, 1846), 85; N. Hawthorne, *The Marble Faun* [1860] (Boston/New York, 1899), 1:160–65; O. Respighi, *Fontane di Roma*, 1917; F. Fellini, *La Dolce Vita*, 1960. While in Rome Hawthorne lived just behind the Trevi on the Via di Poli.

15. C. Fontana, *Utilissimo trattato dell'acque correnti* (Rome, 1696). Fontana's treatise provides a summary of the hydraulic mechanics employed by Salvi.

16. E. Mariotte, *Traité du mouvement des eaux et des autres corps fluides* (Paris, 1686), and *Raccolta d'autori che trattano del moto dell'acque, divisa in tre tomi* (Florence, 1723).

17. L. Callari, *Le fontane di Roma* (Rome, 1945), 71–72, reports that it was a cafe at which Salvi's detractors gathered. See E. Scerbo, *Fontan de Trevi* (Rome, 1980), 142–43 for a discussion of this anecdote.

18. See T. K. Kitao, *Circle, Square and Oval in the Square of Saint Peter's* (New York, 1974), 49–52; and this author's review of Kitao's book in the *Journal of the Society of Architectural Historians* 35 (1976): 234–35.

19. See D. Metzger Habel, "Piazza S. Ignazio, Rome, in the 17th and 18th Centuries," *Architettura* 11 (1981): 31–65.

20. B. Brunelli, ed., *Tutte le opere di Pietro Metastasio* (Milan), vol. 1 (1943), 53.

21. Vatican Library, Cod. Lat., 8235, 23.

22. The earliest suggestion I have found that the Piazza di Trevi should be enlarged occurs in an undated manuscript by Francesco Cancellieri (1751–1826) entitled "Il forastiere istruito per vedere ordinatamente e con metodo le rarità più antiche e moderne di Roma," Vatican Library, Cod. Lat. 9676, 51r.

23. See F. Boyer, "Le Panthéon et la Fontaine de Trevi dans les projets romains de Napoléon," *Études Italiennes*, n.s. 1 (1931): 210–16; and Marconi, Cipriani, and Valeriani, *I disegni*, 2:2683–84.

24. A. Cederna, *Mussolini urbanista* (Rome/Bari, 1980), 80, and A. Bianchi, "La sistemazione di Piazza Trevi," *Capitolium* 1 (1925–26): 563–68.

6. The Construction of the Trevi

1. E. Luzi, "La fontana di Trevi e Nicola Salvi," *Annali della Società degli Ingegneri ed Architetti Italiani* 20 (1905): 137–69.

2. See P. Visconti, *Città e famiglie nobili e celebri dello Stato Pontificio* (Rome), vol. 2 (1847), 889–91.

3. See N. A. Mallory's articles transcribing the references to painting, sculpture, and architecture from the *Diario Ordinario*, in *Bollettino d'Arte* 59 (1974): 164–77; 61 (1976): 102–13; and 67, no. 13 (1982): 109–28; no. 15, 127–47; no. 16, 119–34.

4. V. Giuntella, *Roma nel settecento* (Bologna, 1971), 5.

5. Archivio Segreto Vaticano, Miscellanea, Arm. XV, n. 239.

6. See J. D. Draper, "The Lottery in Piazza Montecitorio," *Master Drawings* 7 (1969): 27–34.

7. Biblioteca Corsiniana, Cod. Cors. 1168, 63–66.

8. Archivio di Stato di Roma, Presidenza degli acquedotti urbani, Acqua Vergine, busta 64, Pagamenti fatti per l'Ornato di Fontana di Trevi, p. 1.

9. G. Brunel, "Recherches sur les débuts de Piranèse à Rome: Les Freres Pagliarini et Nicola Giobbe," in *Piranèse et les Français*, ed. G. Brunel (Rome, 1978), 77–146.

10. Translated by D. Nyberg, ed., *Piranesi Drawings and Etchings* (New York, 1972), 118. Also see P. L. Ghezzi's enthusiastic assessment of Giobbe's talents inscribed on drawing Kdz. 16924 in the Berlin Kupferstichkabinet.

11. See E. Pistolesi, *Modello della Fontana di Trevi ridotto al 15mo dell'originale attribuito a Niccola Salvi discritto da Erasmo Pistolesi esistente nella galleria del Conte Zeloni al Palazzo Albani in Roma* (Rome, 1855). Both Schiavo (*Fontana di Trevi*, 127) and V. Minor, "The Roman Works of Filippo Della Valle" (Ph.D. diss., University of Kansas, 1976), 178–81, convincingly dismiss the authenticity of these *bozzetti*.

12. Rome, Gabinetto Nazionale delle Stampe, F.N. 6719. See Cooke, "The Documents," 152, fig. 25.

13. Archivio di Stato di Roma, Presidenza degli acquedotti urbani, Acqua Vergine, busta 69, 63.

14. See F. Bartolotti, *La medaglia annuale dei romani pontifici, 1605–1967* (Rimini, 1967), 151; and N. T. Whitman and J. L. Varriano, *Roma Resurgens: Papal Medals from the Age of the Baroque* (Ann Arbor, 1983), 183. The die was cut by Eremegildo and Ottone Hamerani.

15. Archivio Segreto Vaticano, Fondo Boncompagni, protocollo 682, 16; and Biblioteca Corsiniana, Cod. 1168, 53–62.

16. Letter of 8/19/1738 from Maini to his brother cited by G. Colombo, "Lo scultore Giambattista Maino," *Rassegna gallaratese di storia dell'arte* 25 (1966): 29–45.

17. See the relevant documents in the Archivio Capitolare di S. Maria Maggione, particularly *Giustificazioni*, 69 (1737–39).

18. Luzi, "Fontana di Trevi," 150.

19. G. D. Campiglia, *Il quinto libro del nuovo teatro delle fabbriche et edifici, fatte fare in Roma e fuori di Roma dalla Santità di Nostro Signore Papa Clemente XII* (Rome, 1739), 12. A second state of Vasi's print, depicting Maini's models in place, was issued at a later date.

20. As early as 1732 the pope was virtually blind.

21. Luzi, "Fontana di Trevi," 151.

22. Biblioteca Corsiniana, Cod. Cors. 1168, 67.

23. Biblioteca Corsiniana, Cod. Cors. 1168, 68.

24. Letter from G. B. Maini to his brother in date of 4/1/1741, cited by Colombo, "Lo scultore G. B. Maino," 37–38.

25. "Un pajo di milioni vinti al lotto, ed impiegati in sassi." E. Morelli, ed., *Le lettere di Benedetto XIV al Card. De Tencin* (Rome, 1955–65), 1:101.

26. Vatican Library, Cod. Ottob. Lat. 3118, 139.

27. Cassio, *Storia*, 308–09.

28. Berlin, Kupferstichkabinett, Kdz. 16924, called to my attention by Elisabeth Kieven. For a photograph of the same site, see Quilici, "Sull'acquedotto Vergine," 155, fig. 55.

29. Appendix 1. 84. Panini's *veduta* is in the Pushkin Museum in Moscow. See F. Arisi, *Gian Paolo Panini* (Piacenza, 1961), 1:204–05, where it is erroneously dated 1750–55. Also see *Il settecento a Roma* exh. cat. (Rome, 1959), 265, no. 1141, for a copy.

30. The inscription is transcribed in V. Forcella, *Iscrizioni delle chiese e d'altri edifici di Roma* (Rome, 1879), 13:175.

31. In 1746, for example, the mason Matteo Caramaschi was paid for setting in place the watering trough visible at the lower right of Piranesi's frontal *veduta*.

32. F. Strazzullo, ed., *Le lettere di Luigi Vanvitelli della Biblioteca Palatina di Caserta* (Galatina, 1976), 1:18.'

33. Maini died on July 29, 1752.

34. Giuiseppe Panini's signature approving bills for repairs to the Acqua Vergine begins to appear in the accounts on 3/12/1751. Archivo di Stato di Roma, Presidenza degli

acquedotti urbani, Acqua Vergine, busta 75, no. 59. For Vanvitelli's comments on Panini's appointment of 9/1/1753, see Strazzullo, *Le lettere*, 1:259–60.

35. Pierpont Morgan Library, 1973.51. V. Carlson, *Hubert Robert, Drawings and Watercolors* (Washington, D.C., 1978), 46. G. K. Loukomski, *La Rome d'Hubert Robert* (Paris, 1930), no. 42, reproduces a counterproof of the Morgan drawing in the Bibliothèque Municipale de Besançon.

36. Gradara, *Pietro Bracci*, 109–12.

37. P. Rossini, *Il Mercurio Errante* (Rome, 1760), 336–37.

38. Vatican Library, Cod. Lat. 8235, 4r.

39. G. Corsetti, *Acquedotti di Roma dai tempi classici al giorno d'oggi* (Rome, 1937), 104–33; and "Il servizio di inaffiamento nella capitale ed il nuovo serbatoio di Via Eleniana," *Capitolium* 11 (1935): 76.

40. Once a week the Trevi is drained and cleaned, and the water changed.

7. Salvi's Design for the Trevi

1. Museo di Roma, Gabinetto comunale delle stampe, Inv. no. GS 880. See *Il settecento a Roma*, no. 1140, and *Roma Sparita. Mostra di disegni e acquerelli dal sec. XVI al XX dalla donazione della Contessa Anna Laetitia Pecci Blunt al Museo di Roma* (Rome, 1976), no. 37.

2. Biblioteca dell'Istituto Nazionale d'archeologia e storia dell'arte, Coll. Lanciani, Roma XI, Cartella 162, IV, p. 20/15. See V. Cianfarani, *Mostra di disegni dell'Istituto Nazionale d'Archeologia e Storia dell'Arte* (Rome, 1956), 55, no. 257, and Schiavo, *Fontana di Trevi*, 136.

3. Museo di Roma, Gabinetto Comunale delle Stampe, inv. no. 16.620.

4. These drawings were called to my attention by Hellmut Lorenz, who also supplied me with photographs of them.

5. See J. Kroupa, ed., *František Antonín Grimm, Architekt XVIII. Stoleti* (Kroměříž, 1982), which reproduces Grimm's elevation of the Fontana di Trevi on page 18, and Hellmut Lorenz's informative review of this exhibition in *The Burlington Magazine* 124 (1982): 727–28.

6. For a discussion of Grimm's copies of Salvi's project for the Lateran facade, see Lorenz, "Unbekannte Projekte," 183–87.

7. Lorenz, "Unbekannte Projekte," 184.

8. "Grund Riess von der F . . . / ist von meinen Architectten Nicola Salvi ein Romer in das / werk gestellet worden und alles in accuraten Mass nach / dem Palmo Romano abgemessen worden."

9. Private collection, Switzerland. Jennifer Montagu called this drawing to my attention.

10. Berlin, Kupferstichkabinett, Kdz. 16374. See H. Voss, "Berninis Fontänen," *Jahrbuch der Königlich Preuszischen Kunstsammlungen* 31 (1910): 127. The Berlin drawing is much stronger than the sketch in Switzerland, leading me to believe that the latter may be a studio copy.

11. G. L. Barbiellini, ed., *Roma moderna distinta per rioni* (Rome, 1741), vol. 2, inserted between pages 198 and 199. Piranesi seems to have reworked an earlier plate by Jean-Laurent Legeay, which is included in some copies of the 1741 edition. While Legeay is quite general in his treatment of the sculpture and basin, Piranesi is much more informative and precise. For a reproduction of Legeay's print, see G. Erouart, "Jean-Laurent Legeay. Recherches," in *Piranèse et les Français, Colloque*, ed. G. Brunel (Rome, 1978), 199–208, fig. 11. Also see H. Millon's essay "Vasi-Piranesi-Juvarra" in the same volume, esp. p. 352, n. 26.

12. Appendix 2.

13. Appendix 1.69.
14. Cyril Humphris, London. Formerly in the Camuccini collection, 270 × 390 mm. The inscription reads: Profilo del Ripiano della / Fontana di Trevi / Faccia dell'Oceano è di Proportione pmi 2 ½ / Alta pmi 25 detta statua / Faccia delli Tritoni è di proportione pmi. 2 ¼ / Ferro dietro l'Oceano p. concatenare li pezzi di marmi / dela Figura, e p. reggere il marmo dello suolazzo / fatto fare alle Ferriere di Conca / grosso in quadro ⅓ cioè ⁴⁄₁₂.
15. Gradara, *Pietro Bracci*, pl. XXX.
16. Arisi, *Panini*, 1:204.
17. London, Sir John Soane's Museum, Adam Collection, Miscellaneous Sketches, Drawer 70, nos. 55–57. These drawings were called to my attention by Sir John Summerson.
18. J. Fleming, *Robert Adam and his Circle in Edinburgh and Rome* (London, 1962), 152.
19. The statues in the lateral niches and the bas-reliefs were not yet in place. The artist has taken liberties in representing the chiaroscuro mock-ups that were visible.
20. Third state, after 1762.
21. R. Wittkower, *Art and Architecture in Italy, 1600–1750* (Baltimore, 1973), 440.
22. Vatican Library, Cod. Lat., 8235, 46r–v.
23. Wittkower, *Art and Architecture*, 440.

8. *Salvi's Iconographical Program for the Trevi*

1. Vatican Library, Cod. Lat. 8235, a bound volume of 168 fols. A second, incomplete version of this manuscript is in the Biblioteca Nazionale Centrale Roma, Fondo Vittorio Emanuele, ms. 580. On the title page of the Vatican codex is the note "seconda copia corretta," which doubtless explains the relationship of the two versions. That the Vatican manuscript was intended for publication can be deduced from a note on fol. 86r, which explains that "gli affari di chi voleva pubblicarle colla stampa non hanno ancora permesso."
2. This date appears in the dedication on fol. 9v. See Garms, "Beiträge zu Vanvitelli's Leben, Werk und Milieu," 158–59, concerning the author of the codex.
3. "Queste due scritture le copiai fedelmente dagli Originali di quel grande Architetto, li quali voi potrete riscontrare a vostro agio dagli eredi." Vatican Library, Cod. Lat. 8235, 9r.
4. Cooke, "The Documents," 169–71.
5. Ibid.
6. Plato's description of the contending steeds of the soul in *Phaedrus* 253c–57b may have suggested this feature.
7. Piccolomini, *Memoirs*, 193.
8. Focillon no. 22. Piranesi's *Grotteschi* were first published in the *Opere Varie* in 1750, but probably were executed several years earlier.
9. J. Scott, *Piranesi* (London/New York, 1975), 51–52.
10. F. Milizia, *Principi di architettura civile* (Milan, 1847), 10.
11. G. Poleni, *De motv aqvae mixto libri dvo* (Padua, 1717). Poleni's paper was presented to the Royal Society in London in 1723.
12. *Iliad* 14.200–01, 244–48; 21.195–97. Aristotle suggests that the Homeric allusion to Oceanus is an early reference to the doctrine that water is the animating principle of material life, a doctrine that Aristotle attributes to Thales of Miletus. See Aristotle, *Metaphysics* 983b.
13. *Phaedo* 110b–13c.
14. Aristotle, *Meteorologica* 2.2, trans. E. W. Webster (Oxford, 1931).
15. *Meteorologica* 1.10.

16. T. Tasso, *La Gerusalemme Conquistata*, 12.20–34, *Opere*, (Florence, 1724), 1:361–62. For a general discussion of the topos of the source, see D. Quint, *Origin and Originality in Renaissance Literature, Visions of the Source* (New Haven/London, 1983).

17. N. Comes, *Mythologiae* (Paris, 1627; repr. New York, 1976), 2.841–44.

18. G. P. Lomazzo, *Trattato dell'arte della pittura, scoltura et architettura*, 7:15, in *Scritti sulle arti*, ed. R. P. Ciardi (Florence, 1973), 2:507.

19. C. Ripa, *Iconologia* (Rome, 1603), 354.

20. Bernard De Montfaucon, *L'antiquité expliquée et représentée en figures*, 6 vols., 2d ed. (Paris, 1722–57). Montfaucon's work was first published in Paris in 1719, and this was followed by an English edition printed in London in 1721–22.

21. *Iliad* 18.606–07.

22. A. Minto, *Il vaso François* (Florence, 1960), 101.

23. Sichtermann, "Oceanus," 620.

24. See A. Furtwängler, *Die Antiken Gemmen* (Munich, 1900), vol. 2, 177, 257, 287, 290; and O. Navarre, s.v. "Oceanus," *Dictionnaire des antiquités grecques et romaines*, ed. C. Daremberg and O. Saglio (Paris, 1907), 4:143–44.

25. Oceanus figured prominently on other imperial nymphaea in Antioch and Adrianople in Thrace. See Tedeschi Grisanti, *Trofei di Mario*, 19.

26. Virgil, *Georgics* 4.374–81: "in thalam pendentia pumice tecta."

27. Colossal bust: Rome, Villa Albani, inv. no. 588; colossal relief: the so-called Bocca della Verità, Rome, S. Maria in Cosmedin.

28. See H. Jones, *The Sculpture of the Palazzo Conservatori* (Oxford, 1926), fig. 40.

29. Ostia, Terme Marittime, rms. C and D. See J. R. Clarke, *Roman Black and White Figural Mosaics* (New York, 1979), figs. 93–94.

30. Mildenhall Treasure, British Museum. See J. M. C. Toynbee, *Art in Roman Britain* (London, 1962), pl. 117.

31. See L. Guerrini, *Marmi antichi nei disegni di Pier Leone Ghezzi* (Vatican City, 1971), cat. nos. 38, 39, 94, 112.

32. The Salvi manuscript in the Biblioteca Nazionale Centrale contains five rather crude drawings of Roman antiquities accompanied by extensive captions. Both the drawings and the explanatory texts are copied from Pier Leone Ghezzi's manuscripts in the Vatican Library (Cod. Ottob. Lat. 3106–09). Judging from the analysis of style, the drawings are not by Salvi.

33. See G. De Luca, *I monumenti antichi di Palazzo Corsini in Roma* (Rome, 1976), no. 57.

34. Guerrini, *Marmi antichi*, 110.

35. G. Rodenwaldt, ed., *Die Antiken Sarkophagreliefs* (Berlin, 1939), vol. 5, no. 116.

36. The Vatican mosaic was excavated in 1780. See B. Nogara, *I mosaici antichi conservati nei palazzi pontifici del Vaticano e del Laterano* (Milan, 1910), 24–25. For other, similar mosaics which have come to light more recently, see G. Becatti, *Scavi di Ostia IV. mosaici e pavimenti marmorei* (Rome, 1961), tavs. 129, 130.

37. See B. Wiles, *The Fountains of the Florentine Sculptors and their Followers from Donatello to Bernini* (Cambridge, Mass., 1933), 48–54.

38. Wiles, *Fountains*, 61–62. Professor Campbell kindly allowed me to consult the unpublished paper on Giovanni Bologna's fountain he read in Edinburgh.

39. See D. Coffin, *The Villa D'Este at Tivoli* (Princeton, 1960), 17; and C. Lamb, *Die Villa D'Este in Tivoli* (Munich, 1966), 50–52.

40. Coffin, *The Villa D'Este*, 145.

41. An earlier allusion to Bernini's snake appears on Filippo Barrigioni's fountain in Piazza della Rotonda (1710–11).

42. R. Preimesberger, "Obeliscus Pamphilius," *Münchner Jahrbuch der bildenden Kunst*, 25 (1974): 137–46.

9. The Trevi and Its Place in the History of Art

1. G. Bottari, *Dialoghi sulle arti del disegno* (Rome, 1772), 170, 201. First published in 1754 but written in the early 1730s.
2. Vatican Library, Cod. Lat. 8235, 53–85v.
3. Milizia, *Memorie, Opere Complete,* 5:378. The *Memorie* were first published in 1768.
4. J. Forsyth, *Remarks on Antiquities, Arts and Letters during an Excursion in Italy in the Years 1802 and 1803* (London, 1816), 174.
5. M. Prunetti, *Viaggio pittorico-antiquario d'Italia e Sicilia* (Rome, 1820), 2:85–86.
6. A. Nibby, *Roma nell'anno 1838* (Rome, 1841), 2:47–55.
7. J. Burckhardt, *Der Cicerone* (Leipzig, 1869), 1:394.
8. Voss, "Berninis Fontänen," 127–129; K. Escher, *Barock und Klassizismus. Studien zur Geschichte der Architektur Roms* (Leipzig, 1910), 91; M. S. Briggs, *Barock-Architektur* (Berlin, 1914), 53; and Muñoz, *Roma Barocca,* 397–99.
9. Fraschetti, *Il Bernini,* 127–36; Brauer and Wittkower, *Die Zeichnungen,* 1:147–50.
10. Cooke, "The Documents."
11. D'Onofrio, *Fontane,* 225–62.
12. D'Onofrio, *Acque,* 526–62. See P. Portoghesi's review in *Palladio* 7 (1957): 146–47.
13. Wittkower, *Art and Architecture* (1973), 380, 439–40.
14. Ibid., 369–73.
15. Neither am I comfortable with the term *Barocchetto,* which has been employed with increasing frequency to describe the Italian version of the Rococo style, for the intrinsic connotations of the term suggest that the works to which it is applied are diminutive and qualitatively inferior. See R. Enggass, "Tiepolo and the Concept of the Barocchetto," *Atti del Congresso internazionale di studi sul Tiepolo* (Venice, 1970), 81–86; Mallory, *Roman Rococo Architecture* (1977); and A. Blunt, *Guide to Baroque Rome* (London, 1982), xvii.
16. E. H. Gombrich, "The Style *all'antica:* Imitation and Assimilation," *Acts of the Twentieth International Congress of the History of Art* (Princeton, 1963), 2:31–41.
17. Nash, *Pictorial Dictionary,* 1:83–87. While this arch was demolished in 1662 the relief plaques survived on the Capitol. Salvi could have known the arch through printed representations, which continued to be issued in the eighteenth century.
18. Salvi's combination of ribs and coffering was anticipated by Pietro da Cortona, particularly in the dome of SS. Luca e Martina.
19. Vitruvius, 1.3.
20. Lione Pascoli refers to Salvi's "antico gusto": *Vite,* 2:477.
21. If one takes into account Michelangelo's intentions, which were altered in execution, the comparison between the Senators' Palace and the Trevi may be pursued even further. Dupérac's engraving of 1568 shows that Michelangelo's facade was to be divided horizontally by a string course running behind the pilasters of the colossal order. Set within the compartments formed by the resulting grid of verticals and horizontals were to have been pedimented windows with balconies projecting below. See J. S. Ackerman, *The Architecture of Michelangelo* (London, 1961), vol. 1, pl. 37, fig. 8.
22. Rovere, Viale and Brinckmann, *Juvarra,* 19, 23.
23. Pinto, "Filippo Juvarra's Drawings," 608–12.
24. P. Portoghesi, *Roma Barocca* (Rome, 1966), 429–34.
25. A. Venditti, *La Loggia del Capitaniato* (Vicenza, 1969).
26. J. Connors, *Borromini and the Roman Oratory. Style and Society* (Cambridge, Mass./London, 1980), fig. 17; and S. Gianini, ed., *Opera del Cav. Francesco Boromini Cavata da Suoi Originali cioè L'Oratorio, e Fabrica per l'Abitazione De P.P. dell'Oratorio di S. Filippo Neri di Roma* (Rome, 1725), pl. 56. Borromini also allowed window frames to break into the entablature of the Lateran nave.
27. Paolo Portoghesi has gone so far as to suggest that Salvi's niche may be seen as an

inversion of the portico before S. Andrea al Quirinale. See Portoghesi, *Roma Barocca*, 430.

28. Two relevant examples are the interior of SS. Luca e Martina and the narthex of S. Maria in Via Lata; a third source, the Villa Pignetto Sacchetti, is discussed below.

29. Bottari, *Dialoghi.*

30. A. Blunt, "Roman Baroque Architecture. The Other Side of the Medal," *Art History* 3, no. 1 (1980): 61–80.

31. S. Benedetti, "L'architettura dell'Arcadia: Roma 1730," *Bernardo Vittone e la disputa fra classicismo e barocco nel settecento* (Turin, 1972), 1:337–91.

32. K. Blauensteiner, *Georg Raphael Donner* (Vienna, 1947), 33–41; and A. Pigler, *Georg Raphael Donner* (Leipzig/Vienna, 1929), 62–66.

33. Nationalmuseum, THC 4426.

34. A. Stavenow, *Carl Hårleman. En studie i Frihetstidens Architektuchistoria* (Upsala, 1927), 50–51.

35. See F. E. Keller's entry on the Du Ry family in *The Macmillan Encyclopedia of Architects* (New York, 1982), 1:614–17.

36. Graphische Sammlung, Staatliche Kunstsammlungen Kassel. This drawing was kindly called to my attention by Cristoph Dittsheid.

37. Soane Ms., Part I; see B. Little, *The Life and Work of James Gibbs, 1682–1754* (London, 1955), 25.

38. London, Sir John Soane's Museum, Drawer xxii, 2.

39. Print Room, Chambers Sketchbook, 93.B.21/5172, no. 155.

40. Quoted by J. Harris, *Sir William Chambers, Knight of the Polar Star* (London, 1970), 22.

41. Harris, *Chambers,* 100.

42. M. Filler, "The Magic Fountain. Piazza d'Italia, New Orleans," *Progressive Architecture* 59 (1978): 81–87.

43. C. W. Moore, "Water and Architecture" (Ph.D. diss., Princeton University, 1957), 4–5.

Select Bibliography

This selection does not include all the titles cited in the notes, which complement the references given here. The entries are arranged under the following headings:

General Works   Salvi's Trevi: Design and Meaning
Urban Context   Guidebooks and Descriptions
Unexecuted Projects

General Works

Ashby, Thomas. *The Aqueducts of Ancient Rome.* Oxford: Oxford University Press, 1935.

Bellonzi, Fortunato. *La Fontana di Trevi.* Milan: Aldo Martello Editore, 1962.

Brigante Colonna, Gustavo. "L'Acqua Vergine e la fontana di Trevi." *Capitolium* 9 (1933): 559–72.

Callari, Luigi. *Le fontane di Roma.* Rome: Apollon, 1954.

Cassio, Alberto. *Corso dell'acque antiche portate da lontane contrade furi e dentro Roma sopra XIV acquidotti; e delle moderne e in essa nascenti coll'illustrazione di molte antichità che la stessa città decoravano.* 2 vols. Rome: Puccinelli, 1756–57.

Colasanti, Arduino. *Le fontane d'Italia.* Milan/Rome: Bestetti e Tumminelli, 1926.

Corsetti, Giampelino. *Acquedotti di Roma dai tempi classici al giorno d'oggi.* Rome: Fratelli Palombi, 1937.

D'Onofrio, Cesare. *Acque e Fontane di Roma.* Rome: Staderini, 1977.

———. *Le Fontane di Roma.* Rome: Staderini, 1957.

Elling, Christian. *Rome: The Biography of her Architecture from Bernini to Thorvaldsen.* Boulder, Colo.: Westview Press, 1975.

Fea, Carlo. *Storia I. Delle acque antiche sorgenti in Roma, perdute, e modo di ristabilirle. II. Dei condotti antico-moderni delle Acque Vergine, Felice, e Paola, e loro autori.* Rome: tip d. Rev. Cam. Apos., 1832.

Gasponi, G. *Roma. La Pietra e l'Acqua.* Trento, 1982.

Gherardi, Filippo. "La Fontana di Trevi." *L'Album* 10 (1843): 337–38.

Marchetti, Raffaele. *Sulle acque di Roma, antiche e moderne.* Rome, 1886.

Mastrigli, Federico. *Acque, acquedotti e fontane di Roma.* 2 vols. Rome: Enzo Pinci, 1928.

Morton, Henry Canova Vollam. *The Fountains of Rome.* New York: Macmillian, 1966.

Pastor, Ludwig Friherr von. *The History of the Popes from the Close of the Middle Ages.* 40 vols. London: K. Paul, Trench, Trubner & Co., 1923–53.

Scatassa, E. "Fontana di Trevi in Roma." *Arte e Storia* 31 (1912): 267–72.

Scerbo, Ercole. *Fontan de Trevi*, Rome: I Dioscuri, 1980.

Valesio, Francesco. *Diario di Roma*. 6 vols. Edited by G. Scano and G. Graglia. Milan: Club del Libro, 1977–79.

Van Deman, Esther Boise. *The Building of the Roman Aqueducts*. Washington, D.C.: Carnegie Institution, 1934.

Urban Context

Bianchi, A. "La sistemazione di Piazza Trevi." *Capitolium* 1 (1925–26): 563–68.

Boyer, Ferdinand. "Le Panthéon et la Fontaine de Trevi dans les projects romains de Napoléon." *Études Italiennes* 1 (1931): 210–16.

Carta archeologica di Roma, 2. Ministero della Pubblica Istruzione. Florence, 1964.

Conforti, Claudia. "Piazza di Trevi." In *Monumenti d'Italia: Le Piazze*, edited by Franco Borsi and Geno Pampaloni, 388–91. Novara: De Agostini, 1975.

Dudley, Donald. *Urbs Roma*. London: Phaidon, 1967.

Egger, Hermann. *Römische Veduten*. 2 vols. Vienna/Leipzig: F. Wolfrum & Co., 1911–31.

Evans, Harry B. "Agrippa's Water Plan." *The American Journal of Archaeology* 86 (1982): 401–11.

Fabretti, Raffaele. *De aquis et aquaeductibus veteris Romae dissertationes tres*. Rome: G. B. Bussotti, 1680.

Fagiolo, Marcello, ed. *La Roma dei Longhi. Papi e architetti tra manierismo e barocco*. Rome: DeLuca, 1982.

Falda, Giovanni Battista. *Il nuovo teatro delle fabriche, et edificii, in prospetiva di Roma moderna, sotto il felice Pontificato di N.S. Papa Alessandro VII*. Rome: G.G. Rossi alla Pace, 1665.

———. *Il terzo libro del'novo teatro delle chiese di Roma date in luce sotto il felice pontificato di Nostro Signore Papa Clemente IX*. 4 vols. Rome: G. G. Rossi alla Pace, 1667–69.

Fontana, Domenico. *Delle trasportatione dell'obelisco vaticano e delle fabbriche di Nostro Signore Sisto V fatte dal Cavaliere Domenico Fontana*. Rome: D. Basa, 1590.

Frontinus, Sextus Julius. *De Aquis Urbis Romae Libri II*. Loeb Classical Library, no. 174. Cambridge: Harvard University Press, 1961.

Frutaz, Amato Pietro. *Le piante di Roma*. 3 vols. Rome: Ist. di Studi Romani, 1962.

Gatti, Guglielmo. "Caratteristiche edilizie di un quartiere di Roma del II secolo d. Cr." *Quaderni dello istituto di storia dell'architettura* 6–8, fasc. 31–48 (1961): 49–66.

Gregorovius, Ferdinand. *History of the City of Rome in the Middle Ages*. 8 vols. Translated by A. Hamilton. London: G. Bell, 1894–1902.

Grelle, Anna, ed. *Palazzo Poli. Sede dell'Istituto Nazionale per la Grafica*. Rome: De Luca, 1979.

Huelsen, Christian. *Die Thermen des Agrippa*. Rome: Loeschner & Co., 1910.

Krautheimer, Richard. "Alexander VII and Piazza Colonna." *Römisches Jahrbuch für Kunstgeschichte* 20 (1983): 195–208.

———. "*Il porton di questo giardino*: An Urbanistic Project for Rome by Alexander VII (1655–1667)." *Journal of the Society of Architectural Historians* 42 (1983): 35–42.

————. *Rome, Profile of a City 312–1308.* Princeton, N.J.: Princeton University Press, 1980.

————, and R. B. S. Jones. "The Diary of Alexander VII: Notes on Art, Artists and Buildings." *Römisches Jahrbuch für Kunstgeschichte* 15 (1975): 199–233.

Lanciani, Rodolfo. *Forma Urbis Romae.* Milan: Hoepli, 1893.

————. *The Destruction of Ancient Rome.* New York: Houghton & Mifflin, 1899.

————. *Topografia di Roma antica. I commentarii di Frontino intorno le acque e gli aquedotti.* Rome: Salviucci, 1880.

Lloyd, R. B. "The Aqua Virgo, Euripus and Pons Agrippae." *The American Journal of Archaeology* 83 (1979): 193–204.

Lugli, Giuseppe, and Italo Gismondi. *Forma Urbis Romae Imperatorum Aetate.* Novara: De Agostini, 1949.

Muntz, Eugene. *Lers arts à la cour des papes pendant le XVe et le XVIe siècle, Recueil de documents inedits.* 3 vols. Paris: E. Leroux, 1878–98.

Nash, Ernest. *A Pictorial Dictionary of Ancient Rome.* 2d ed. London: Thames & Hudson, 1968.

Neuerburg, Norman. *L'architettura delle fontane e dei ninfei nell'Italia antica.* Memorie dell'Accademia di Archeologia, Lettere e Belle Arti di Napoli, vol. 5. Naples, 1965.

Orbaan, Johannes A.F. *Documenti sul Barocco in Roma.* Rome: Società romana di storia patria, 1920.

Pace, Pierantonio. *Gli acquedotti di Roma e il De Aquaeductu di Frontino.* Rome, 1983.

Patetta, Luciano. *I Longhi, una famiglia di architetti tra Manierismo e Barocco.* Milan: clup, 1980.

Pecchiai, Pio. *Acquedotti e fontane di Roma nel cinquecento.* Rome: Staderini, 1944.

Peto, Luca. *De restitutione ductus Aquae Virginis.*, Rome, 1570.

Pierro, M. "Il Palazzo della Stamperia." *Capitolium* 4 (1928): 237–49.

Pinto, John. "The Trevi Fountain and its Place in the Urban Development of Rome." *AA Files* 8 (1985): 8–20.

Piranesi, Giovanni Battista. *Campus martius antiquae urbis.* Rome, 1762.

————. *Le antichità romane.* Rome, 1756).

————. *Le rovine del castello dell'Acqua Giulia.* Rome, 1761.

Pius II, Pope. *Memoirs of a Renaissance Pope: The Commentaries of Pius II.* Translated by F. A. Gragg, New York: Putnam, 1959.

Platner, Samuel B., and Thomas Ashby. *A Topographical Dictionary of Ancient Rome.* Oxford: Oxford University Press, 1929.

Pollak, Oskar. *Die Kunsttätigkeit unter Urban VIII.* 2 vols. Vienna: B. Filser, 1927–31.

Quilici, Lorenzo. "Sull'acquedotto Vergine dal Monte Pincio alla sorgente." *Studi di topografia romana*, 125–60. Rome, 1968.

Salerno, Luigi, "L'ambiente di Palazzo Carpegna." In *L'Accademia Nazionale di San Luca*, edited by V. Crocetti, 58–77. Rome, 1974.

————, Luigi Spezzaferro, and Manfredo Tafuri. *Via Giulia, una utopia urbanistica del 500.* Rome: Staderini, 1975.

Schiavo, Armando. "Palazzo Poli e il Palazzetto Schiavo a Fontana di Trevi." *L'Urbe* 42, fasc. 5 (1979): 19–27.

Shipley, Frederick W. *Agrippa's Building Activities in Rome.* St. Louis: Washington University Press, 1933.

Tedeschi Grisanti, Giovanna. *I "Trofei di Mario," Il ninfeo dell'Acqua Giulia sull'Esquilino.* Rome: Studi Romani, 1977.

Varriano, John. "The Roman Ecclesiastical Architecture of Martino Longhi the Younger." Ph.D. diss., University of Michigan, 1970.

Vasari, Giorgio. *Le Vite de'più eccellenti pittori scultori ed architetti.* 9 vols. Edited by G. Milanesi. Florence: Sansoni, 1878–85.

Unexecuted Projects

Berckenhagen, Ekhart. *Architektenzeichnungen 1479–1979.* Berlin: Speiss, 1979.

Bianchi, Lidia. "Disegni del Vanvitelli e del Fuga al Gabinetto Nazionale delle Stampe." *Atti dell'VIII Congresso Nazionale di Storia dell'Architettura*, 115–25. Rome, 1956.

———. *Disegni di Ferdinando Fuga e di altri architetti del settecento.* Rome: Farnesina alla Lungara, 1955.

Braham, Allan, and Hellmut Hager. *Carlo Fontana. The Drawings at Windsor Castle.* London: Zwemmer, 1977.

Brauer, Heinrich, and Rudolf Wittkower. *Die Zeichnungen des Gianlorenzo Bernini.* 2 vols. Berlin: H. Keller, 1931.

Calmet, Dom, Abbé de Senones. *Bibliothèque lorraine, ou l'histoire des hommes illustres.* Nancy, 1751.

Cassirer, Kurt. "Die Handzeichnungsammlung Pacetti." *Jahrbuch der Preussischen Kunstsammlungen* 43 (1922): 63–96.

Chattard, Giovanni Pietro. *Nuova descrizione del Vaticano osia del Palazzo Apostolico di San Pietro.* 3 vols. Rome: Eredi di Barbiellini, 1762–67.

di Stefano, Roberto, ed. *Luigi Vanvitelli.* Naples: Edizioni scientifiche italiane, 1973.

Egger, Hermann. *Römische Veduten.* 2 vols. Vienna/Leipzig: F. Wolfrum & Co., 1911–31.

Eisler, William. "Concorso Clementino of 1706." In *Architectural Fantasy and Reality. Drawings from the Accademia Nazionale di San Luca in Rome, Concorsi Clementini 1700–1750*, edited by H. Hager and S. Munshower, 53–63. University Park: Pennsylvania State University Press, 1982.

Fichera, Francesco. *Luigi Vanvitelli.* Rome: Reale Accademia d'Italia, 1937.

Fraschetti, Stanislao. *Il Bernini, la sua vita, la sua opera, il suo tempo.* Milan: Hoepli, 1900.

Garms, Jörg. "Beiträge zu Vanvitellixs Leben, Werk und Milieu." *Römische Historische Mitteilungen* 16 (1974): 107–90.

Gigli, Giacinto. *Diario Romano, 1608–1670.* Edited by G. Ricciotti. Rome: Tumelli, 1958.

Gradara, Costanza. *Pietro Bracci scultore romano, 1700–1773.* Milan: Alfieri & Lacroix, 1920.

Hager, Hellmut. "Puntualizzazioni su disegni scenici teatrali e l'architettura scenografica del periodo barocco a Roma." *Bollettino del Centro Internazionale di Studi di Architettura Andrea Palladio* 17 (1975): 119–25.

Jacob, Sabine. *Italienische Zeichnungen der Kunstbibliothek Berlin: Architektur und Dekoration 16. bis 18 Jahrhundert.* Berlin: Staatl. Museen Preuss. Kulturbesitz, 1975.

Kieven, Elisabeth. "Revival del Berninismo durante il Pontificato di Clemente XII." In *Gian Lorenzo Bernini Architetto e l'architettura europea del Sei-Settecento,* edited by Gianfranco Spagnesi and Marcello Fagiolo, 459–68. Rome: Ist. d. Enciclopedia Italiana, 1984.

Kommer, Bjorn R. "Nicodemus Tessin und das Stockholmer Schloss." Ph.D. diss., University of Heidelberg, 1974.

Marconi, Paolo, Angela Cipriani, and Enrico Valeriani. *I disegni di architettura dell'Archivio Storico dell Accademia di San Luca.* 2 vols. Rome: De Luca, 1974.

Millon, Henry A. *Filippo Juvarra: Drawings from the Roman Period 1704–1714.* Part 1. Rome: Edizioni dell'Elefante, 1984.

Montaiglon, Anatole de Courde de, ed. *Correspondance des directeurs de l'Académie de France a Rome.* 17 vols. Paris: Charavay frères, 1887–1908.

Oechslin, Werner. *Bildungsgut und Antikenrezeption des frühen Settecento in Rom.* Zurich: Atlantis, 1972.

———. Review of S. Jacob, *Italienische Zeichnungen der Kunstbibliothek Berlin. Kunstchronik* 31 (1978): 187–207.

Pascoli, Leone. *Testamento politico d'un Accademico Fiorentino.* Cologne: Eredi di C. d'Egmond, 1733.

———. *Vite de'pittori, scultori ed architetti moderni.* 2 vols. Rome: A. de'Rossi, 1730–36.

Pinto, John, and Elisabeth Kieven. "An Early Project by Ferdinando Fuga for the Trevi Fountain in Rome." *The Burlington Magazine* 125 (1983): 746–49.

Pinto, John. "An Early Project by Nicola Michetti for the Trevi Fountain." *The Burlington Magazine* 119 (1977): 853–57.

———. "The Trevi Fountain: Unexecuted Projects from the Pontificate of Clement XI." In *Projects and Monuments in the Period of the Roman Baroque, Papers in Art History from the Pennsylvania State University,* Volume 1, edited by H. Hager and S. Munshower, 101–27. University Park: Pennsylvania State University Press, 1984.

Roserot, Alphonse. "La vie et l'oeuvre d'Edme Bouchardon en Italie." *Gazette des Beaux-Arts* 40 (1908): 17–37.

Rotili, Mario. "Il progetto vanvitelliano per la Fontana di Trevi." *Samnium* 27, nos. 1–2 (1954): 54–64.

———. "I progetti di Luigi Vanvitelli per la Fontana di Trevi." *Studi Romani* 21 (1973): 314–31.

Schiavo, Armando. "Un ignoto progetto di Innocenzo XIII per la piazza di Trevi." *Strenna dei Romanisti* 20 (1959): 197–201.

Schmitz, Hermann. *Baumeisterzeichnungen des 17. und 18. Jahrhunderts in der Staatlichen Kunstbibliothek zu Berlin.* Berlin/Leipzig: Verlag für kunstwissenschaft, 1937.

Vanvitelli, Luigi, Jr. *Vita di Luigi Vanvitelli.* Edited by M. Rotili. Naples: Società editrice napoletana, 1975.

Vogel, Lisa. *The Column of Antoninus Pius.* Cambridge: Harvard University Press, 1973.

———. "The Column of Antoninus Pius: *Antiche Memorie* in the Eighteenth Century." In *Studies Presented to George M. A. Hanfmann,* 189–95. Cambridge: Harvard University Press, 1971.

Voss, Hermann. "Berninis Fontänen." *Jahrbuch der Königlich Preuszischen Kunstsammlungen* 31 (1910): 99–129.

Weber, Gerold. "Edme Bouchardon, Studien zu seiner Stellung in der französischen Plastik des 18. Jhs." Ph.D. diss., University of Vienna, 1965.

Salvi's Trevi: Design and Meaning

Bottari, Giovanni Gaetano. *Dialoghi sulle arti del disegno.* Naples: presso i Simoni, 1772.

Brunel, Georges. "Recherches sur les débuts de Piranese à Rome: Les Frères Pagliarini et Nicola Giobbe." In *Piranèse et les Français, Colloque*, edited by Georges Brunel, 77–146. Rome: Edizioni dell'Elefante, 1978.

Campiglia, Giovanni Domenico. *Il quinto libro del nuovo teatro delle fabbriche et edifici, fatte fare in Roma e fuori di Roma dalla Santità di Nostro Signore Papa Clemente XII.* Rome: Pie di Marmo, 1739.

Cianfarani, Valerio. *Mostra di disegni dell'Istituto Nazionale d'Archeologia e Storia dell'Arte.* Rome: Modenese, 1956.

Colombo, Giulio. "Lo scultore Giambattista Maino." *Rassegna gallaratese di storia dell'arte* 25 (1966): 29–45.

———. "Sulle tracce di G. B. Maino." *Rassegna gallaratese di storia dell'arte* 27 (1968): 25–34.

Cooke, Hereward Lester. "The Documents Relating to the Fountain of Trevi." *Art Bulletin* 33 (1956): 149–73.

Del Lungo, A. "La flora nelle sculture della Fontana di Trevi." *Capitolium* 22, no. 8 (1957): 18–21.

Domarius, Kurt von. *Pietro Bracci, Beiträge zur römischen Kunstgeschichte des XVIII Jährhunderts.* Strasbourg: Heitz, 1915.

Du Jardin, L. "Del simulacro tiberino di Marforio e delle statue affini." *Atti della Pontificia Accademia Romana di Archeologia, Memorie* 3 (1932–33): 35–80.

Enggass, Robert. "Bernardo Ludovisi—The Early Work." *The Burlington Magazine* 110 (1968): 438–44.

———. *Early Eighteenth-Century Sculpture in Rome.* 2 vols. University Park: Pennsylvania State University Press, 1976.

Fleming, John, and Hugh Honour. "Giovanni Battista Maini." In *Essays in the History of Art Presented to Rudolf Wittkower*, edited by D. Fraser, H. Hibbard, and M. J. Lewine, 255–58. London: Phaidon, 1967.

Forcella, Vincenzo, *Iscrizoni delle chiese e d'altri edifici di Roma.* 14 vols. Rome: Tip. delle scienze matematiche e fisiche, 1869–84.

Giuntella, Vittorio Emanuele. *Roma nel settecento.* Bologna: L. Capelli, 1971.

Gradara, Costanza. "Il diario dello scultore Pietro Bracci." *Rassegna d'Arte* 15 (1915): 242–52.

Kroupa, Jiri, ed. *František Antonin Grimm, Architekt XVIII. Stoleti.* Kroměříž, 1982.

Letarouilly, Paul. *Édifices de Rome moderne.* 4 vols. Paris: Bance, 1856–60.

Lorenz, Hellmut. "Kroměříž, Franz Anton Grimm." *The Burlington Magazine* 124 (1982): 727–28.

———. "Unbekannte Projekte für die Fassade von San Giovanni in Laterano." *Wiener Jahrbuch für Kunstgeschichte* 34 (1981):183–87.

Luzi, E. "La Fontana di Trevi e Nicola Salvi." *Annali della Società degli Ingegneri ed Architetti Italiani* 20 (1905): 137–69.

Mallory, Nina A. "Notizie sull'architettura nel settecento a Roma, 1718–1760." *Bollettino d'Arte* 67, no. 13 (1982): 109–28; no. 15, pp. 127–47; no. 16, pp. 119–34.

———. "Notizie sulla scultura a Roma nel XVIII secolo, 1719–1730." *Bollettino d'Arte* 59, nos. 3–4 (1974): 164–77.

Mariani, Valerio. "Lo stile *pittoresco* nella Fontana di Trevi." *Architettura e arti decorative* 8 (1928–29): 3–30.

Mariotte, Edme. *Traité du mouvement des eaux et des autres corps fluides.* Paris: E. Michallet, 1686.

Matthiae, Guglielmo. "Nicola Salvi minore." *Palladio* 4 (1954):161–70.

Meis, Domenico Maria de. *Fontana di Trevi.* Rome, 1935.

Metastasio, Pietro. *Dido Abbandonata, Tutte le opere di Pietro Metastasio.* 2 vols. Edited by Bruno Brunelli. Milan: Mondanori, 1943–54.

Millon, Henry A. "Vasi-Piranesi-Juvarra." In *Piranèse et les Français, Colloque*, edited by Georges Brunel, 345–54. Rome, 1978.

Milizia, Francesco. *Memorie degli architetti antichi e moderni, Opere Complete.* 9 vols. Bologna: Cardinali e Frulli, 1826–28.

Minor, Vernon H. "Della Valle and G. B. Grossi revisited." *Antologia di Belle Arti* 2 (1978): 233–47.

———. "The Roman Works of Filippo Della Valle." Ph.D. diss., University of Kansas, 1976.

Montfaucon, Bernard de. *L'antiquité expliqueé et representeé en figures.* 2d ed. 6 vols. Paris: F. Delaulne, 1722–57.

Morelli, Emilia, ed. *Le lettere di Benedetto XIV al Card. De Tencin.* 2 vols. Rome: Edizioni di storia e letteratura, 1955–65.

Moschini, V. "La prima opera di Nicola Salvi." *Roma* 7 (1929): 345–47.

Passerini, Luigi. *Genealogia e storia della famiglia Corsini.* Florence: M. Cellini, 1858.

Pistolesi, Erasmo. *Modello della Fontana di Trevi ridotto al 15° dell'originale attribuito a Niccola Salvi descritto da Erasmo Pistolesi esistente nella galleria del Conte Zelone al Palazzo Albani in Roma.* Rome: G. Olivieri, 1855.

Poleni, Giovanni. *De motv aqvae mixto libri dvo.* Padua: I. Comeni, 1717.

Portoghesi, Paolo. *Roma Barocca, Storia di una civiltà architettonica.* Rome: C. Bestetti, 1966.

Quint, David. *Origin and Originality in Renaissance Literature. Versions of the Source.* New Haven/London: Yale University Press, 1983.

Ripa, Cesare. *Della più che novissima iconologia.* Padua: Donato Pasquardi, 1630.

Roma Sparita. Mostra di disegni e acquerelli dal sec. XVI al XX dalla donazione della Contessa Anna Laetitia Pecci Blunt al Museo di Roma. Rome: Fratelli Palombi, 1976.

Scalabroni, Luisa. *Giuseppe Vasi, 1710–1782.* Rome, 1981.

Schiavo, Armando. *La Fontana di Trevi e le altre opere di Nicola Salvi.* Rome: Ist. Poligrafico dello Stato, 1956.

———. "La Fontana di Trevi." *Le vie d'Italia* 44 (1938): 694–705.

Il settecento a Roma. Exhibition Catalogue, Museo di Roma. Rome: De Luca, 1959.

Tasso, Torquato. *La Gerusalemme Conquistata, Opere.* Vol. 1. Florence: nella stamperia di S.A.R. per li Tartini, e Franchi, 1724.

Vasi, Giuseppe. *Della magnificenze di Roma antica e moderna.* 10 vols. Rome: Chracas, 1747–61.

Whitman, Nathan T., and John L. Varriano. *Roma Resurgens. Papal Medals from the Age of the Baroque.* Ann Arbor: University of Michigan Press, 1983.

Wiles, Bertha. *The Fountains of the Florentine Sculptors and their Followers from Donatello to Bernini.* Cambridge: Harvard University Press, 1933.

Wittkower, Rudolf. *Art and Architecture in Italy, 1600–1750.* Baltimore: Penguin, 1973.

Guidebooks and Descriptions

Albertini, F. *Opusculum de mirabilibus novae & veteris urbis Romae.* Rome: Jacobum Mazochium, 1510.

Baedeker, Karl. *Central Italy and Rome.* Leipzig/London: K. Baedeker, 1890.

Blunt, Anthony. *Guide to Baroque Rome.* New York: Harper and Row, 1982.

Brosses, Charles de. *Lettres familières sur l'Italie.* 2 vols. Paris: Firmin-Didot, 1931.

Burckhardt, Jacob. *Der Cicerone.* 2 vols. Leipzig: A. Seeman, 1869.

Clark, Eleanor. *Rome and a Villa.* New York: Atheneum, 1962.

Donati, Alessandro. *Roma vetus ac recens.* Rome: Maneiphi, 1639.

Felini, Pietro Martire. *Tratado nuevo de las cosas maravillosas de la alma cividad de Roma.* Rome: Bartolomeo Zanetti, 1610.

Forsyth, Joseph. *Remarks on Antiquities, Arts and Letters, during an Excursion in Italy in the Years 1802 and 1803.* 2d ed. London: J. Murray, 1816.

Franzini, Giovanni Domenico, ed. *Descrittione di Roma antica e moderna.* Rome: Andrea Fei, 1643.

Gaddi, Giambattista. *Roma nobilitata nelle sue fabbriche della Santità di N.S. Clemente XII.* Rome: A. de'Rossi, 1736.

Hawthorne, Nathaniel. *The Marble Faun.* 2 vols. New York/Boston: Houghton Mifflin, 1899.

Justi, Karl. *Briefe aus Italien.* Bonn: F. Cohen, 1922.

—————. *Winckelmann und seine Zeitgenossen.* 3 vols. Leipzig: F. C. W. Vogel, 1923.

Lanciani, Rodolfo. "Il codice barberiniano XXX, 89 contenente frammenti di una descrizione di Roma del sec. XVI." *Archivio della Società Romana di Storia Patria* 6 (1883): 223–240, 445–96.

—————. "L'itinerario di Einsiedeln e l'ordine di Benedetto Canonico." *Accademia Nazionale dei Lincei, Monumenti Antichi* 1, part 3 (1891): 438–551.

Lees-Milne, James. *Roman Mornings.* London: A. Wingate, 1956.

Micheli, Benedetto. *Sonnetti romaneschi, 1750–67.* Edited by E. Celani. Rome, 1889.

Martinelli, Fioravante. *Roma ornata dall'architettura, pittura e scoltura.* Biblioteca Casanatense Ms. 4984. Transcribed by Cesare D'Onofrio, *Roma nel Seicento.* Rome: Staderini, 1968.

Nibby, Antonio. *Roma nell'anno 1838.* 2 vols. Rome: Tipografia delle Belle Arti, 1841.

Prunetti, Michelangelo. *Viaggio pittorico-antiquario d'Italia e Sicilia.* 2 vols. Rome: L. Contadini, 1820.

Roisecco, Gregorio, ed. *Descrizione di Roma moderna.* 2 vols. Rome: G. Roisecco, 1739.

—————, ed. *Roma antica e moderna.* 3 vols. 1745. Reprints: 2 vols. Rome, 1750; 3 vols. Rome, 1765.

Roma moderna distinta per Rioni, e cavata dal Panvinio, Pancirolo, Nardini, e altri Autori. Ornata di vari Ramj diligentemente intagliati rappresentanti le Basiliche, e altre insigni Fabbriche fino all'anno MDCCXL. Rome: G. L. Barbiellini, 1741.

Rossini, Pietro. *Il Mercurio Errante.* Rome: Fausto Amidei, 1760.

Scotto, Francesco. *Itinerario d'Italia.* Rome: Bernabo e Lazzarini, 1747.

Stael-Holstein, Anne Louise Germaine. *Corrinne, ou l'Italie.* Paris: Firmin Didot frères, 1845.

Stendhal [Marie Henri Beyle]. *Promenades dans Rome.* Sceaus: J. J. Pauvert, 1955.

Totti, Pompilio. *Ritratto di Roma moderna.* Rome: Mascardi, 1638.

Vasi, Giuseppe. *Indice istorico del gran prospetto di Roma.* Rome, 1765.

————. *Itinerario istruttivo, diviso in otto giornate per ritrovare con facilità tutte le antiche e moderne magnificenze di Roma.* Rome: A. Casaletti, 1777.

Venuti, Ridolfino. *Accurata, e succinta descrizione topografica e istorica di Roma moderna.* 2 vols. Rome, 1766.

Index

Page numbers in italic refer to illustrations.